SECRET WEAPONS OF WORLD WAR II

SECRET WEAPONS OF WORLD WAR II

THE UNDERCOVER INNOVATIONS IN MILITARY ARMAMENTS, 1939–45

CHRIS McNAB

Chris McNab

Over the course of his two-decade career as an author and editor, Chris McNab has written more than 100 titles, primarily focused on historical and military topics. His titles include: *Weapons of War: AK47, 20th-Century Small Arms, A History of the World in 100 Weapons, The Illustrated History of the Vietnam War, A History of War* and *J. Robert Oppenheimer*. In addition to his writing work, Chris has made regular contributions on radio and television.

This edition published in 2025 by Arcturus Publishing Limited
26/27 Bickels Yard, 151–153 Bermondsey Street,
London SE1 3HA

Copyright © Arcturus Holdings Limited

All rights reserved. No part of this publication may be reproduced, stored in a retrieval system, or transmitted, in any form or by any means, electronic, mechanical, photocopying, recording or otherwise, without prior written permission in accordance with the provisions of the Copyright Act 1956 (as amended). Any person or persons who do any unauthorised act in relation to this publication may be liable to criminal prosecution and civil claims for damages.

AD012261UK

Printed in the UK

Contents

INTRODUCTION

9

CHAPTER 1

Smatchets and Liberators
– Hand-Held Weapons of the Special Forces

27

CHAPTER 2

Coal Bombs and Deadly Rats – Explosive Devices

53

CHAPTER 3

Mice and Monsters – Armour and Anti-Armour Weapons

67

CHAPTER 4

Salamanders and Grass Snakes –
German and Japanese Secret Aircraft

85

CONTENTS

CHAPTER 5
Vampires and Bat Bombs – Allied Aerial Innovations
107

CHAPTER 6
Autumn Winds and Blazing Typhoons – Air Defence
119

CHAPTER 7
From Flying Bombs to Superguns
– German Vengeance Weapons and Guided Missiles
139

CHAPTER 8
Tallboys and Disney Bombs –
Allied Ordnance and Missiles
157

CHAPTER 9
Limpets and Pigs
– The Small-Boat War
173

CONTENTS

CHAPTER 10
Hedgehogs and Electroboats – The Submarine War
197

CHAPTER 11
Fat Man and Little Boy – The End of Secret Weapons
221

ENDNOTES
235

BIBLIOGRAPHY
243

INDEX
249

Introduction

'...war is completely permeated by technology and governed by it.'[1]
MARTIN VAN CREVELD

On 3 March 1945, one Eugene T. Jensen, a B-17 Flying Fortress pilot of the 349th Bomb Squadron, 100th Bomb Group, pointed the nose of his aircraft towards a distant target in Germany. Hope as well as fear was on the horizon. Hitler's empire now stood on tottering legs, the Third Reich shrinking as Soviet forces advanced from the east and Western Allied armies pressed in from the west. By the spring of 1945, United States Army Air Forces (USAAF) bombing missions carried reduced risk of death compared to the harrowing missions of 1943, when unescorted bomber formations were hacked and slashed by relentless swarms of German fighters. But there was no room for complacency, not least because the Third Reich still bristled with 50,000 anti-aircraft (AA) guns and thousands of fighters. On the last day of 1944, the 100th Bomb Group lost 12 out of 35 aircraft in a single mission. Accidents were frequent, and, as Jensen put it, 'Death and an empty bunk simply became a part of our lives.'[2]

This mission was a big one – 1,102 bombers and 743 fighters from the Eighth Air Force set out to strike key strategic targets across northern and eastern Germany. The threats were now familiar: bursting clouds of AA fire, enemy Bf 109 and Fw 190 fighters (though in reduced numbers), and the ever-present risk of mechanical failure. As Jensen and his crew neared the target on a beautiful, blue-skied day, they braced for action. Their designated role was to fly ahead of the miles-wide, miles-deep bomber stream and deploy chaff – metallic strips dispensed in the air, designed to confuse enemy radar.

INTRODUCTION

As they released the chaff, Jensen noticed something unusual – a single P-51 Mustang in the far distance. Fixing his eyes on the aircraft as it rapidly closed the gap, he started to reassess what his eyes were telling him: 'Our lone P-51 evolved into an aircraft unlike anything we had ever seen. No propeller!' This was no friendly escort:

As we watched it made a tight high-speed circle, coming in from behind our little formation of three bombers. It became evident that we were to have a new and unpleasant experience. The pilots of the three aircraft abandoned the 'chaff' formation and pulled in close together to give us maximum firepower, wingtips only a few feet apart.

Our gunners were fooled by the speed of the aircraft, and despite our massed firepower, we did no apparent damage. The jet flew through our already tight formation so close that we could see the pilot, the rivets in the aircraft skin and the 200mm cannon firing.

The wing of our lead aircraft was cut free from the rest of the aircraft almost as if by a giant chain saw, and the aircraft began its lethal tumble to earth. We saw no parachutes.[3]

The crew didn't know it at the time, but they had just encountered the German Messerschmitt Me 262, the first jet fighter to reach combat status in World War II. Powered by two Junkers Jumo 109-004B-4 turbojets, each producing 900 kg (1,984 lb) of thrust, and armed with four plane-ripping MK 108 30 mm (1.18 in) cannons, the Me 262 was a revolutionary machine. Cutting the air in a futuristic swept-wing profile, it could hit a top speed of 870 km/h (541 mph) and had a climb rate of 1,200 m (3,937 ft) per minute. By comparison, the P-51D Mustang – one of the best-performing Allied fighters – had a maximum speed of 704 km/h (437 mph) and a climb rate of around 1,036 m (3,400 ft) per minute. It was clear that in the war's final months, Allied bomber and fighter crews would face a technological threat that had performance levels beyond anything they could match.

Jensen recalled, 'The development and deployment of a super fighter by the German Air Force had been rumoured but air crew had not been briefed on the profile or performance characteristics of the aircraft.'[4] The Me 262's long and secretive development had indeed kept it hidden from enemy view, at least until the moment it tore across the skies. It was the perfect example of a *Wunderwaffe* or 'secret weapon' – a tactical or strategic game-changer, meant to tip the balance in at least one domain of warfare.

But like many of the secret weapons released during World War II, the Me 262's impact was ultimately limited. It was too late, too insufficient in numbers, to change the outcome of a war that was already set. Mechanically mercurial, it was prone to crashes, particularly during take-off and landing. The wily Allied fighter pilots also soon worked out its vulnerabilities, explored in depth in Chapter 6. Individually, it was revolutionary, but it could not overcome the Allies' greatest advantage – mass.

The struggle between technological innovation and sheer numbers is a recurring theme of this book. It can be framed by a simple question: Is it better to produce large quantities of basic weapons or smaller numbers of superior ones? Of course, the answer is not always an either/or choice, but during World War II, different combatants approached the answer to that question in different ways. Every so-called secret weapon in this book was built on the belief that a technological leap could bring local, or even ultimate, victory.

THE ARMS RACE

The world truly turned during the Industrial Revolution of the 18th and 19th centuries. This imperial, inventive age was the convergence of many great technological revolutions – in manufacturing, machine productivity, transportation (especially railways and macadamized roads), metallurgy, communications, printing, agriculture, electricity generation and chemical production (from artificial dyes to dynamite). The unrestrained spirit of innovation both fed and depended on Enlightenment thinking. Human endeavour could now be adjusted through scientific progress and social engineering.

The Industrial Revolution didn't just influence war, it reshaped it from the grass roots up. Strategy and tactics were reformulated as weapons design took off at an unprecedented pace, multiplying the capacity for killing and destruction. Advances came thick and fast: smokeless powder and the percussion cap; rifled breech-loading artillery; centre-fire cartridge firearms; bolt-action and repeating rifles; mechanical and self-loading machine guns; semi-automatic handguns; high explosives; armoured, steel-hulled, steam-powered battleships; early submarines and torpedoes; rotating naval gun turrets; mechanical artillery predictors; land mines; field telephones and telegraphy (for co-ordinating military operations).

The world was now locked in a technological arms race. This competition in steel and explosives kept its momentum into the 20th century, driven not just by government and military institutions but by capital-rich military-industrial corporations like Krupp and Vickers. Humanity had fully entered the age of industrial warfare, transforming battlefields into factories of death.

War itself turned up the heat under innovation. The Russo-Japanese War (1904–05) became a proving ground for advances in land warfare, naval warfare and logistics. That conflict demonstrated the power of long-range naval artillery paired with armoured ship hulls, a lesson that led directly to Britain's design and construction of HMS *Dreadnought* in 1906. With its revolutionary 'all-big-gun' armament layout and steam turbine propulsion, it rendered every other battleship instantly obsolete, firing a starting gun on a separate naval arms race.

The Russo-Japanese War, however, was merely a prelude to the global convulsion of World War I (1914–18). This was a conflict of contrasts, depending on the theatre. On the Eastern Front, large-scale force manoeuvres played out over vast distances; on the Western Front,

INTRODUCTION

The British battleship HMS Dreadnought, *when it entered service in 1906, changed the global naval arms race overnight with its new 'all-big-gun' design. Credit: US Navy Historical Center.*

opposing armies were locked into static trench lines stretching for hundreds of miles. It was a war that drove technological innovation, though some areas advanced more rapidly than others. The greatest leaps came in air warfare and submarine warfare. At the war's outset, 'combat aircraft' meant crude, juddering biplanes with pilots or observers firing pistols or rifles from open cockpits. By the end, all sides operated large fleets of aircraft purpose-built for war – bombers, fighters and ground-attack types in both biplane and monoplane configurations. Submarines, too, evolved from an experimental curiosity into a nation-level strategic threat. German and Austro-Hungarian submarines alone sank 5,000 Allied merchant ships, at a cost of 15,000 lives.

World War I was not a quick war, settled by one side rolling out incontestable military hardware. Instead, it became a hideous four-year grind. The problem wasn't a lack of advanced technology – quite the opposite. Both sides possessed cutting-edge weaponry, but rather than delivering decisive victories, this balance of force only cranked up the death toll. As Winston Churchill, then Minister of Munitions, put it: 'The war will be ended by the exhaustion of nations rather than the victories of armies.'[5]

World War I offers many salutary lessons about the possibilities and limitations of technology. When both sides possess similar technology, two ways to gain a *tactical* edge are: 1) to acquire a subsequent technology that is decisively superior to anything the enemy possesses; 2) to outmatch the enemy in sheer mass of firepower, through superior concentration, deployment or manoeuvre. The latter, I would argue, is easier to achieve than the former in a conflict between peer opponents; scientific or technological breakthroughs are comparatively rare, whereas the military effects of mass production are well attested.

THE BUILD-UP

The 'dark valley' of the 1920s and the 1930s set the conditions of the coming world war, politically, ideologically but also technologically. The first decade after the end of World War I in 1918 bought the predictable rush to demobilization, with accompanying reductions in military investment. Money was tight, driven by post-war austerity and debt repayments, plus periodic crises in economics and employment. The United Kingdom, France, Italy, Japan and the United States all reduced their military expenditure significantly and voluntarily. In Germany, by contrast, the compulsions of the Versailles Treaty – a 100,000 soldier limit on the German Army; a navy with only six battleships and no submarines; no tanks or military aircraft permitted – eviscerated one of Europe's greatest militaries. There were also efforts to restrict elements of a future naval arms race. On 6 February 1922, the United States,

United Kingdom, Japan, France and Italy signed the Washington Naval Treaty (also known as the Five-Power Treaty), which committed the signatories to restricting both the tonnage and the numbers of their battleships, battle cruisers and aircraft carriers.

Consequently, the 1920s were a decade of relative stagnation in military innovation. If we take the United States as an example, the research and development (R&D) budget was only about 1 per cent of total armaments expenditure; today it is about 10–15 per cent.[6]

But retreating waters were simply a prelude for the tsunami to come. Everything changed in the 1930s. Rising extreme nationalism in Germany and Japan, feverishly proclaimed in the language of expansion, militarism and race theory, raised the spectre of global conflict once again. In 1933, Adolf Hitler took power as the German Chancellor, his Nazi Party the dominant force in Germany both ideologically and electorally. The chancellorship quickly became a dictatorship, and Hitler set about loosening the shackles of the Versailles Treaty. He took a first step towards rebuilding an air force by establishing the Reichskommissariat für die Luftfahrt ('Reich Commissariat for Aviation') on 27 April 1933, masking aircraft development programmes under the activities of the Deutscher Luftsportverband (DLV; 'German Air Sports Association') and Deutsche Luft Hansa civil airline. In the same year, Hitler formally withdrew Germany from the League of Nations, and with growing confidence set his nation on the path to full rearmament. The gloves truly came off in 1935, when he formally and publicly rejected the military limitations of Versailles, announcing the formation of the new German Air Force, the Luftwaffe, plus the reintroduction of conscription. During this decade, Germany also took pole position as a pioneer in the development of tactical aircraft and armoured vehicles. Both were key technological elements in the Wehrmacht's ('Defence Forces') new guiding doctrine of warfare: the *Bewegungskrieg* ('War of Movement'), an ambitious new take on manoeuvre warfare, one that has historically and inaccurately being labelled as *Blitzkrieg* ('Lightning War').

INTRODUCTION

Wider Europe was slow to respond, at first directed and manipulated by the desire to appease Hitler, later eager to postpone war as long as possible to provide a window of opportunity for rearmament. On 18 June 1935, the UK and Germany signed the Anglo-German Naval Agreement, which set a 35:100 tonnage ratio between the Kriegsmarine (German Navy) and the Royal Navy respectively. What it did, in effect, was to give Germany another green light for rearmament. Also in that year, Japan began its own sprint towards intensive and unlimited military expansion, particularly focusing on naval construction (which in itself threatened US and European influence in the Pacific), new designs of combat aircraft and tanks, and infantry mechanization.

As the 1930s progressed, the United Kingdom, France and the Soviet Union were eventually shaken from their complacency and began a breathless rearmament. Like Germany and Japan, these countries had to address new technological parameters, not just the need to build up volumes of men and materiel. The biplanes of World War I, for example, were now sliding into obsolescence, overtaken by faster and tougher monoplanes. Battleships still represented the apogee of naval power, but new classes of submarine and the first generations of aircraft carrier augured a changing struggle for mastery of the waves. Armoured vehicles were no longer the clunking plate steel boxes seen on the Somme or at Cambrai, but had become genuine lead elements in the war of manoeuvre, offering speed, armoured protection and mobile firepower. The motorization and mechanization of infantry forces was now a realizable possibility through mass-produced light armoured vehicles and soft-skinned trucks and cars. Advances in radio offered freedom from the curse of the cut field telephone wires, and the tactically transformative possibility of the wireless co-ordination of troops, aircraft and tanks on the battlefield, and ships at sea.

By the time war began in 1939, therefore, the world was once again bristling with gun barrels. It had been an uneven race, however. The UK, for example, boasted the world's largest navy (a superlative it had admittedly boasted for more than a century) and had 2,000 military aircraft, but on land it possessed only 17 infantry divisions and two armoured divisions. By way of comparison, the accelerated rearmament of Germany meant that by 1939 the country had 86 infantry divisions, six Panzer divisions, 3,000 aircraft and 57 submarines. (Despite the size of its navy, of the latter Britain had just 38.) Similarly, the United States might have been an industrial giant, but when it came to pre-war military production that giant was mostly sleeping, the country's isolationism keeping it comparatively weak in relation to a power such as Germany. The Soviet Union had the largest land army, but sheer size hid weaknesses in technology and professionalism.

MILITARY R&D

As the prospect of war loomed, all future combatants joined, to varying degrees, a technological arms race. The pre-war era saw the foundation or expansion of military scientific and engineering organizations dedicated to applied research and technology prototyping, both within and outside the usual big beasts of service procurement. In the United States, for example, both the Naval Research Laboratory (NRL) and the Aberdeen Proving Ground (a test and evaluation facility for ordnance and related delivery systems, plus armoured vehicles) expanded their scale and remit significantly during the 1930s. Breakthroughs of the NRL alone during the decade included the first US radio Identification Friend-or-Foe (IFF) system and one of the first operational radars installed on a battleship. On 27 June 1940, prior to US entry into the war, the federal government also established the National Defense Research Committee (NDRC), a pure R&D national security institution dedicated 'to coordinate, supervise, and conduct scientific research on the problems underlying the development, production, and use of mechanisms and devices of warfare'.[7] The NDRC was in turn superseded on 28 June 1941 by the Office of Scientific Research and Development (OSRD), an organization that would grow to acquire enormous centralized influence over weapons development,

INTRODUCTION

Sir Henry Thomas Tizard was one of the leading minds behind the development of radar for air defence during the interwar years. He was also the man who helped create the modern 'octane rating' used to classify petrol. Credit: Chronicle/Alamy

not least through its administrative control of the initial stages of the Manhattan Project.

Britain had its own collection of research centres, some of them world-leading. The British government was preoccupied by the doom-mongering predictions of future strategic bombing, and thus in 1934 it formed the Committee for the Scientific Survey of Air Defence (CSSAD), informally known as the Tizard Committee after its chairman, Henry Tizard. The Tizard Committee was created to advance the development of Britain's air defences, particularly early radar technologies, for the detection of incoming threats and the vectoring of defensive aircraft or AA artillery to meet them. In 1936, the Tizard Committee established the Bawdsey Research Station (BRS) radar research group, so called on account of its headquarters north-east of London at Bawdsey Village, Suffolk. Multiple changes to name and location followed, the BRS eventually mutating into the Air Ministry Research Establishment (AMRE), the Ministry of Aircraft Production Research Establishment (MAPRE) and, in November 1940, the Telecommunications Research Establishment (TRE). Other important R&D centres for British weapon development included the Design Department of the Research Department, Royal Arsenal Woolwich (which concentrated on artillery, ordnance and explosives), and the Admiralty Research Department with a remit of naval technologies (such as submarine detection). Pioneering the tactics and technologies of irregular warfare was the Military Intelligence (Research) department of the British War Office, with its MIR(c) branch dedicated to weapons research. From July 1940, the infamous Special Operations Executive (SOE) was formed, a covert operations group tasked by Churchill 'to set Europe ablaze'.[8] In December of that year, most of the MIR divisions were moved under the SOE umbrella, except MIR(c), which went to the Ministry of Defence (MOD) as MD1.

As one might expect given its rapid focus on rearmament, Germany also committed to weapons R&D. Much of this was contained within the major centralized organizations of the Wehrmacht – the Reichsluftfahrtministerium (RLM; 'Ministry of Aviation') for the Luftwaffe; the Heereswaffenamt (HWA; 'Army Ordnance Office') for tanks, artillery and small arms; and the Marinewaffenamt (MWa; 'Naval Weapons Department'), later (from 1939) the Marinewaffenhauptamt ('Naval Weapons Head Department') of the Oberkommando der Marine (OKM; 'Upper Command of the Navy'), which oversaw the Kriegsmarine. All these organizations identified a weapons requirement and issued specifications to the big industrial weapon developers (Messerschmitt, Heinkel Krupp, Rheinmetall, etc.), who worked to provide the solutions. Adolf Hitler himself, as we shall discover, remained an influential and intrusive figure in this whole process. Hitler's Germany also had some specialist research centres. Most notorious was the Heeresversuchsanstalt Peenemünde (HVP; 'Peenemünde Army Research Centre'), established in the Baltic in 1937 as one of the HWA's proving grounds, this one specializing in the secret development of rocket weapons. Another experimental weapon research organization was already in operation at the Kummersdorf 25 km (15.5 miles) south of Berlin; here the R&D activities also included the testing of advanced German Army vehicles.

The Soviet Union also had its own research centres, although much of their effort was dedicated to producing conventional weapons or components for them. The Main Artillery Directorate (GAU) was a 19th-century organization that by the 1930s focused its attention on ordnance, artillery, rockets and tank guns. Two other groups were also dedicated to missile and rocket research: the Group for the Study of Reactive Motion (GIRD) and the Reactive Scientific Research Institute (RNII), the latter the brains behind the Katyusha rocket launcher. Both of these organizations were founded in the early 1930s; clearly and correctly, the Soviet Union saw rockets and missiles as the future of warfare. The Central Aerohydrodynamic Institute (TsAGI), meanwhile, was an aircraft design and research bureau, one that later investigated jet propulsion.

We will in due course hear much more about the activities of these and other organizations in the effort to design, develop, test and field new generations of secret weapons. They were populated by an unusual spectrum of individuals, leaning of course towards engineers, physicists, chemists and military officers, but sometimes including figures with more tangential specialisms, including artists, psychologists, even actors and magicians. While their pre-war activities were taken seriously, peacetime conditions meant that the momentum of output was steady, even relaxed at times. Not for long.

In September 1939, disquieting fears became hard reality when Germany invaded Poland, triggering a war that quickly drew in Europe's major powers. The conflict spread from northern Europe to southern Europe, to North Africa, sub-Saharan Africa and the Middle East. With the Japanese attack on Pearl Harbor on 7 December 1941, and Imperial Japan's assault on the Pacific and East Asia (adding to its already long-running war in China), the United States entered the fray and the war became a fully global affair.

In six compressed years, World War II became one of the most scientifically and technologically innovative periods in human history. The visionary outputs were not only weapons, but also devices and principles that reframed much of the modern world. Even a non-exhaustive list of the inventions is extensive, and includes (randomly) jet engines, key advances in radar and radio, electronic computers, high-level encryption and deciphering, blood plasma transfusions, space rocketry, superglue, synthetic rubber and oil, autonomous guidance systems, duct tape and atomic power. In the field of weapons research, the subject of this book, the innovations were broad and diverse. They ranged from near-silent assassination rifles to ballistic missiles, from nerve agents to guided missiles, rocket planes to atomic bombs. The pace of innovation was fast because it had to be. Projects that might have taken years or even decades in peacetime were pushed through within weeks or months in war.

Why was this so? Innovation was driven hard by the extremity of the conflict. World War II was an ideological and physical fight to the death. It became the fullest expression of 'total war', the conceptual framework coined in 1935 by the German general Erich Ludendorff in his publication *Der totale Krieg* ('The Total War'). Under apocalyptic conditions, any innovation that could, potentially, find the path to victory or at least ensure survival was to be vigorously pursued. Seen in this light, we can draw a logical line of innovation between a new assault rifle designed to increase infantry firepower to an atomic bomb that wiped cities from the map. Each was a technological contribution to total war, the breadth of innovations matching the desperation and moral collapse of a planet fighting for survival.

THE SECRET WEAPONS

What do I mean by 'secret' weapons? It's a term with dramatic weight, tailor-made for blockbuster novels and cinematic intrigue. It suggests a weapon so transformative that the mere revelation of its development would upend the existing arms race. A secret weapon is designed and built under strict conditions of non-disclosure, hidden from enemy eyes until that sweet-spot moment when it is unleashed, sweeping the board and delivering victory.

The pathways of weapons innovation in World War II, however, varied between the combatants, being conducted under different procurement processes and engineering philosophies. Generally speaking, Germany, the United Kingdom and the United States became the leading innovators in the more experimental and advanced fields of science. The Soviet Union certainly made important advances in key weapon types – think the T-34/85 tank or the IL-2 *Sturmovik* ground-attack aircraft – and the Japanese made signal advances in warship design and light tanks (if only in the 1930s and the early years of the war), but comparatively neither made the leaps in groundbreaking science.

We must reinforce a point made earlier: the truly significant struggle between opposing armies was more a matter of mass than technology. This is not to say, of course, that those two elements are mutually exclusive – there were plenty of mass-produced weapons intelligently and even exquisitely designed (think the Spitfire). But we can make the point by considering armoured vehicles. From 1933 until 1945, Germany produced a total of 49,777 tanks and self-propelled guns (SPGs). The bulk of these were Panzer III and IV vehicles, 59 per cent of the total, while the prestige vehicles – the Tiger I and II, the Panther and the *Elefant* – constituted 8,584 units, a mere 17 per cent of the total. Now consider that the Allies collectively manufactured 230,000 tanks and SPGs between 1939 and 1945 (the USA, for example, made *c.*49,000 Sherman tanks alone), and it becomes clear that there was almost no technological advance that would have been capable of winning the German armoured battle.

The example of AFVs can be replicated with similar disparity in almost every domain of weaponry during World War II, largely made possible by the awakened industrial might of the United States. The German and Japanese war machines were ultimately drowned under a torrent of Allied steel and ordnance. But although investments in secret weapons programmes were costly diversions of resources away from mainstream weaponry, we could argue that from 1944 onwards a technological breakthrough might well have been one of the few life rafts the Nazis could cling to.

On the Allied side, the outcome of the war was touch and go for many years, but even after the tide turned in their favour from 1943, the sheer human cost of combat still drove the effort to design war-winning technologies.

So, the term 'secret weapon' needs a bit more rigour if it's going to serve as the foundation of this book. The concept has problems. For one, almost all weapons development, to some degree, begins under conditions of secrecy. Take the Soviet T-34, for example. Early prototypes were developed, tested and refined under strict institutional secrecy. They represented high innovation – some were fitted with 45 mm (1.8 in) guns, others with high-velocity 76.2 mm (3 in) guns; they had steeply sloped armour for shell deflection; extra wide tracks allied to the Christie suspension gave them superb off-road mobility. But given that more than 57,000 T-34s were produced between 1939 and 1945, forming the backbone of Soviet armoured divisions, calling it a 'secret weapon' feels a bit of a stretch.

The endgame of T-34 development was to manufacture and field a standard-issue, mass-produced armoured vehicle. From that moment on, secrecy would be lost, as the enemy would without doubt inspect destroyed or captured examples. Also, the T-34 was not necessarily superior to all the other AFVs it would fight against; indeed, taking crew performance into account, it was inferior on a one-to-one basis in many encounters. One German PzKpfw V Panther tank, for example, might typically destroy four or five T-34/85s in a concentrated engagement before it was itself overwhelmed by numbers and destroyed (if it was). Likewise on the Western Front, Allied Sherman tanks had a $3/5$–1 loss ratio against German Tiger tanks. But weight of numbers meant that such losses could be sustained without affecting the final victory. The sweet spot of innovation, therefore, was to produce weapons that were *both* technologically advanced *and* capable of mass production and distribution.

So, we need some rules for establishing how we will select 'secret weapons'. Here I offer four criteria:

1. Weapons that represented advances in science, technology or engineering significant enough to warrant conditions of secrecy not only during development, but also during subsequent service.
2. Weapons designed specifically (sometimes exclusively) to fulfil a tactical or strategic mission that was itself secret.
3. Weapons that held the potential to change the course of the war, or at least the course of specific aspects, without necessarily relying upon mass production.
4. Weapons that took an unusually novel approach to solving a specific problem, the design and development conducted beyond the normal routes of armaments procurement.

None of these categories are entirely watertight within and amongst themselves, but they narrow down our choice to a manageable level. Even with these selecting principles, the demands of space mean that we cannot be exhaustive in our inclusions. Rather, I will concentrate on judicious and representative types, pulling out the inspiration and innovation from their development, and the triumphs and disasters of their use.

As we shall see, some technologies in this book were highly consequential, a genuine leap forward in weapons design and combat effects. This category can include proximity-fused AA shells, radar-guided missiles and jet aircraft. Sometimes the full potential of the technology was, admittedly, only realized after World War II, when there was the time and luxury to develop it properly – think here of the way that the V-2 ballistic missile programme formed the bedrock of the Cold War space race and the development of nuclear missiles. Other secret weapons were, by contrast, woefully unconvincing.This book will also explore some of the mad fringes of secret weapons programmes, projects so misguided one wonders how they secured funding in the first place. (Bat bombs is my winner in this category, but see where your judgement leads you.) But even in their absurdities, secret weapons reveal intriguing truths about science and engineering, if only through their failure. All these weapons sit at the dynamic intersection between curiosity, knowledge and extreme pressure.

Chapter 1

Smatchets and Liberators – Hand-Held Weapons of the Special Forces

***

Armies have always had their elites. Governments have always had their spies. But World War II gave birth to a new type of unit, and a new type of soldier – what we today call special operations forces (SOF).

THE SECRET WAR

Total war meant just that – all options were open. Many of the combatants of World War II not only looked to defeat their enemies on the open battlefield but also undermine and sabotage them deep within their own territories. This operational focus required not large land armies, but small, secretive, exhaustively trained units, equipped with the most advanced and specialized weapons.

Of necessity, Britain led the way. From the outset of the war, the UK never had the capacity to defeat Germany unilaterally, so quickly sought unorthodox means and missions to take the fight to the enemy. In 1940, the new Prime Minister Winston Churchill remarked with visceral turn

Chapter 1

of phrase that '[We need] specially trained troops of the hunter class, who can develop a reign of terror down these coasts [of occupied Europe], first of all on the butcher and bolt policy... leaving a trail of German corpses behind them.'[9] To this end, new units of elite troops were formed to act as raiders, assassins, saboteurs and reconnaissance experts. First up were the Commandos, an all-volunteer British Army force founded in June 1940 under the umbrella of the Special Service Brigade; in 1942, the Royal Marines also converted its infantry battalions to Commando battalions. Others soon followed, from little-known units with mouthful titles such as the Royal Marines Boom Patrol Detachment (RMBPD) and Combined Operations Pilotage Parties (COPP) to what are today regarded as the world's leading SOF units, the Special Air Service (SAS) and Special Boat Service (SBS).

The challenge of clandestine missions in occupied territories went principally to the Special Operations Executive (SOE); then a secret, today lauded for its covert exploits. It was formed in July 1940 from a fusion of Section D (sabotage) of MI6 (the UK's foreign intelligence service), the MI(R) research branch of the War Office, and Department Electra House (EH), a propaganda/subversive warfare branch of the Foreign Office. It grew big – peak personnel strength was about 13,000 in mid-1944 (including 3,000 women), supported in foreign operations by the audacious skill and bravery of about 40,000 crew and ground personnel from the Royal Air Force Special Duties (SD) Service. But it remained one of the most secretive organizations of the war. Its field operatives conducted missions of appalling risk deep in enemy territory, their work ranging from liaising with resistance groups to conducting raids and sabotage on key installations.

Other countries bought into the SOF concept and by war's end the influence of shadow soldiers had spread like oil across water. The United States stood up a broad range of light infantry forces with tactical specialisms in raiding and reconnaissance, or with theatre or terrain expertise (e.g. jungle or amphibious warfare). They included the First

Special Service Force (FSSF; a joint US-Canadian commando unit), US Army Rangers, 5307th Composite Unit (Merrill's Marauders), Marine Raiders, Alamo Scouts and the US Navy Underwater Demolition Teams (UDTs). But the biggest clandestine operations organization, equivalent to the British SOE, was the Office of Strategic Services (OSS).

Created on 13 June 1942 via Presidential Order from President Franklin Delano Roosevelt, the OSS was primarily an intelligence organization, instructed to 'collect and analyze such strategic information as may be required'. But its remit widened as the war progressed. It came to perform the same range of combat and support operations as SOE. In fact, the two organizations liaised closely. An example would be the three-man 'Jedburgh teams', consisting of one SOE and one OSS trooper plus a single Free French agent, formed to conduct operations alongside the French resistance before, during and after the *Overlord* landings in Normandy in June 1944.

Looking to the Soviet Union, Stalin wielded less SOF and more a fearsome security apparatus, most notoriously embodied in the People's Commissariat for Internal Affairs, the NKVD, headed by the invariably cruel Lavrenti Beria. Although the NKVD's reputation is forever linked to the persecution, exile and murder of the USSR's own people, during World War II select NKVD units also conducted sabotage operations in German-occupied portions of the country. Often they performed these duties in liaison with Soviet partisans, which also came to constitute an informal branch of Soviet SOF. The Red Army also formed the precursors to the elite Spetsnaz, beginning in August 1941 with 'Unit 9903', intended as a 'special purpose reconnaissance troop'.[10] During the war, Spetsnaz troops had three main operational purposes: infantry raiders, reconnaissance troops and engineer sabotage specialists. They conducted missions of great depth, sometimes penetrating enemy lines to hundreds of kilometres' depth, even crossing national borders.

Axis special forces never grew to the scale of those employed by the Allies. The reason for this state of affairs was partly cultural – both Nazi

Chapter 1

Germany and Imperial Japan saw covert operations as a low priority in comparison to the nation-carving business of conventional campaigns, and their hierarchical militaries were also sceptical of forming elite, independent offshoots. For Japan, clandestine warfare had the scent of dishonour about it. Furthermore, there was the matter of reduced need. Both Germany and Japan secured, for a time, vast empires – they were the conquerors, not the resisters.

Such is not to say that there were no Axis special forces, though. Germany's premier elite was the 'Brandenburgers', a pure commando unit formed in 1939 and subordinated to the Abwehr (the German military intelligence and espionage service). The Brandenburgers were trained to fight behind enemy lines, often in civilian clothes and speaking foreign languages. From 1943, however, Germany began its long descent to defeat, and greater interest in covert operations took hold. The SOF units formed in the last two years of the war included the SS-Jäger-Bataillon 502 and elements of the SS-Panzer Brigade 150; the latter made their reputation by donning US uniforms and impersonating American troops during the 1944–5 Ardennes campaign, which more often than not led to the soldiers being captured, tied to a post, and shot as spies.

In Japan, SOF often took on a twisted, suicidal angle. Examples include the Fukuryu kamikaze frogmen, trained to attack US landing craft with underwater mines at the cost of their own lives. Similarly, naval personnel were trained to man the Kaiten suicide torpedoes. (Both these weapons will be studied in the book.) Given that their sole purpose was to terminate their mission in death, it is rather challenging to brand them special forces.

What all SOF troops needed were weapons. In most cases, especially in the Soviet Union and Germany, they were equipped from standard-issue military stocks, albeit the best of the arsenal, including submachine guns (SMGs) and advanced generations of selective-fire battle/assault rifles. (A selective-fire weapon allows the user to choose between semi-automatic fire – one shot per trigger pull – and fully automatic fire – continuous fire until the trigger is released.) But among the Allies, whole new R&D branches and organizations were created, devoted to the design and production of secret weapons. On 27 June 1940, for example, President Roosevelt issued the order to form the National Defense Research Committee (NDRC). Headed by the engineer, inventor and industrialist Vannevar Bush, the NDRC received substantial funding ($6 million in its first year) to energize innovation in weapons research. On 28 June 1941, however, the NDRC was subordinated within the much larger Office of Scientific Research and Development (OSRD), which by 1945 had a half a billion dollar budget (equivalent to about $9 billion today). As we shall see, the OSRD and the NDRC oversaw a vast R&D enterprise, designing weapons large and small. Regarding the OSS, its main research branch was the NDRC's Division 19 (Miscellaneous Weapons).

Weapons R&D for the British SOE, meanwhile, came mostly from its own Station IX (Research Section) and from Station XII. The former was established in 1941 at a private hotel called The Frythe in Welwyn Garden City in Hertfordshire, south-eastern England, the latter at the 17th-century Aston House near Stevenage, also in Hertfordshire. Collectively they worked on a marvellous array of technologies to aid operations, including camouflage, rations and spy devices. In terms of weapons specifically, however, they focused on explosives, incendiaries and detonating mechanisms, but also extended their thinking to projects as ambitious as miniature submarines, these being explored through Station IX subsections based in Middlesex and Pembrokeshire. As the weapons emerged into prototype stage, they were often demonstrated to agents and authorities in the Demonstration Room in the Natural History Museum, South Kensington, known as Station XVb.

The inventiveness of these and other research groups, stimulated by the pressures of war, was prodigious. Freewheeling minds met ample funding and the absolute necessity for finding solutions.

Chapter 1

EDGED WEAPONS

For those interested in military history and in offbeat inventions, the OSS weapons catalogue is a gift that keeps giving. Published in June 1944, it was a handy reference guide for OSS operatives, laying out the full range of secret weapons available for clandestine missions. The dozens of weapons listed and illustrated are of wildly different type and design, mostly purposed for sabotage, assassination and self-defence, but also for less direct objectives, such as psychological warfare. Some are relatively conventional weapons, albeit with limited distribution or specialist modifications. Others seem straight out of a James Bond movie, courtesy of Q branch.

The early pages of the catalogue explain the two primary OSS edged weapons. The first is the classic Fairbairn–Sykes fighting knife (shortened to 'F-S knife' or 'F-S dagger'), the blade that today graces the official emblem of the Royal Marine Commandos. The knife was designed by two legends in the history of close-quarter combat theory and practice, William Ewart Fairbairn and Eric Anthony Sykes. While serving with the Shanghai Municipal Police in China before World War II, a tough posting, they sought to develop a truly practical combat knife. The two men would subsequently take leadership roles in the wartime SOE, SAS and British Commandos, and they took their knife with them. It migrated to the OSS but was also adopted by the US Rangers and the Marine Rangers during the war.

The knife had a slender blade of diamond cross-section, made from high-grade steel, sharpened on both sides and terminating in an acute point. Its design made it lethal in both the cut and the thrust. The OSS catalogue stated that the knife was 'excellent for stealthy attack', the operator holding it 'lightly between thumb and next finger, end of handle lying between the fatty tissues of the palm'.[11] It recommend that the warrior target the enemy's main artery groups; the catalogue's illustrations show a US soldier dispatching a German sentry by restraining him in a rear left-hand choke hold, while driving the knife into his throat using his right hand.

Strictly speaking, the OSS knife was a copy of the Fairbairn–Sykes blade, but manufactured by Landers, Frary & Clark, of New Britain, Connecticut. They received an initial order for 10,000 knives, but a problem with soft steel meant that some had to be recalled and heat-treated again to improve their hardness.

The OSS blade wasn't the only American combat knife based on the Fairbairn–Sykes. In July 1942, the FSSF, a joint Canadian-American special operations unit, was formed at Fort William Henry Harrison, Montana. Its all-volunteer personnel were known as 'The Forcemen' and their punishing training regime and behind-the-lines operational mindset laid the foundations for subsequent US SOF. The force commander, Lieutenant Colonel (later Major General) Robert T. Frederick liaised with other FSSF personnel to design what they saw as the perfect fighting knife. The subsequent 'Knife, Fighting, Commando Type, V-42' was recognizably of the Fairbairn–Sykes stable, but had a slightly longer blade, a grip formed from serrated leather washers, and a sharp point on the pommel designated as a 'skull crusher'. (This feature was in debt to the Mark I trench knife issued to the soldiers of the American Expeditionary Force during World War I.) The V-42 became a popular and prestigious knife among those to whom it was issued. Like its Fairbairn–Sykes siblings, it was *only* a combat knife; other knives and daggers were frequently used as utility tools, for opening cans, cutting foliage, etc. Do that with an F-S-type dagger, and you would likely wreck either the point or the cutting edges.

Another OSS edged weapon was the evocatively titled 'Smatchet'. This was another design from Fairbairn, who took his inspiration from the Royal Welch Fusiliers trench knife of World War I. The Smatchet appeared as a cross between a hand-held paddle, a machete and the knife. (The OSS catalogue describes it as a mix between a machete and a bolo, the latter being a broad-bladed weapon/tool indigenous to the

Philippines.) It had a particularly wide but thin blade profile – the blade being fully sharpened along one edge and half-sharpened along the other. From tip to hilt, the weapon measured 419 mm (16.5 in). It was also heavy, at 0.71 kg (1 lb 9 oz). The combination of sharp point, heavy blade and double edge meant it was a stab-and-slash weapon of gruesome force, the catalogue noting that 'When properly used it will readily penetrate thin sheets of metal, such as is used in ordinary steel helmets.' The tactical illustrations show the warrior using the Smatchet to slash at inner elbows or wrists, or the exposed neck, stab to the stomach, and even use the pommel to deliver an augmented uppercut to the chin. For Fairbairn, the Smatchet also imbued the user with the warrior spirit. He wrote:

The psychological reaction of any man, when he first takes the Smatchet in his hand, is full justification for its recommendation as a fighting weapon. He will immediately register all the essential qualities of a good soldier – confidence, determination, and aggressiveness. Its balance, weight and killing power, with the point, edge or pommel, combined with the extremely simple training necessary to become efficient in its use, make it the ideal personal weapon for all those not armed with a rifle and bayonet.[12]

Combat might seem a strange category of secret weapon, given their non-mechanical nature, but they represented the elite mindset. The development of SOF, their emphasis on stealth and covert killing, the dismissal of traditional rules, scorned 'gentlemanly' warfare. Winston Churchill himself once said that: 'It's not just the good boys who win wars, but the cheats and the stinkers as well.'[13] An acceptance of underhand combat was reflected in SOE's nickname – 'The Ministry of Ungentlemanly Warfare' – and that of the London Controlling Section (a secret government department dedicated to strategic deception), the 'Dirty Tricks Committee'. Under conditions of total war, such epithets

The Liberator pistol was a secret weapon based on the inverse of advanced technology. Its purpose was mass distribution as an assassination weapon. Credit: Musée de l'Armée

became acceptable, to be encouraged, thus few weapons were out of bounds. All that mattered was to win.

OSS FIREARMS

Obviously, it would take more than knives and daggers to win engagements. The SOF community, therefore, sought to design and develop firearms better suited to clandestine operations. As noted, the bulk of firearms used by SOF were those of the conventional military, albeit leaning towards equipment that was more easily concealed and more convenient to handle in close-quarters engagements: think handguns and SMGs

Chapter 1

rather than rifles and heavy machine guns. But for some missions, especially those involving lone or small groups engaged behind the lines in occupied countries, some specialist firearms were added to the arsenal.

Four firearms, of sorts, were featured in the OSS catalogue. The first was the FP-45 Liberator, a firearm that on the scale of crudeness ranks only just above homemade weapons. Its primitive cheapness was intentional. Looking somewhat like a pressed-steel and boxy cartoon ray gun, it was designed as a single-shot .45-calibre handgun for mass production and distribution into occupied countries, the hope being to produce nations of underhand assassins. Its rudimentary design meant that a) it could be produced quickly in large volumes without sophisticated machinery; and b) its cost wouldn't place undue strain on war budgets.

The Liberator was developed co-operatively by the US Army Joint Psychological Warfare Committee and the German-American gun designer George Hyde, employed by the Inland Manufacturing Division of the General Motors Corporation in Dayton, Ohio. It measured 152 mm (6 in) overall and was delivered in a carton that contained the gun, a packet of ten .45 ACP rounds, a cartridge ejection rod and a set of step-by-step visual instructions; the latter meant that the weapon could be operated by anyone, regardless of whether they spoke English or not. The clunky operating procedure involved manually opening the breech by withdrawing and twisting the bolt group to one side, raising the breech cover and inserting a single cartridge, closing the breech cover and bolt group, firing the weapon, then repeating the breech opening process and ejecting the spent cartridge by inserting the provided rod (or an available stick) down the barrel and poking the cartridge out. Given that this process would take many seconds, the operator had to be sure of using his first shot with maximum effect. The catalogue description acknowledges that 'The low accuracy of the pistol [the weapon had an unrifled barrel] and useful range of approximately 25 yards limit it to close-proximity anti-personnel use.' The range figure is actually quite optimistic; the gun would be better applied with the muzzle pressed hard against the target. In fact, one of the aims of the Liberator was that the insurgent might kill an enemy soldier or armed official with the pistol, then retrieve the more capable weapon from its former owner. The catalogue also expressed the view that 'Besides its physical use, this weapon, if discovered by the enemy, carries the psychological factor of inducing fear in enemy troops in occupied countries.'

The Liberator was a curious low-tech weapon, designed for mass production and distribution deemed to be secret. In official documentation, it was referred to as a 'flare pistol' or 'flare projector' – hence the 'FP' in its title – which given its chunky profile was quite believable at first glance. The plan was for tens of thousands of Liberators to be dropped over occupied territories in Europe and the Pacific. Approximately 1 million of the pistols were indeed manufactured by General Motors' Guide Lamp Division, and some 450,000 went to OSS, but the weapon appears to have had limited distribution. Evidence suggests that some of them went to Greece, China, the Philippines and Guadalcanal, but in all likelihood the majority of the Liberators were destroyed by the US authorities at the end of the war, as few of the original million produced have survived.

The idea of a small, cheap assassination firearm found its way into other OSS designs. The Stinger, for example, didn't even resemble a firearm, but looked more like a cigar tube with a hinged lever fitted to the top. It was, in fact, a one-shot disposable firearm. The metal tube was the barrel and a basic firing mechanism, pre-loaded with a small .22-calibre round. A spring-loaded lever lying flush with the barrel was raised upwards to cock the weapon, and when it was squeezed down again between palm and fingers the weapon fired. Its ballistic properties were woeful, but again it was intended for close-range use only, and had the advantage of being wonderfully concealable: it was only 82.5 mm (3.25 in) long and 12.7 mm (0.5 in) in diameter. As the catalogue stated: 'Its extremely small size is an advantage for concealment, and it can be fired from the palm of the hand at a person sitting in a room or passing in a crowd. It is inexpensive, available in large quantities, and can be distributed widely among native patriots of occupied countries.' It came in two subtle variants, the T1 and T2, and was delivered in units of ten Stingers in a moisture-proof envelope, in turn packed inside a wood and cardboard box. Like the Liberator, evidence about actual use and distribution is scant. Even in wartime, there were security issues about sending hundreds of thousands of durable assassination devices out into a world in great political and social upheaval.

Before moving on to other secret firearms, we should note another OSS hand-held projectile weapon of a very different kind. Coyly titled 'Who, Me?' – surely the most informal weapon name in history – the catalogue description explains its design and its purpose:

DESCRIPTION: Who, Me? is a soft metal tube with a screw cap on a projecting tip. When the cap is removed and the tube squeezed it squirts a liquid chemical of violent, repulsive, and lasting odor. Each tube is covered by a cardboard sleeve for protection of the operator.

PURPOSE: Who, Me? is a psychological harassing agent. It is to be squirted directly upon the body or clothing of a person a few feet away. The odor is that of occidental feces, which is extremely offensive to the orientals. Very good use of this agent can be made by native patriots in crowded markets and bazaars to create disturbances, attack morale of enemy guards, and to divert attention from other activities.

The development of 'Who, Me?' was actually prompted by a November 1943 request to Division 19 by the OSS director of R&D, Stanley P. Lovell, for a liquid that among civilian populations would 'produce unmistakable evidence of extreme personal uncleanliness'[14]. The tactical purpose of this foul contaminant was varied, but included dispersing crowds, confusing enemy personnel and hostile civilians, and polluting enemy rations and supplies. Its main theatre of operations was deemed the Pacific, assaulting Japan's deep cultural and spiritual reverence for cleanliness. Several potions were concocted, the final mixture consisting of alpha-ionone, butyric acid and amyl mercaptan, emitting a gross faecal stench. We know that some 500 glass tubes were issued in February 1945. We do not know of any malodorous operational results.

Returning to the firearms, OSS also made good use of the United States Submachine Gun, Cal. .45, M3, known informally as the 'Grease Gun'. The basic M3 (and M3A1 variant) was the antithesis of a secret weapon. It was a mass-produced submachine gun developed and adopted by the US Army as a super-cheap alternative to the expensive M1928A1 Thompson SMG. It was a crude affair, all welding and pressed sheet steel, but it worked and could be churned out in large volumes: more than 600,000 of the type were rattled off during the war years, each unit costing $c.\$3$ compared to $20 for a Thompson.

Although the M3 was a standard-issue SMG, the fact that it had a detachable barrel meant that the OSS saw its potential for developing a suppressed weapon. (Technical note: although devices attached to firearms to reduce the noise of their firing report are popularly referred to as 'silencers', the correct term is 'suppressor', not least because even the best suppressor rarely renders the weapon completely noiseless.) The special operations M3 was manufactured by the High Standard firearms company. The prototype was unveiled in 1943 and production commenced the following year. The weapon had a two-stage suppressor: one stage was wrapped around the perforated barrel, while the forward second stage projected in front of the muzzle. Both stages contained and diffused the propellant gas via screens or sheets of wire mesh. Reducing the gas pressure resulted in significant noise reduction, amplified by the fact that it also made the bullet subsonic; much of a firearm's report is caused by the bullet splitting the sound barrier as it leaves the muzzle. (This being said, the heavy .45 ACP round is often subsonic even when fired from non-suppressed weapons.) The reported result was a gunshot of 89

Chapter 1

decibels (dB), which was actually quieter than the mechanical action of the gun cycling through the shots. Thus OSS operatives could deliver full-auto SMG fire without attracting too much attention.

The OSS also received the 'Bushmaster' remote firing device, which could be fitted to the M3, but also to most other weapons. The device was essentially a remotely operated firing mechanism, used to convert a secured firearm (i.e. one tied to a tree or a post) into a blazing booby trap. The body of the device was clamped on to the trigger guard of the firearm. A floating tube ran through the housing and via a hook connected at one end to the trigger. The other end of the tube was threaded so that it could connect to a spring-loaded pressure mechanism. (Some Bushmasters had two sets of threads: one for fitting to British mechanisms and the other for American types.) The spring-loaded mechanism was cocked and connected to a tripwire; the gun was aimed at the intended point of intersection with the enemy. Should an enemy soldier catch the tripwire, the firing mechanism was released, which in turn drove the Bushmaster tube on to the trigger and held it down. If it was attached to an M3, the weapon would then run through its entire 30-round magazine, indiscriminately shooting down whoever was in its line of sight.

Another suppressed weapon used by the OSS was the '.22 Caliber Automatic Pistol'. This weapon was actually a High Standard H-D .22 sporting handgun, a semi-automatic handgun feeding from a ten-round magazine and fitted with an integral suppressor. The .22 LR cartridge is not a loud round anyway, but the OSS catalogue claimed a further '90 per cent noise reduction' and clarified what that meant in practical terms: 'The amount of noise audible is merely that of metal contacts and not audible enough to attract attention in normal conditions above traffic noises, doors closing, and other activities of everyday life. This pistol is excellent for use in a closed room or for eliminating sentries. The muzzle is flashless, even in the dark. The range and accuracy are unaffected and remain the same as the normal piece.' In total, OSS acquired 2,600 of these weapons.

BRITISH SOF FIREARMS

The British clandestine services were equally busy developing suppressed firearms during World War II, with two classic types standing out. The first was the Welrod pistol. The 'Wel' part of its name was actually a common suffix for several weapons developed by Station IX; it referred to Welwyn and, in the case of the Welrod, 'rod' was gangland slang for 'gun'. The inventor of the weapon was Major Hugh Quentin Alleyne Reeves, a productive and innovative member of the R&D fraternity.

Looking largely like a section of plumbing or a bicycle pump, the Welrod was a bolt-action suppressed pistol, firing either the .32 ACP or the 9×19 mm Parabellum cartridge, fed from an eight-round or six-round magazine respectively. An interesting design feature was that the gun magazine, once seated in the housing, actually acted as the pistol grip. Its mechanism was a rotary bolt, operated between each shot by manipulating a knurled knob at the rear of the weapon. The bolt mechanism helped keep the weapon super-quiet, as it avoided the noisy clatter of a semi-automatic action cycling under gas, blowback or recoil pressure. In terms of firing noise, the Welrod has been referred to as 'Hollywood quiet'[15], akin to a BB gun fired under a cushion. The suppressor lowered the gas pressure by passing the bullet through a sequence of rubber wipes (essentially solid rubber disks) – the first shot from the gun punched a hole through the wipes, hence that first shot was the quietest of them all. After 15 shots, the wipes would begin to lose their noise-abating efficiency. Effective range was cited up to 23 m (25 yd) in the daytime or 7 m (7.7 yd) at night (the weapon was fitted with fluorescent night sights), but like many suppressed handguns it was best used as close as possible.

The Welrod was a sound design, so much so that while 2,800 were made during World War II, the British produced another 11,000 during the Cold War; kills were made with the Welrod as late as the 1991 Gulf War. The weapon was also used by the OSS, the SAS and post-war US special forces.

Chapter 1

The Welrod was not the only output from Major Reeves. In similar fashion to the OSS M3, he fitted a suppressor to the standard British Sten Mk II SMG to produce the carbine, m/c Sten, 9 mm Mk2(S). Suppressed versions of later Sten prototypes and variants were also produced, specifically the Mk IVA(S) and the Mk VI(S). The suppressed Sten was widely used by SOE and some captured examples were even rebranded by the Germans as the MP 751(e). One enthusiastic German adopter was none other than Otto Skorzeny, the newsworthy Waffen-SS commander who led numerous special operations, including the rescue of the Italian dictator Benito Mussolini from his captivity on the Gran Sasso in September 1943. He is said to have remarked of the weapon: 'What splendid possibilities the use of these silencers offered, I thought enthusiastically. What losses they might save and what dangers they might avert! How wonderful, in case of an unexpected meeting with an enemy detachment, to be able to fire without the reports attracting the attention of other enemy groups!'[16] It was not a perfect weapon, though. Firing just a single magazine on full auto would result in problematic overheating, therefore it was better used as a single-shot repeater.

Another of Reeves' whispering inventions was the Welwand 'sleeve gun'. This was similar to the Welrod but was a single-shot weapon without a pistol grip and the handgun's awkward trigger mechanism. It was basically a suppressed firearm tube, designed to be hidden easily inside clothing. The SOE scientist Douglas Everett tested its efficacy by concealing one up his sleeve during an evening in the staff bar; at the opportune moment, he whipped it out and fired a round into a nearby sandbag, apparently without alerting anyone around him.

Having thrown his ingenuity into Britain's war effort, Reeves himself was not destined to live long after the war. On 25 October 1955, he was accidentally sucked into the engine of a Hunter Mk V jet aircraft, during his investigations into methods for reducing engine noise. He was killed instantly.

The De Lisle carbine remains one of the quietist military firearms in history. The technology within its suppressor was kept confidential for many years after the war. Credit: Atirador/CC BY-SA 3.0

Then there was the De Lisle carbine. This weapon originated not in SOE but was actually a private design from William Godfrey de Lisle, an Air Ministry engineer. A keen hunter, he spent some time in his workshop rustling up a .22 suppressed rifle through a conversion of a Browning semi-auto sporting rifle. In 1943 he approached and demonstrated the rifle to Major Sir Malcolm Campbell, an officer in the Combined Operations Headquarters of the War Office; Combined Operations oversaw joint Army and Navy raiding missions in Europe. The demonstration apparently involved firing the weapon from the roof of the New Adelphi building in London into the River Thames, the two men observing that passers-by were none the wiser.

The weapon was patented and accepted in principle, although it went through significant subsequent redesign. It eventually emerged as a suppressed .45 ACP conversion of the bolt-action Short, Magazine, Lee–Enfield Mk III* rifle. The subsonic round and the highly effective suppressor meant that the De Lisle had roughly the same auditory output as the Welrod, but with an effective range of $c.200$ m (219 yd). Feed was a 7- or 11-round detachable magazine. The De Lisle was used by SOE operationally, included in recorded assassinations of German officers. Like the Welrod, it went on to have a life beyond the war, including service with the US Army Special Forces in Vietnam and with SAS operators in Northern Ireland during the 'Troubles'.

Chapter 1

LITTLE JOE

Crossbows might have been ancient history by the 1940s, but that didn't stop some enterprising American engineers revisiting them as a potential secret weapon. For if you wanted truly quiet firepower, how about using a weapon that didn't make a bang in the first place? On 27 October 1942, the NDRC received a request for a 'silent, flashless weapon' for use by behind-the-lines operatives. The requirement was for a covert assassination device with a muzzle velocity of 328 m/sec (1,000 ft/sec) and with a maximum reloading time of 30 seconds. Thinking laterally, the NDRC engineers reinvestigated crossbows and in February 1943 demonstrated a prototype, opaquely titled the 'Little Joe Penetrometer'. Just 330 mm (13 in) long, 203 mm (8 in) high and 51 mm (2 in) wide, and weighing just 1 kg (2 lb 3 oz), it was a single-handed, vertical-profile crossbow pistol. Its frame was made from heat-treated aluminium alloy and power came from a bowstring composed of 50 rubber bands at each end, holding in the middle a section of graphite-coated linen. Its projectile was a stubby flighted bolt that featured a broad penetrating head and weighed 30 g (1 oz). To cock the weapon, the user pulled the pivoted upper arm up and back until the string engaged with the release-mechanism. The pistol had a disc or bead front sight and a rear leaf sight, the latter being adjustable for ranges of 14 or 23 m (15 or 25 yd).

As produced, Little Joe failed to meet the velocity requirements: the bolt left the device at just 52 m/sec (170 ft/sec). But it had many plus points. It was quiet (only 72 dB) and accurate (152 mm/6 in groups at 18 m/20 yd). It could kill out to 30 m (33 yd) and at point-blank range had deep penetration: in tests the bolts went through a 1,276-page phone book. It also had a 4 rpm rate of fire. Yet it and the subsequent models were, ultimately, crossbows in a firearms age. The suppressed firearms were a more practical and efficient option, hence Little Joe never went into field service. The NDRC nevertheless invested time developing a shoulder-mounted senior brother, called Big Joe 5, which not only fired longer, heavier bolts over greater distances, but could also launch incendiary weapons. It, too, failed to move from prototype to operational field weapon.

AROUND THE BEND

Germany had its own special forces units, but the Wehrmacht and the Nazi intelligence services never had the busily productive relationship with clandestine weaponry as seen on the Allied side. This being said, some of their firearms innovations – either weaponry or accessories – need mentioning, as they bordered on the category of secret weapons, certainly during their development phase.

Here I am thinking specifically about the new generations of semi-auto and selective-fire infantry weapons developed in Germany during the war years. With the exception of the United States – whose military forces adopted the .30-06 M1 Garand semi-automatic rifle as a standard-issue weapon between 1936 and 1940 – most of the world's infantry fought World War II with bolt-action rifles or SMGs. In crude summary, military bolt-action weapons fired what we call 'full-power' cartridges, emphasizing long range, accuracy and terminal ballistics. There were at least a dozen such cartridges, ranging from 6.5×55 mm Swedish at the small end up to 8×50 mm R Lebel at the opposite end.

Bolt-action rifles offered accuracy, super-dependable reliability and long reach; the effective range of such weapons with iron sights was *c.*600 m (656 yd), and when the rifles were fitted with scopes, a steady and well-trained marksman could be firing out past 800 m (874 yd). They were also easy and cheap to manufacture, so they could be turned out en masse. The problems with bolt-action rifles, however, were legion in modern warfare:

- They were physically long and cumbersome to handle, even in carbine versions, which made them unwieldy when fighting at close quarters.
- They required manual reloading between each shot; cycling the

Chapter 1

bolt by hand took only about a second or so, but that's a long time when an enemy is bearing down on you.
- They had a low magazine capacity, typically between five and ten rounds.
- They had a thumping recoil. This, combined with operating the bolt handle, meant the soldier was continually having to rediscover the point of aim (POA) between shots.
- The long range of a bolt-action rifle was great for a sniper, but for most soldiers that range was well in excess of what they actually needed – it's hard to even see a human-sized target beyond 400 m (437 yd), let alone accurately shoot at one.

In contrast to the bolt-action rifle was the SMG. These weapons, issued with varying ratios among infantry forces, fired pistol-calibre cartridges at semi-auto or full-auto from capacious magazines; the typical box magazine held about 30 rounds, while some drum magazines could hold up to 100 rounds. Cyclical rates of fire were anywhere from about 450 rpm up to a scorching 900 rpm or more. They were also designed to be compact and convenient to handle, meaning that they were ideal for fast-moving close-quarters combat, not least because you could keep firing just by pulling the trigger. Recoil was perfectly comfortable. But there were definite trade-offs. The combination of basic sights, pistol-calibre rounds and the short barrel meant effective range was low – 200 m (218 yd) was an optimistic upper limit, albeit one comfortably within human visual acquisition. Penetration of cover was limited. They were also generally inaccurate. Hits on target were often attained less by carefully aimed shots than by 'walking' the visible impacts of a burst of fire on to the target.

Attentive or informed readers will spot a logical gap between rifles and SMGs – a weapon that offers magazine-fed selective fire with manageable recoil; decent accuracy over *practical* combat ranges of up to 400 m (437 yd); convenient dimensions for better handling. The

Germans became aware of this sweet spot during the interwar years. A 1924 memorandum from the Inspektion der Infanterie (Inspectorate of the Infantry) outlined a requirement for a selective-fire weapon feeding from a 20- or 30-round magazine and with an effective range set around the 400 m (437 yd) mark. Cutting a very long story very short, during the 1930s and the war years this impulse took several lines of evolution, not only focused upon rifle design but also upon developing a new 'intermediate' cartridge sitting between the full-power rifle round and the pistol cartridge.

Two outcomes in particular are relevant to our story here. The first was the Fallschirmjägergewehr 42 (FG 42; Paratrooper's Rifle 42). As the name suggests, this weapon was designed specifically for Germany's elite airborne forces. It proceeded from a 1941 requirement issued by the Luftwaffe's Unterkommission zur Entwicklung von Automatischen Waffen (Sub-committee for the Development of Automatic Weapons) in November 1941. The commission demanded a new man-portable weapon, one that had the firepower of a light machine gun, but which could be handled like a rifle, and which could be carried during a parachute drop using a special body harness. The resulting FG 42 emerged in prototype forms from the spring of 1942 and the winning design went into production in September.

The FG 42 still fired the German 7.92×57 mm rifle round, but everything else was a bold reworking. It was a gas-operated weapon, firing from a closed bolt during semi-auto fire, but switching to an open bolt during full-auto fire.[17] It had a flat-topped 'straight-in-line' layout that sent the recoil more directly into the shooter's shoulder, whose control of the weapon was also augmented by a special flared stock. Felt recoil was also reduced by an internal buffer and a muzzle brake. The pistol grip was canted to a quite extreme angle to make the weapon suitable for firing from the hip (as one might do during a contested parachute descent) and comfortable when firing prone. It also had an integral bipod to support stable and accurate full-auto fire or carefully

Chapter 1

aimed single shots. The magazine port, which accepted 10- or 20-round box magazines, was side mounted on the left of the receiver to make prone reloading accessible. This placement also helped reduce the overall length of the weapon to a comfortable 945 mm (37 in), while also keeping the barrel long (500 mm/20 in), which aided range and accuracy. Full-auto cyclical rate of fire was 900 rpm, with the later Type II weapon increasing that to 1,200 rpm. It could also take a ZFG42 or ZF4 telescopic sight.

The FG 42 was one of the most visionary innovations in personal firepower in World War II, a firearm that could still hold its own even among today's military carbines. Relatively few were produced – c.7,000 – and those that were went into service with German paratroopers fighting in the infantry role in Normandy and Italy. It wasn't perfect by any means. The rifle was complex, heavy and its barrel was prone to overheating on full auto. But it augured a new era in rifle design. The Allies' early impression of the weapon can be seen in the June 1944 issue of *Intelligence Bulletin*, issued by the US War Department:

> *The Germans have a new 7.92-mm automatic rifle, the F.G. 42 (Fallschirmjäger Gewehr 42), which is a light and versatile weapon, especially suitable for use by German airborne personnel. It should be remembered that the 9-mm machine carbines (M.P. 38/40), which are now in general use, were originally introduced as parachutists' weapons; in like manner, the Germans may well put this new 7.92-mm rifle to more general use in the future.*
>
> *The new rifle, which represents a departure in small-arms design, is a close-combat weapon firing any 7.92-mm Mauser rifle ammunition, and combines a relatively light weight with a reasonable degree of accuracy both in single-round and automatic fire. The Germans have struck a balance between the weight limitations of the machine carbine and the power and pressure requirements of the rifle or light machine gun.*[18]

But the FG 42 was not the only specialist firearm to enter the German arsenal in 1944. The other was the Sturmgewehr 44 (StG 44), originally produced as the Maschinenpistole (MP) 43 and 44. The StG 44 was a true game-changer. It was history's first production example of an *assault rifle*, the standard infantry weapon type of the post-war world. Indeed, *Sturmgewehr* can literally translate as 'assault rifle'.

What defines an assault rifle? It is a selective-fire weapon firing an *intermediate* cartridge, a power category between a pistol and rifle round, designed specifically for practical combat ranges of up to 400 m (437 yd), but not much beyond. Back in 1940, the German Polte-Werke company in Magdeburg was experimenting with strategies to fulfil German requirements for a controllable selective-fire rifle. It produced a new 7.92×33 mm *kurz* (short) round, being the same calibre as the standard 7.92×57 mm rifle cartridge, but with a significantly shortened case to reduce power and increase the comfort of handling. Its muzzle velocity was *c*.685 m/sec (2,247 ft/sec), compared to 820 m/sec (2,690 ft/sec) of its older, bigger brother. What it now needed was a weapon to go with it.

Both the Haenal and Walther companies produced rifles for the new *kurz* round, the MKb 42(H) and the MKb 42(W) respectively. The former held most promise and in 1943 it was rebranded the MP 43, with authorities in the Heereswaffenamt urging its full-scale production. The blocker was Hitler. For reasons best known to him, he took exception to the MP 43 and, even after convincing demonstrations, banned its further development. But persistence paid off, and by the end of the year Hitler's opinions had swung in favour of the gun and it entered production. With tweaks and adjustments, it became the MP 44 and then, in December 1944, Hitler himself rebranded it as the StG 44, showing his talent for tactically fearsome weapon names.

The StG didn't have all the internal bells and whistles innovations of the FG 42, but it still stood out from the crowd. It was another gas-operated weapon, feeding from a distinctively curved 30-round box

Chapter 1

magazine and offering a 500 rpm rate of fire. It was a heavy gun, but that and its medium-power cartridge made it highly controllable, even on full auto. It gave pitch-perfect combat performance across a practical range, from close-quarters combat out to several hundred metres.

The chief problem for the StG 44 was that it came late in the war, and thus its production was squeezed between numerous other competing demands on the collapsing German war effort. About 426,000 were made, distributed to a mix of Heer (Army) and Waffen-SS units and, in the final months of the war, to some Volkssturm civil defence forces. It could be fitted with optical sights (the 1.5× Zf 41 or the 4× Zf 4), and it even occasionally featured in combat with a bulky Zielgerät 1229 *Vampir* infrared sight, enabling aimed shooting in low-light conditions. (This substantial item, however, took the total weight of the gun up to 15 kg/33 lb, a heavy load for even the most strong-armed soldier.)

But there was one secret accessory that stood out from the rest – the Krummlauf attachment. This was nothing less than an attempt to enable soldiers to shoot around corners while remaining under cover. It consisted of an outlandish-looking curved barrel married to a forward-mounted Vorsatz J prismatic aiming device, which allowed the user to view and aim at targets out of his line of sight. Initially, this system had been developed for machine guns firing the standard 7.92×57 mm rifle cartridge, but this was found to be too bruising a round to turn the corner. The StG 44, with its intermediate round, seemed a more promising candidate. It was first tested, in July 1944, with a wildly ambitious barrel that arced a full 90 degrees, but this was reined back in to 30 degrees. An equivalent device was also developed for fitting to armoured vehicles, so the crew inside could shoot at blind spots around the vehicle; this was known as the Vorsatz Pz. The term Krummlauf was applied to the combined fittings.

The German testers of the Krummlauf would doubtless have noticed that bullets want to go straight, not around corners. The new weapon was incredibly punishing on the barrels – in some tests, barrels were literally blown off after the weapon had fired about 170 rounds. But it sort of worked, and small numbers made their way into combat. On 18 July 1945, the US Office of the Chief Ordnance Officer issued a testing report about the weapon, a document that also included information obtained via an interrogation of the inventor, Colonel Hans Schaede, who was an assistant in the research division of Rheinmetall-Borsig, and of Major Fred Hartmann, who had worked in the German Ministry of Armament, Division of Infantry Units, in Berlin, supervising research on small arms. While the report noted that 'The *Krummlauf* (bent barrel) is an entirely new idea in controlling and changing the direction of the delivery of a bullet', the physical testing of the devices showed that new ideas are not necessarily good ideas:

> **Data and comments on the 30-degree barrel:** *According to the inventor, the Krummlauf has an expected life of 6,000 rounds, but this is greatly doubted. Test firing indicates that the strain on the barrel in diverting the normal straight-line course of the barrel is great, and it is believed that it would enlarge, erode, and pocket, both in the auxiliary throat and in the curved area. All bullets test fired were seriously distorted, and this was verified by interrogation of Major Hartmann.*
>
> *On test firing the 30-degree barrel, the "jump" or climb was greatly accelerated by the change in the direction of the bullet, but it was not too uncomfortable to shoot. The release of the gas through the auxiliary barrel ports relieved much of the apparent strain on the mechanism.*
>
> *[...]*
>
> *As the bullet hits the curve in the barrel there is a violent reaction in the opposite direction. There is a combination of normal recoil, a tremendous torque as the rotating bullet undergoes the punishment of taking the new rifling with gas pressure relief, and a vicious sideways recoil. Approximately 150 rounds were fired in testing the weapon.*

Chapter 1

Single shots and burst fire were tried, and, despite the attempts of several shooters to hold the weapon rigidly at the hip, more than three shots in automatic fire proved dangerous as shooter and weapon were spun almost 90 degrees. Firing tests into sawdust produced more fragments than intact bullets.[19]

The Krummlauf device, the German innovations in small arms, and the strange killing devices of Allied SOF all belong to a specific category of secret weapon. Each weapon was an effort to amplify individual lethality, either by boosting firepower or by giving covert means of bringing a firearm to the fight. But to do more serious damage in combat, it would take bigger bangs.

Chapter 2

Coal Bombs and Deadly Rats – Explosive Devices

***

SOF were particularly good at destroying things. And in World War II, the list of enemy targets that could be blown up or otherwise wrecked was near endless – bridges, locomotives and train tracks, vehicles, radar and radio stations, shipyard equipment, warships and merchant ships, workshops, industrial machinery, tool production plants, pumping stations, weapons research facilities, enemy headquarters, aircraft, and many others. Of course, important logistical or infrastructural targets could be and were attacked from the air via bombing raids, many of those massive in scale. But on occasions, on-the-ground sabotage or demolition was required, either to protect nearby civilians or valuable assets, ensure a precise effect (air raids were notoriously imprecise), move quickly on a target of opportunity, or to identify and attack a target with greater accuracy. Sometimes the target also required a small and localized bang, not the roar and destruction of an air-dropped bomb. For this reason, much ingenuity was devoted to producing explosive devices and detonating mechanisms.

Chapter 2

PLASTIC POSSIBILITIES

Standard military explosive packs and demolition charges were widely available and commonly used by SOF. But sometimes the covert nature of the mission and the physical demands of the target required more specialist instruments of sabotage, and the Allied research organizations in particular showed impressive ingenuity.

From a design perspective, their work was aided by steady improvements and diversification in plastic explosives. Beginning with the invention of gelignite in 1875 by Alfred Nobel, plastic explosives combined high explosives with plasticizers and phlegmatizers, the former rendering the explosive hand-malleable while the latter stabilized it against accidental explosion. (Plastic explosives can only be initiated by a detonator mechanism.) Plastic explosives were also immensely powerful for their weight and volume.

The advantages of plastic explosive can be seen in some rare wartime SOE demonstration videos, now in the collection of the Imperial War Museum but also viewable on YouTube (links are provided in the Bibliography). The compounds could be shaped, moulded or packaged to direct the explosive force with considerable precision for controlled effects. In one of the videos, SOE scientists mould an open circle of plastic explosive, stick it to a steel panel, then insert a detonator. When the explosives are blown, the blast cuts a perfect circular hole through the plate. The only limit to applications was imagination.

One of the classic plastic explosive types used by SOE was another Nobel invention: Explosive No. 808, a gelignite-type compound that apparently had the colour and resistance of green plasticine and the smell of almonds. 'Explosive 808' was probably the type of explosive used in the attempt to kill Adolf Hitler on 20 July 1944 at his Wolf's Lair headquarters in East Prussia; the explosives in the briefcase planted by Count Claus von Stauffenberg were likely from SOE stocks. Another popular explosive was RDX, standing for 'Research Department eXplosive' or 'Royal Demolition eXplosive', although strictly speaking this was a powerful base explosive mixed with other explosives and/or with plasticizers and phlegmatizers. RDX was the central ingredient of many of the Anglo-British 'Composition' family of explosives used during World War II and beyond, including Composition B (59.5 per cent RDX, 39.5 per cent TNT, 1 per cent paraffin wax) and Composition C (88.3 per cent RDX plus oil-based plasticizer and phlegmatizer).

The properties of plastic explosive meant that the secret weapon designers could let their creativity run riot. Let's illustrate this first by looking selectively at some devices developed for SOE and UK SF. SOE weapon designers realized that they could package plastic explosive into all manner of everyday items, making them perfect for planting in plain sight of the enemy. For example, SOE files describe the design of an explosive wine bottle:

The Chianti bottle is made of thick celluloid, and is in two sections. The lower section is bowl shaped, the top section represents the neck and shoulders of the bottle, and has the base of the neck closed by means of a diaphragm of celluloid so that the neck may be filled with wine to complete the camouflage when the bottle is assembled. Each section is filled with PE [and] a detonator.

The two sections are fixed together and the joint sealed with acetone and buffed up, the inside of the celluloid having first been treated with transparent green paint, so that when the two portions are fixed together the whole takes on the appearance of green glass as used in wine bottles. Next the raffia cover is attached to the bottle together with authentic labels. The effect is that of a genuine bottle of Chianti.[20]

The explosive bottle would have been easy to place, one can imagine, on a table in a French cafe frequented by German occupiers. The SOE files also describe an explosive brass cylinder that could be fitted into the body of a bicycle pump, its initiating mechanism attached to the

Chapter 2

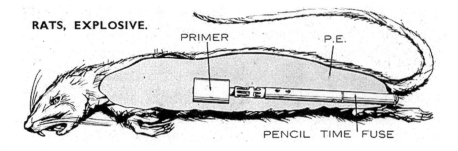

The rat bomb seems like the most implausible weapon of war, but it had an operational purpose and a certain degree of logic on its side. This diagram is from an SOE manual. Credit: TBC

pump handle. The plan was that the agent should deflate an enemy's tyres and replace the existing pump with the lethally modified version; the enemy would be killed or seriously injured the moment he withdrew the pump handle for the first compression.

Looking to the Pacific, meanwhile, one of the most astonishing efforts in explosive design was to form mock Balinese wood carvings from plastic explosive and trade them to the Japanese: 'These are faithful reproductions of the famous Balinese wood carvings, [but] cast in solid explosive [and] mounted on a wooden base, and equipped for initiation by a time delay. It is intended to use these through native agents posing as hawkers frequenting the quaysides, and selling them to Japanese troops about to embark.'[21]

The fact that plastic explosive could be moulded into something as ornate as Balinese wood carvings indicates its versatility. Explosives were squeezed into all manner of objects: books, food cans, fake logs, cigarette packets. Two more leaps in imagination are 'exploding rats' and 'coal bombs'.

These two weapons were united by a common objective: to destroy locomotive engines, ship boilers, power stations or industrial machinery – basically anything that ran from a furnace and a boiler. The exploding rats were, quite literally, dead rats that were skinned and stuffed with plastic explosive. A No. 6 primer was also inserted into the body cavity, connected to a pencil time fuse inserted into the middle of the converted creature. The idea was that the dead rat would be placed within or around a pile of boiler coal. One of the workers, eager to be rid of the corpse, would throw it into the fire box, thus triggering an explosion that would destroy the machinery. Apparently about 100 exploding rats were produced (the bodies of the creatures came from a London supplier who had no idea about their purpose) and were moved to occupied France. Unfortunately, the rodent consignment was intercepted by the Germans, but according to SOE reports this fact actually had an 'extraordinary moral effect', producing a hunt for 'hundreds of rats the enemy believed were distributed on the continent'.[22]

We should note in passing that the time pencil detonator was also one of the great secret ordnance inventions of World War II. These slender devices were convenient, concealable means for controlling the detonation of explosives with specific time delays, ranging from a few minutes to 24 hours or more. They worked on chemical principles, the user initiating the mix of a corrosive chemical compound that over a controlled period of time ate through a restraining wire holding back a spring-loaded striker. When the wire broke at the set time, the striker was released, hitting a percussion cap, which in turn initiated the detonator attached to the explosives. The British led the way in time pencil design, albeit drawing on some earlier Polish models, but other versions were developed by industrial chemist and Harvard professor Stanley Lovell for OSS use.

The 'coal bomb' worked on similar principles to the exploding rats but was far more plausible. The core idea was to create explosive pieces of coal and place them among the regular coal waiting to the fed into a boiler furnace. All being well, the explosive would be shovelled into the flames, where it would eventually detonate. It was not an original concept. Back in the American Civil War (1861–5), Captain Thomas Edgeworth Courtenay of the Confederate Secret Service invented a weapon called the 'coal torpedo' for attacking Union steamships. It was a lump of iron, roughly cast with the contours of a piece of coal. A hollow internal cavity was filled with a gunpowder charge, the filling aperture sealed with a threaded plug. Then the whole item was covered in beeswax and rolled in coal dust for disguise. The extent of their operational use and their effectiveness is unclear, but they are credited with damaging or even destroying several Union vessels.

The SOE coal bomb was essentially a modern reworking of the idea, and several design approaches were taken. In 1940, SOE began producing a coal boring device, a tool for creating a hollow cavity in a real piece of coal without (hopefully) fracturing the coal into smaller pieces. The cavity could then be filled with plastic explosive, fitted with a detonator, and the handiwork disguised with coal dust. This was fiddly and time-consuming work, so a new solution was found – one that involved a pre-moulded fake piece of coal made from dyed Herculite plaster, coated with coal dust for disguise. The device even came with a kit of paints and brushes, so that the operator could touch up the bomb's appearance with the colour and texture of local coal.

The next step in the design evolution was to make the weapon more convenient to use. The modified variant was described in the SOE's own Descriptive Catalogue of Special Devices and Supplies:

A hollow cast of a piece of coal is made in two sections. The interior is filled with plastic explosive, in a 1 oz. Primer, Field, is set. The two sections are then clamped together and the join sealed. The coal is finished off with a coating of black shellac which is garnished with coal dust. A length of dowelling keeps the passage to the Primer clear until the insertion of the initiation unit. Initiation is by means of a match headed safety fuse to which a No. 27 Detonator is crimped, or by means of a length of safety fuse with a No. 27 Detonator crimped on one end and a Copper Tube Igniter crimped on the other end. The match end is dusted over with coal dust prior to operational use.[23]

Later, SOE improved again on the design by creating the bomb casing in one-piece metal (which removed the visible seam) and then disguising it by wrapping it in plaster, which was then coloured up to resemble coal.

As outlandish as the coal bomb sounds on first encounter, there was definite logic behind both its design and its purpose. Indeed, coal bombs had wide international appeal. OSS developed a form of coal bomb created by casting Pentolite high-explosive directly into coal shapes, reinforcing the object with a coating of tough scrim fabric coated with black enamel. There is evidence that some of these devices were used against locomotives, barges and ships in Yugoslavia, Germany and China. The German Abwehr produced their own types of coal bomb for operational use. Between 12 and 17 June 1942, the Abwehr II sabotage section launched Operation *Pastorius*, in which eight German agents were landed, via U-boat, on the coasts of New York and Florida. All were exposed soon after their deployment, and subsequent searches of their safe houses revealed German-produced coal bombs and detonators. Apparently, the mission objective was to place the bombs into the coal cars of US locomotives, with the intention of damaging US industrial facilities.[24] The Abwehr also issued coal bombs to the British-turned double agent Edward Arnold Chapman – aka 'Agent Zigzag' – with the intention of sabotaging the British merchant ship *City of Lancaster* in March 1943. With Chapman's compliance, the bombs were 'discovered' by a British search party.

INCENDIARY DEVICES

Turning back to the OSS catalogue, we see an even wider range of possibilities for the design of secret explosive devices, particularly at a miniature scale. A special focus was given to incendiary devices. Starting a fire involved less drama and collateral damage than a bomb going off, plus it might be blamed on innocent accidental causes rather than deliberate sabotage, restraining the punitive backlash from the occupiers. For example, the 'Incendiary Packet' was a 'pocket-size, olive drab metal box' containing three cartons of chemicals: powdered potassium chlorate, powdered sugar and a slender ampule of sulphuric acid, consisting of an outer plastic casing around a thin glass container holding the acid. The Incendiary Packet was designed to start fires 'where it has combustible materials to kindle', such as 'woodwork, upholstery, draperies and furniture in offices and dwellings'. To use the device, the operator would mix equal amounts of the potassium chlorate and the sugar, then crush two or more of the sulphuric acid ampules and insert them into the mixture. The action of crushing the ampule released the acid from the fractured glass container, and then over the course of one to four hours (different time delays were available) the acid would eat through the plastic and eventually ignite the powder mixture.

A more aggressive form of incendiary device was the 'Small Thermit Well'. This was designed specifically for the destruction of heavy machinery. Its appearance was innocuous: a simple 'pasteboard box' on the outside, roughly the size of a grocery packet or lubricant can. Inside, however, it contained a ceramic liner holding a thermite mixture. Thermite was a ferocious incendiary composition of metal powder and metal oxide, which could burn with a temperature of around 2,700 °C (5,000 °F), enough to cut through steel casings and warp, melt or fuse moving parts such as 'gears, pistons, bearings and shafts'. The OSS catalogue was liberal in the application of the device: 'It is easily concealed and installed. This Small Well has unlimited uses in factories, power houses, machine shops, or on vehicles. It can destroy transformers, electric motors, lathes, engines, differentials and transmissions.' A Large Thermit Well was also developed for more ambitious targets.

SPECIAL PURPOSES

The coal bomb and Small Thermit Well illustrate how explosive secret weapons were often designed for a narrow band of missions. The OSS catalogue abounds in such special-purpose weaponry. There was the 'Mole', for example, which was 'designed for the special purpose of derailing and destroying an enemy railroad train after it enters a tunnel'. It was a sophisticated piece of kit, essentially a photoelectric detonator mechanism, featuring a light-sensitive photo cell and magnets for attaching to a metal surface. The Mole would trigger an attached explosive charge with 'the sudden and complete shutting off of all light to the photo cell', such as would occur when a train went into a dark tunnel. (The device was calibrated so that subtle or slowly graded changes in light levels, such as light flickering through trees or the change from daylight to night-time, would not initiate the detonation sequence.) The intention was for the device to be installed covertly against the axles or wheels of locomotives or railroad cars. A delay of 5–10 seconds after the Mole device entered the tunnel ensured that the explosive derailment of the train car would occur deep inside the tunnel, augmenting the chaos.

When it came to destroying aircraft, the OSS field operator could of course use basic methods of military vandalism – shooting up the airframe or blowing up the engines with grenades or standard demolition charges – but for more scheming destruction there was the 'Anerometer'. Measuring 152 mm (6 in) by 38 mm (1.5 in) in diameter, the Anerometer consisted of a triggering mechanism sensitive to atmospheric pressure, connected to a booster charge, which was in turn linked to a flexible container designed to hold a charge of plastic explosive. Typically, the charge would weigh 0.45 kg (1 lb). It was advised that the device be installed into a wing or the tail assembly of the target aircraft. Once the device was armed, it would automatically explode at an altitude of $c.457$ m (1,500 ft), the explosive charge being 'sufficient to destroy a wing or tail assembly on a large heavy craft, and to cause medium and light craft to disintegrate completely in mid-air'. Given their operational characteristics, Anerometers were ideal for targeted assassination attempts against high-value personnel using aircraft, although there appear to be few details of operational use.

The sheer variety of clandestine explosive devices developed during World War II is sufficient to have warranted thick catalogues for their

Chapter 2

listing. The OSS and SOE catalogues alone include pressure-activated devices for blowing train tracks, incendiary suitcases, devices for setting fire to oil slicks on water, palm-sized fuel tank bombs, and the 'Caccolube', a 'small thin-rubber sac (prophylactic sheath), containing a gritty chemical compound that damages and destroys any type of internal combustion engine' (once slipped into the oil intake). We bring our reflection on secret explosive weapons to a conclusion with a special British type, the No. 82 Grenade, better known as the 'Gammon Bomb' after its inventor, Captain R.S. 'Jock' Gammon of the 1st Parachute Battalion, Parachute Regiment.

The Gammon Bomb was an intended replacement for an earlier British weapon, the Grenade, Hand, Anti-Tank No. 74, which also went by the name 'Sticky Bomb'. It was designed in 1940 by the Ministry of Defence 1 (MD1), a division of MI(R). In our story of secret weapons, MD1 is important. It was formed in early 1939 as a group purposed to design weapons for irregular warfare, headed by a Major Millis Jefferis. In 1940 it came under the direct authority of the Minister of Defence, Winston Churchill; Churchill actually created this post and became its first office-holder in May 1940, at the same time as he became prime minister. For this reason, MD1 garnered the nickname 'Churchill's toyshop'. It was initially based at 35 Portland Place, London, but during the Blitz moved out to the village of Whitchurch in Buckinghamshire, operating out of a mansion house called 'The Firs'.

During the war years, MD1 showed a lively aptitude for military inventions. The Sticky Bomb was designed as an infantry-launched anti-armour weapon. It was essentially a glass-sphere hand grenade covered in stockinette fabric and then slathered in birdlime adhesive, to make the device supremely glutinous. (The sticky outer face of the grenade was shielded until use by a split spherical sheet-metal casing.) The theory was that the grenade would be thrown or smashed against the side of an enemy AFV, the weapon's adhesive qualities meaning

No. 74 'Sticky Bombs' are assembled somewhere in Britain in 1943. The worker is assembling the protective cover that would enclose the adhesive-coated bomb until it was ready for use. Credit: IWM/Getty Images

that it stuck to the vehicle and detonated in direct contact with the armour plate, making it more destructively effective.

The No. 74 was produced and distributed at scale (about 2.5 million were manufactured between 1940 and 1943), and it would prove effective in combat. Its users included the FSSF and the French Resistance. But it also had its problems. When the casing was removed, the bomb could just as easily stick to its users as to the enemy tank. (There is an account of a Home Guard soldier getting a primed Sticky Bomb glued to his trousers, only being saved by a quick-thinking comrade who pulled off the trousers and threw the sticky bundle to a distance, where it safely detonated.[25]) Often it failed to stick on the target, especially if the vehicle was muddy or dusty. Tactically, it required high-risk manoeuvres, such as running headlong at an enemy tank.

The Gammon Bomb was an attempt at improving on this device. It had an ingenious design. The main body of the grenade was actually an elasticized stockinette bag. This was delivered empty; it was up to the user to fill it with the amount of plastic explosive required: smaller amounts for close-in anti-personnel work; larger amounts for anti-armour attacks from behind cover. The maximum weight of explosive it could hold was 0.9 kg (1.98 lb), and users could also include pieces of metal, small stones or ball bearings to add a shrapnel or fragmentation effect. The neck of the bag was capped with a fuse mechanism. When the bomb was intended to be used, the operator unscrewed and removed a protective cap from the fuse. This revealed a length of linen tape connected to the fuse, the tape having a section of lead weight attached to one end. As the user threw the grenade at the target, the inertia of the lead weight pulled the tape from the fuse, releasing a safety pin and activating an impact mechanism. The striker within the fuse was now held by only a weak creep spring, with a heavy ball bearing on top of the striker. When the grenade hit the target, the resulting impact would jolt the ball bearing, and this shock would overcome the creep spring retention, releasing the striker to hit a percussion cap, which in turn would initiate a detonator that triggered the explosion instantaneously.

Gammon Bombs were another fine example of the innovation within the secret weapon industry. While regular British infantry relied on the standard No. 36 'Mills bomb' hand grenade, the Gammon Bombs were manufactured in far smaller numbers, hence were issued primarily to paratroopers and to special forces from 1943. Known as 'hand artillery' to such troops, they could be highly effective if deployed correctly. They were most productively applied against German armour during the Battle of Normandy in 1944, where the close urban and bocage terrain allowed cover and concealment on the approach to enemy armoured vehicles.

In hand-deployed weapons alone, the ingenuity of engineers and designers during World War II was exceptional. But as we shall see, there is a fine line between something being innovative and being practically useless. It was the 19th-century Prussian field marshal Helmuth von Moltke who imparted the wisdom that 'No plan of operations reaches with any certainty beyond the first encounter with the enemy's main force', often shortened to 'No plan survives first contact with the enemy.'[26] As we shall see, the same perspective can often be applied to secret weapons.

Chapter 3

Mice and Monsters – Armour and Anti-Armour Weapons

***

In World War I, battlefield armour was largely peripheral, scarce and novel when seen in the context of the whole conflict. In World War II, armour was central, abundant and advanced. Operating alongside motorized and mechanized infantry, armoured fighting vehicles (AFVs) were often the pointed tip of the spear in land warfare, providing a unique tactical package of powerful and accurate firepower, cross-country mobility and heavy armour in one ground-shaking unit.

Japan is somewhat the exception to our story of armoured warfare. It invested poorly in AFV design beyond light and medium tanks and tankettes, and even those it did produce were regarded as little more than adjuncts to infantry formations. Between the rest of the combatants, by contrast, a tank vs tank and tank vs anti-tank arms race raged and did not stop until the end of hostilities. We see two quite different philosophies at play. The Germans, by and large, had an armour-clad martial psychology. Tanks were central to the new German doctrines of manoeuvre warfare, and the country's advanced industry was well-placed to design, develop and manufacture high-quality vehicles. Consequently, the Germans came to have excellent tanks and equally excellent crews. Its well-documented

Chapter 3

problem, however, was the over-proliferation of advanced AFV types. Too little central co-ordination, lots of scattered funding and plenty of competing engineering talent resulted in individual vehicles that often outclassed the enemy's, but weren't produced in sufficient numbers or, worse still, created an unmanageable and wasteful maintenance and spare parts supply situation.

The Allies, by contrast, sought to ensure that their armies had the best tanks their engineers could design, but also that the front-line units had a choice few AFV types distributed as widely as possible. Thus the Soviets, British and Americans developed workaday tanks en masse, the armoured battlefield being a clash of philosophies as much as technologies.

So where in this picture was the opportunity for innovation, for the secret AFV projects' equivalent to the development of jet fighters or V-weapons? The fundamental proposition of the tank was, by 1940 at least, well established – it was a tracked vehicle with a turreted gun and heavy sloped armour. That proposition, notwithstanding the development of turretless tank-destroyers (which were in essence budget tanks), changed little throughout the war, thus many of the new types were incremental improvements over what had gone previously. There were examples, however, when the engineers explored altogether more ambitious propositions.

GERMAN SUPERTANKS

The armoured war began to slip from Germany's grasp in 1943–4. The German AFVs and their crews were still killing enemy tanks in great numbers. At the Battle of Kursk – the greatest armour engagement in history, fought in July–August 1943 – the Germans destroyed approximately 2,471 Soviet AFVs; in return the Germans lost about 1,536 tanks and self-propelled assault guns.[27] But the blunt fact was that the Soviets could endure even this scale of loss and return to the fight, whereas the German armoured force was progressively being depleted below production or fielding rate. (For example, in August 1943, the Germans had 2,555 AFVs on the Eastern Front, while the Soviets had 6,200. In June 1944, those ratios were even more skewed: the Germans had 4,470 while the Soviets had 11,600.[28]) For all their technological sophistication, the excellent German armour remained vulnerable to the many barrels of T-34 medium tanks and KV-1 heavy tanks.

In response, Hitler became increasingly drawn to the idea of what we might call the 'supertank'. The supertank was a vehicle that would take a tank's size, firepower and armoured protection to absolute extremes. These battlefield monsters would be invulnerable to enemy fire, regardless of calibre, and their guns would open up any armoured opponent or fortification like a cheap tin can. Our understanding of Hitler's psychology suggests why the supertank principle was appealing. Much like his rocket-powered *Vergeltungswaffen* ('vengeance weapons'), the supertanks would take his belief in German invincibility and build it a physical weapon, the apotheosis of total war.

By 1943 and 1944, Germany was already fielding some big armoured beasts. The most famous of these was the PzKpfw VI Ausf E Tiger I, which went into service in late 1942. It weighed 55 tonnes (54.1 long tons), much of that weight accounted for by armour that, in places, was up to 110 mm (4.3 in) thick. It was powered by a 522 kW (700 hp) Maybach HL 230 P-45 12-cylinder petrol engine and was armed with a superior 8.8 cm (3.46 in) KwK L/56 gun. The Tiger I was slow and it suffered from frequent mechanical problems, but its survivability and lethality meant it was a bogeyman in the minds of Allied tank crews. Furthermore, it provided the platform for an extended range of heavy tanks. The fearsome PzKpfw VI Ausf E Tiger II took the total weight up to 69.7 tonnes (68.6 tons) and had the even more potent 88 mm (3.46 in) KwK 43 L/71 gun. There were also two behemoth tank-destroyer variants, the Panzerjäger Tiger (P) SdKfz 184 *Ferdinand/Elefant*, at 65 tonnes (64 tons) and, the greatest of them all, the Panzerjäger Tiger Ausf B *Jagdtiger* ('Hunting Tiger'), a casemated tank that tipped the scales at 70.6 tonnes (69.5 tons). The latter was the heaviest AFV fielded in World War II, but

Chapter 3

its great size limited its reliability, production numbers and tactical versatility. This illustrative lesson didn't remove the idea of the supertank from the drawing board.

One of the earliest iterations of a titanic, omnipotent AFV began in the 1930s. Engineer Edward Grote was at the time an employee of Rheinmetall, working in the Soviet Union to develop a new heavy tank. While there, he also played with the concept of the *Festungs Panzer* ('fortress tank'), an outsized tank with demolishing firepower and clad in impenetrable armour. Nothing went further, and details about the precise design vision are sketchy, but Grote took the bare idea back to Germany in the late 1930s.

It would re-emerge in 1942, but this time on an altogether greater scale. On 23 June 1942, Grote (by this time serving as a performance testing expert within the OKM) submitted to Hitler a proposal for a *Landkreuzer* ('land cruiser'). The titular fusion between land warfare and naval warfare was intentional. Grote proposed creating a vast armoured vehicle weighing approximately 1,000 tonnes (984 tons), crewed by up to 60 personnel. Firepower would come from twin full-bore naval guns – the type of firepower only seen otherwise on battleships. Multiple powerplants would be required to grind it forward on its enormous tracks.

Remarkably, Hitler actually gave permission for the idea to be taken further, despite the fact that most engineers and tacticians saw it as a complete non-starter. The Krupp concern drew up design blueprints for the Landkreuzer P1000 *Ratte* ('Rat'). Its 1,000-tonne (984-ton) weight reflected its absurd ambition. It was armed with a turret bearing two 280 mm (11 in) SK C/34 L/54.4 guns, the same type found on the *Scharnhorst*-class battle cruisers, plus at the rear another turret for a 128 mm (5 in) PaK 44 anti-tank gun. There were multiple secondary weapons, including machine guns and anti-aircraft cannon. At its thickest, the armour would be 250 mm (9.5 in). Moving this dead weight would be the responsibility of either two MAN V12Z32/44 24-cylinder marine diesels or eight Daimler-Benz MB 501 20-cylinder marine diesel engines; total power output required to grind the tank along would be 12,000 kW (16,000 hp).

The P1000 *Ratte* seems absurd now, and to many back then. Its crushing weight meant that it would be unsuitable to travel across many of the Earth's surfaces; using bridges of any description was definitely out. A recognition of this fact was that the *Ratte* was designed to be able to cross deep rivers almost fully submerged, using a snorkel apparatus for air supply. Furthermore, level heads saw that the sheer size of the vehicle – 35 m (114 ft 10 in) long and 14 m (45 ft 11 in) wide – would make it the juiciest of slow-moving targets for Allied air power, which could, with persistence and heavy bombs, destroy it.

Albert Speer cancelled the *Ratte* project in January 1943, before it made it to approval and, God forbid, production. We should add there was another Krupp proposal for an even larger vehicle, the unapologetically named Landkreuzer P1500 *Monster,* weighing approximately 2,500 tonnes (2,460.5 tons) and armed with the 800 mm (31.5 in) Dora/Schwerer Gustav K (E) railway gun, plus assorted howitzers and cannon. It is hard to see why this might be considered a reasonable idea; Speer shut it down by the spring of 1943.

The P-series tanks remained implausible visions, but other supertank ideas gained some traction. In the autumn of 1941, the indefatigably inventive Krupp and Wa Prüf 6 (the Waffenamt department responsible for the development and testing of armoured and motorized vehicles) began the process of designing what would become the PzKpfw VII *Löwe* ('Lion'), initially known as tank project VK 70.01. The purpose was to create an AFV capable of slugging it out with the heavyweight Soviet KV-1 and KV-2 tanks. The design specification was for a tank that could weigh a maximum of 90 tonnes (89 tons) and had frontal armour up to 140 mm (5.5 in) thick, with a correspondingly heavy gun fitted. Krupp designed a 'light' version at 77.2 tonnes (76 tons) and a heavy version at the ceiling weight, both equipped with a 105 mm (4.1

Chapter 3

Adolf Hitler, accompanied by Ferdinand Porsche, makes an inspection of one of the prototype Maus *tanks in the summer of 1943. Credit: Ullstein bild Dtl./ Getty*

in) L/70 gun. Hitler's subsequent feedback, however, led to the heavy version becoming the sole design focus, its weapon now the 150 mm (5.9 in) KwK 44 L/38.

Many different variations of the *Löwe* were proposed during the first half of 1942, the main wrestling points being the armament and the powerplant. But in July 1942, the whole project was cancelled, principally because there was a bullish new design in town, the PzKpfw VIII *Maus* ('Mouse'). Today we tend to associate the Porsche brand name with luxurious sports cars, but during the 1930s and '40s Ferdinand Porsche's company was heavily involved in weapons R&D. In March 1942, Porsche was commissioned to design a heavy tank weighing a magisterial and rounded 100 tonnes (98.4 tons). The design was designated the VK.100.01, which mutated into the Porsche Type 205. While the 100-tonne specification might seem an upper limit, as 1942 progressed discussions between Porsche, Speer and Hitler raised the bar. The first design to emerge, in June 1942, was therefore for a 120-tonne (118-ton) vehicle. This was already looking outlandish, but with Hitler's endorsement and interventions the project specifications just kept on growing. With progressive irony, the tank was at first called the *Mammut* ('Mammoth'), then from December 1942 it became the *Mäuschen* ('Little Mouse'), and finally settled on *Maus* ('Mouse') in February 1943.

The final *Maus* had a designed empty weight of 152.4 tonnes (150 tons). Add fuel, ammunition and a crew, plus further technical additions, and the weight climbed to about 188 tonnes (185 tons). Firepower was now a 128 mm (5 in) KwK 44 L/55 gun with a coaxial 75 mm (3 in) KwK 44 L/36.5 (this was Hitler's personal preferred configuration), with the prospect of upgrading the main weapon to a 150 mm (5.9 in) KwK 44 L/48 or even a 170 mm (6.7 in) KwK 44. Giant innovations abounded. The powerplant was to be an 894 kW (1,200 hp) Daimler-Benz MB 517 diesel engine, which provided power to an electric-drive system. Armour was to be 220 mm (8.7 in) on the turret front. Like the *Ratte*, the *Maus* would have with a snorkel system for submerged river crossings.

Beyond the design stages, the *Maus* had a strange evolution. The HWA approved the vehicle for production in May 1943, then did an about turn the following October and cancelled the programme, but while allowing the advance of six prototypes. The first two were designated V1 and V2. V1 was fitted with a dummy turret only, and tested an MB 509 engine in the petrol-electric drive configuration. V2, completed in June 1944, had a fully functioning turret with the KwK 44 L/55 and KwK 44 L/36.5 combination, plus the MB 517 diesel-electric drive. In trials, maximum speed was just 20 km/h (12 mph).

The *Maus* project, with only two prototypes completed, simply ran out of war to be pursued any further. It seems unlikely that it was destined for operations anyway. Its immense weight made it supremely impractical from logistical and operational points of view. Observers recounted how if it moved down a street water pipes were split open, windows broken and the road surface torn up. (In balance, drivers reported that its electric-drive system made it smooth and easy to drive.) Even with its heavy firepower, its slow speed would almost certainly lead to it being outmanoeuvred and eventually destroyed. Soviet forces seized the prototypes in April 1945. The Germans had attempted to destroy the vehicles, but in testament to the vehicles' armoured resilience they were not entirely successful – the Soviets managed to take the prototype back home and construct a running composite vehicle, which now sits in Kubinka Tank Museum in Moscow Oblast.

The German love affair with supertanks took several other forms. There was, for example, the E-100 (Gerät 383) design, a super-heavy tank weighing an estimated 140 tonnes (137.8 tons) and armed similarly to the *Maus*. In was to be the heaviest vehicle in the *Entwicklung* (E) series of vehicles, an attempt by the Wa Prüf 6 to rationalize all then current German AFVs into six core classes of vehicle. The broader project failed to get off the ground and the *furthest* the E100 got was a prototype chassis. The German supertanks were intriguing and inventive, but scarcely practical given the war conditions.

ALLIED SUPERTANKS

The Allies largely, and sensibly, turned their backs on the concept of the supertank. During the 1930s, the Soviets were influenced by Grote's extreme visions of armour, resulting in a set of construction drawings for the T-42 super-heavy tank. This would have weighed 101.6 tonnes (100 tons) and had five gun turrets mounting weapons of various calibres. It was so long it looked like a cross between a tank and a set of railway carriages. It did not get past the artwork stage. During the war, the heaviest of the Soviet production tanks, weighing in at 52 tonnes (51 tons), was the KV-2, a profoundly boxy and top-heavy tank with an M-10 152 mm (6 in) howitzer. It was a failure and few were manufactured. (Some of the choice descriptors used by modern commentators on the KV-2 include 'exceptionally dumb', 'cursed by design' and 'Stalin's fridge'.)

The British had some experimental heavy tank designs on the go between 1943 and 1945. The Tank, Infantry, Black Prince (A43), for example, was basically a Churchill Mk VII tank fitted with a powerful QF 17-pounder gun, an installation that required an enlarged turret. The extra weight of gun and turret took the vehicle up to 51 tonnes (50 tons) – reasonable by supertank standards, but still too heavy for the Churchill's 261 kW (350 hp) Bedford 12-cylinder engine. Maximum speed was an almost literally pedestrian 17.7 km/h (11 mph), and the vehicle was also difficult to drive. Several unimpressive prototypes emerged, but the tank's rationale was stolen by the excellent Sherman Firefly, which also had a 17-pounder gun, and the development of the Centurion tank, which had better armour and performance.

The British gave some consideration to what were called 'assault tanks'. These were heavy AFVs designed for attacking fortified defences, a tactical challenge that became increasingly relevant as the Allies conducted more expeditionary campaigns from 1942. A series of vehicles worth a mention is the Assault [also Armoured] Vehicle Royal Engineers (AVRE). These were a broad spectrum of types developed specifically to provide combat engineering solutions in support of assault operations, particularly amphibious landings and attacks on fixed enemy defences. AVREs consisted of an armoured chassis, typically that of a Churchill Mk III or IV, but fitted with all manner of ingenious weapons or contraptions instead of a standard turret. Examples of the functions included: the 'Fascine', a bundle of wooden poles or brushwood dropped into a ditch to facilitate crossing; the 'Bobbin', a reel of steel-reinforced canvas sheet, 3 m (10 ft) wide, unrolled on the ground to form a stable passage across soft terrain; and the 'Small Box Girder Bridge', an assault bridge that could be extended to cross a 9.1 m (30 ft) gap. (The list is not exhaustive.) Weaponized AVREs included the 'Goat', 'Carrot' and 'Onion' vehicles, which via an extendable frame could place demolition charges

Chapter 3

The Sherman DD ('Duplex Drive') tank converted an M4 Sherman into an amphibious vehicle by adding a canvas flotation screen (seen raised here) and fitting a propeller drive. It was used, not entirely convincingly, in support of the D-Day landings in Normandy in June 1944. Credit: Morio/CC BY-SA 4.0

on enemy strongpoints, then retreat before detonating them. It also included a vehicle fitted with a 230 mm (9 in) petard spigot mortar, which launched an enormous 'flying dustbin' explosive charge well suited to destroying strongpoints.

The AVREs came to be part of the suite of innovative vehicles known as 'Hobart's Funnies', named after Major-General Sir Percy Cleghorn Stanley Hobart, the commander of the 79th Armoured Division and the man made responsible for specialist vehicle development to support the *Overlord* landings in Normandy. They included legendary vehicles such as the problematic Sherman DD amphibious tanks, many of which floundered off the shores of Normandy on 6 June 1944, and the Churchill Crocodile, a terrifying flame-throwing variant of the tank.

Another notable armoured vehicle intended for service with Hobart's division was the Tortoise heavy assault tank (A39), developed in 1943–4 by Nuffield Mechanisation & Aero Ltd. The intention behind the Tortoise was to create an AFV for assaulting resilient German defences, such as the Siegfried Line. The tank needed deep armour to shrug off incoming fire and a big gun to blow apart the fortifications. The Tortoise emerged as one of the heaviest tanks ever made by the British, weighing 79 tonnes (78 tons) and with armour up to 225 mm (8.9 in) deep. It was driven by a Rolls-Royce Meteor V12 petrol engine generating 480 kW (650 hp). This was a powerful unit, but the Tortoise – true to its name – had a trundling top speed of 20 km/h (12 mph). It did have an excellent gun though, the Ordnance QF 32-pounder. Production vehicles were ordered in 1944, but the wheels turned slowly (pun intended) and by war's end only six prototypes were in existence. The immense weight and a progressive loss of tactical relevance to other weapon systems meant its destiny was as a fascinating museum piece.

Looking across the Atlantic, one design stands out as approaching the supertank threshold. The T28 super-heavy tank had a similar rationale to the Tortoise, as a fortress-demolition machine, but it was also seen as a tool for killing the latest breeds of German heavy tank. A design was drawn up by March 1945 and it fell to the Pacific Car and Foundry Company to produce the prototypes. Like the Tortoise tank, the T28 did away with a turret in preference for a casemate design; the main gun was a 105 mm (4.1 in) T5E1 gun. The designers did not hold back on dimensions and weight. The T28 measured 11.1 m (36 ft 5 in) long, 4.39 m (14 ft 5 in) wide and 2.84 m (9 ft 4 in) high. Armour depth maxed out at an impressive 305 mm (12 in), which made the largest contribution to the vehicle's total weight – 86 tonnes (85 tons). To cope with that weight, the vehicle actually had four separate track systems.

The T28, therefore, was a real monster. The phrase 'maximum speed' seems almost self-mocking in its context – the tank could do 13 km/h (8 mph) flat out – while its weight brought with it all the associated practical issues in deployment and manoeuvre, not least how it would manage to keep up with the rest of the army. The idea burned out with just two prototypes completed by the end of the war. To this day, the supertank vision has never manifested itself in a practical production vehicle.

KILLING TANKS

While many experiments in armour ran into practical dead ends, the field of anti-tank (AT) warfare, by contrast, established new directions that remain in the field to this day. Most of the combatants began World War II with tanks that had comparatively light armour (at least compared to what was to come) and anti-tank weapons pitched only to defeat such armour. As the war progressed, however, armour became substantially thicker and more intelligently designed in terms of material composition and angle of presentation. (Generally speaking, the practical depth of armour a flat-trajectory shell has to penetrate can be made greater by increasing the armour's angle of slope.) Thus by 1943, say, AT weapons that might have worked in 1939 would now do little more than put a nasty scratch on the outer hull of an AFV. But by this time, new, often secret, solutions were emerging.

Beyond AT mines, there were essentially two different approaches to penetrating armour – shaped-charge warheads and kinetic energy shells. The principle of the shaped-charge warhead had been understood since the late 18th century, although it was only weaponized properly for AT work in the 1930s. A typical shaped-charge warhead has a ballistic cap at the tip, followed by an air cavity. Behind the cavity is a cone-shaped hollow metal liner (typically made of copper), with the larger open end facing towards the target. The outer surface of the liner is surrounded by explosive. When the shell hits the target, the explosives detonate and collapse the liner into a thin hypersonic jet of molten metal particles, of such speed (up to 14 km/9 miles per second) and heat that it can slice through armour with astonishing ease.

The great advantage of the shaped-charge warhead is that is does not rely upon shell velocity at all for penetration: a hand-thrown shaped charge can be as effective as a shaped charge fired from a gun. Shaped charges, therefore, appeared in all manner of weapons during World War II, from conventional tank guns (as High-Explosive Anti-Tank, or HEAT, shells) down to AT hand grenades. Their most influential application, however, was in a whole new generation of man-portable recoilless infantry weapons. The most famous examples of these are the American 'Bazooka' and the German Panzerfaust, but there were many other types. Collectively, these hand-held weapons killed thousands of tanks during the war, cheaply and efficiently. Being short-range weapons, they really came into their own in urban combat; it is estimated that during the city battles for eastern Germany in 1945, about 70 per cent of Soviet tank losses were accounted for by Panzerfaust and the larger Panzerschreck weapons.

Kinetic energy AT weapons, by contrast, rely on firing hard, heavy shot at high velocities, the combined physics of mass, speed and material density punching through the armour barrier. The science behind the kinetic penetration of armour is complex, involving both shell design and gun design, but it was the Germans who made one of the first significant leaps in World War II. This was the taper-bore, or squeeze-bore, gun.

The basic idea was that the barrel of a gun reduced in calibre from breech to muzzle, squeezing down the specially designed shot while maintaining the original gas pressure. The outcome was a much-increased velocity compared to a straight-bore gun. German patents for taper-bore weapons had been filed in both 1903 by Carl Puff and 1932 by Hermann Gerlich (the taper-bore design is sometimes known as the 'Gerlich principle'). The first prominent weapon to utilize taper-bore technology was the 28 mm (1.1 in) schwere Panzerbüsche 41 (s PzB 41; 'Heavy Anti-Tank Rifle'), a diminutive lightweight AT gun with a muzzle velocity of 1,400 m/sec (4,593 ft/sec). Its ammunition had a tungsten penetrator

Chapter 3

core surrounded by a lead sleeve but wrapped in a soft iron alloy that compressed during the transit through the barrel. The resulting penetration was 66 mm (2.6 in) at 500 m (547 yd). The Germans went on to develop several other powerful AT guns using the taper-bore design, such as the 42 mm (1.7 in) Panzerjägerkanone 41 (PaK 41; 'Anti-Tank Gun 41') and the 75 mm (2.95 in) Pak 41. The latter showed where the design could go – it could penetrate 150 mm (5.94 in) of homogeneous armour at 900 m (1,000 yd).

In 1941 the Allies captured an s PzB 41 in the Western Desert, and had their eyes opened to the principle of taper-bore guns; the reason behind the s PzB 41's performance had been successfully kept a secret up to this point. The British, aided by the talented and displaced Czech weapon designer František Janeček, developed their own distinct version of the taper-bore design. Instead of creating a new gun, they produced the 'Littlejohn Adaptor'. This was a tapering smoothbore extension that was attached to the chamber of an existing gun; the extension performed the function of the taper-bore, increasing the muzzle velocity as the shell went into the barrel. Like the German designs, the Littlejohn Adaptor fired a shell that had a tungsten core with a softer, compressible, outer sleeve.

From its service issue in late 1942, the Littlejohn Adaptor was a qualified success. It was first fitted to the QF 2-pounder AT gun and certainly improved velocity and, therefore, penetration. But the 2-pounder was progressively superseded by newer, heavier weapons, and the device found itself mainly attached to small-calibre guns in light armoured cars.

Nevertheless, the Allies began showing an increasing aptitude for AT weapon design, not least because they had to deal with heavily armoured German designs such as the Tiger and the Panther. Another innovation was the 'discarding sabot shot'. Building on pre-war French experiments, engineers at the Research Department, Woolwich Arsenal, began looking at another strategy for improving shell velocity. It involved taking a sub-calibre penetrator and encasing it in a light split jacket, or 'sabot', that filled the bore of the gun. The sabot was designed to fall away from the penetrator just after leaving the muzzle, the unencumbered penetrator now flying on to its target. The principle at work here is that the propellant charge for, say, a 105 mm (4.1 in) gun could be applied to a penetrator of 75 mm (2.95 in) calibre. Artillery specialist Ian Hogg noted the effect of the innovation:

> *By making the shot of tungsten and then shrouding it in a light alloy sabot they [the British designers] were able to step up the velocity obtained from the 6-pounder anti-tank gun from 2600 ft a second to 3500, and the penetration of armour at 1000 yards jumped from 74 mm to 146 mm. They then applied their talents to the 17-pounder and improved the armour penetration from 109 mm to 231 mm at 1000 yards.*[29]

These were astonishing jumps in performance, and from mid-1944 the Germans would be on the receiving end of the new technology, to their cost.

Recoilless weapons was another area of Allied innovation. The majority of guns have a fully closed breech when they are fired, meaning that all the force of the burnt propellant goes forward, pushing the mass of the shell before it. Given that school physics tells us 'for every action there is an equal and opposite reaction', these weapons produce an equivalent rearward force, felt, managed or witnessed as recoil. Recoilless guns, however, provided means by which the rearward recoil could be neutralized by redirecting some of the force forward. The recoilless weapon, therefore, could fire a big shell but with no appreciable movement – that was ideal for a lightweight but powerful AT gun.

The Germans produced several recoilless weapons during the war, led by the design efforts of Rheinmetall-Borsig. Many of these weapons went to airborne forces, who appreciated being able to take their own

Chapter 3

AT firepower with them, despite their role as light infantry. The chosen German technology was to make the base of the cartridge case from a destructible plastic and install a De Laval nozzle (a tube designed to accelerate a fluid or gas) in the breech block. When the gun was fired, the gas both propelled the shell and was vented externally backwards from the gun; the two contrary forces could be balanced to make the weapon recoilless.

It worked, and worked well, expressed in useful weapons such as the 75 mcm (2.95 in) Leichtgeschütz 40 ('Light Gun 40') and larger calibre members of that family. The British, meanwhile took a different path in developing recoilless AT guns. One of the most innovative solutions proceeded from Sir Charles Dennistoun Burney, a man eccentric in both name and personality, who in both world wars exhibited an unstoppable appetite for invention. He privately hit upon a new recoilless principle. The cartridge case was bored through with multiple holes and the case was then wrapped in a thin metallic outer cover. The gun chamber was also pierced, but surrounded by an outer chamber fitted with rearward-facing vent nozzles. When the shell was fired, the pressure inside the case burst through the cover. The gas vented into the chamber and was in turn redirected rearwards through the nozzles. Again, with much fine tuning, the forward and rearward forces could be cancelled out to make the gun recoilless.

Burney's first weapon, the 88 mm (3.45 in) 'Burney gun', looked somewhat akin to a hobbyist's rocket ship with the nose cone cut off. Nevertheless, demonstrators impressed onlookers by firing the weapon comfortably from the shoulder. Two other weapons of larger calibres were intended to complete the series. Burney also added some spice to the idea by creating a 'wallbuster' shell that splattered a large volume of plastic explosive against a concrete wall then detonated it. The resulting shockwaves were so powerful that, in a trial in September 1943, a 183 mm (7.2 in), 63 kg (139 lb) shell was fired at a section of ferro-concrete wall some 1.5 m (5 ft) thick and cut a substantial hole through it without trouble.[30] In time, this type of shell would become known as High-Explosive Squash Head (HESH), which was as effective applied to AFVs as it was to reinforced walls, and thus became a standard Cold War munition.

The Burney gun did not enter service in World War II, owing to problems of breech erosion from the hot gases. All recoilless guns suffered from one common problem, furthermore; the rearward jet blast was not only dangerous to bystanders for many metres from the nozzles, but it also kicked up considerable dust and debris, which provided the enemy with a useful visual locator of the gun team's position. Nevertheless, Burney's innovations would inform practical and successful post-war designs.

The engineers and designers of the United States also explored the recoilless principle and took some of their products into combat before war's end. Between October 1943 and April 1944, the Artillery Section of the Research and Development Service produced the 105 mm (4.1 in) T9 Recoilless Howitzer. It used the same basic operating method as described for the German weapons. But owing to the gas erosion problem, the next US recoilless weapons – the 57 mm T15 RCL [Recoilless] Rifle and the 75 mm (2.95 in) M20 RCL Rifle – applied the Burney design. Both of these weapons proved that recoilless rifles had a secure future in US armed forces (at least until the advent of effective guided missiles). They were deployed to the European and Pacific theatres in 1945, where they delivered precision fire out to 4,572 m (5,000 yd) and 6,400 m (7,000 yd) respectively.

The innovations in AT weaponry during World War II pointed to developments of the Cold War era. Although tanks remained primary killers of other tanks, steadily the bigger threat to armour came from smaller, infantry-operated or vehicle-mounted missiles. As proof of this reality, we need only consider the evisceration of Russia's armoured fleet during the recent conflict in Ukraine.

Chapter 4

Salamanders and Grass Snakes – German and Japanese Secret Aircraft

***

The history of experimental aviation during World War II is certainly one capable of filling an entire volume of its own, and a hefty one at that. It was a war of astonishing advances in monoplane aircraft design, aviation engineers not only perfecting the principles and applications of propeller-driven combat aircraft but also introducing the first generations of jet and rocket aircraft. Some of these played around the edges of the speed of sound, hinting at the dawn of supersonic flight.

Because of the scale of this topic, even when narrowed under the rubric of 'secret weapons', I shall be necessarily selective. My focus will lean heavily towards German secret aircraft projects, although not exclusively so. This is not because the Allies were slouches when it came to aeronautical innovation; far from it. It is rather because Germany's aircraft engineers pushed the envelope to greater extremes, the diversity of solutions reflecting their desperation in the air war. Some of these designs led to nothing more than a couple of ambitious prototypes. Others, however, went into action and changed the face of aerial combat.

Chapter 4

GERMAN JET AND ROCKET FIGHTERS

We tend to associate the German jet and rocket programmes with the final two years of the war, when Germany engaged in its last frantic efforts to meet and reverse the Allied strategic bomber offensive. In reality, many of the Luftwaffe's experiments with jet and rocket propulsion began back in the late 1930s or early 1940s, and were either aborted or remained as prototypes, or were resurrected in 1944 to 1945. Regardless of the status of each aircraft, however, the German engineers embraced unrestricted innovation in terms of design and aeronautical performance. Some the aircraft that emerged were little short of absurd. Others were reckless, but promising. Others were the next steps in the evolution of military aircraft.

Germany takes the honour of developing the first aircraft to fly solely using turbojet power. This was the Heinkel He 178, which as a single prototype first flew on 27 August 1939. The journey began back in 1936, when powerplant engineer Dr Hans Pabst von Ohain began R&D on an aviation gas turbine for the Heinkel company. After several failed efforts to use hydrogen as an energy source, Ohain graduated to a more stable and freely available diesel fuel and produced the HeS 3b centrifugal-flow engine for a new aircraft, the He 178.

Seen in the context of the times, the He 178 had something of the spacecraft about its appearance. It had high shoulder-mounted wooden wings attached to an all-metal semi-monocoque fuselage. (For reference, a monocoque fuselage uses the aircraft skin to hold the skeleton frame together, while a semi-monocoque design has both the skin and the frame working together as load-bearing elements.) The heart of the aircraft was the HeS 3b turbojet, which generated 500 kg (1,102 lb) of thrust. With the air intake in the nose and the exhaust in the tail, the He 178 had a sleek look. Its performance, with later improved engine types, included a maximum speed of 598 km/h (372 mph). Actually, this was scarcely more than early model Spitfires, and the He 178 had a tremendously limited range of just 200 km (120 miles). But these were the early days of jet exploration, and they slowly awakened the German military authorities to the possibilities they offered.

World War II began just days after the first flight of the He 178, and the aircraft remained purely experimental. Heinkel's order book was consumed by production of conventional aircraft, not least the He 111 medium bomber, but its engineers also took time out to design the first purpose-built jet fighter, the He 280. This aircraft took a fresh design direction compared to the He 178. It swapped the single fuselage-mounted powerplant for two wing-mounted turbojets. It also had a tricycle landing gear and twin fins/rudders. Despite the latter, its overall appearance hinted at the future Me 262.

Nine prototypes of the He 280 were built, with the first flight on 2 August 1941. The first of the prototypes was the He 280 V1, powered by two HeS 8 engines each generating 700 kg (1,543 lb) of thrust. Subsequent prototypes experimented with different powerplants and armament arrangements, the weaponry progressing from three nose-mounted 20 mm (0.79 in) MG 151 cannon up to six of the same in later designs. The aircraft was fleet of foot: it achieved top speeds of 900 km/h (559 mph). But it also suffered from problems with handling and structural weaknesses, and administratively it was pushing uphill against a lack of enthusiasm from General Ernst Udet, the Luftwaffe's Chief of Procurement and Supply. Collectively, these problems led to the He 280 being abandoned in favour of the Me 262.

JET THOROUGHBRED – THE ME 262

The Messerschmitt Me 262 remains the most iconic German jet aircraft of World War II, principally because it saw active combat service and thus demonstrated its vices and virtues in the theatre of war. With *c.*1,400 of the type built, furthermore, it managed to advance well beyond the prototype – the stage where so many of the German designs ground to a halt.

Chapter 4

The aircraft had a particularly protracted design and development journey. Initial design work began back in 1938, but the wheels turned slowly: the first prototype did not fly until 18 July 1942. Even then, the Me 262 was not actually introduced into service until April 1944, German panic expediting the production process. Part of the reason for the Me 262's slow progress was Hitler's personal interference. He believed that it should be developed as a fast bomber rather than a fighter, penetrating British air defences at speed to deliver reprisal raids across the Channel and the North Sea. By the end of 1943, this distraction for the designers ceased to be an option to explore – the Me 262 was needed to fight the Allied bomber onslaught – and the block was removed.

The Me 262 gained influential supporters. In April 1943, the lauded German fighter ace General der Jagdflieger Adolf Galland, head of the Luftwaffe's fighter arm, personally tested an Me 262 and was ebullient about its performance. In a famous reference in a 1944 report, Galland stated that:

In the last four months [January–April 1944] our day fighters have lost 1,000 pilots [...] we are numerically inferior and will always remain so [...] I believe that a great deal can be achieved with a small number of technically and far superior aircraft such as the [Me] 262 and [Me] 163 [...] I would at this moment rather have one Me 262 in action rather than five Bf 109s. I used to say three 109s, but the situation develops and changes.[31]

Galland's desire for more Me 262s was fulfilled, but to a limited extent. The first production model, the Me 262A-1a *Schwalbe* ('Swallow') went operational in April 1944. In core performance, nothing on the Allied side could touch it. Its two Junkers Jumo engines propelled it to a maximum speed of 870 km/h (541 mph).[32] By way of comparison, a P-51D Mustang's maximum speed was about 703 km/h (437 mph). It had an endurance of up to 90 minutes with external fuel tanks, which

The Messerschmitt Me 262 was unable to turn the tide of German air defence in the last years of the war, but it demonstrated the viability of operational fighter-jets, with a performance that outclassed its propeller-driven enemies. Credit: Bettman/Getty

wouldn't have been enough for long-ranging operations but gave it sufficient loiter and combat time over German airspace. Its core armament was four MK 108 30 mm (1.18 in) cannon in the nose, but subsequent variants of the aircraft explored heavier weapon loads. These included up to 500 kg (1,102 lb) of bombs in the Me 262A-2a *Sturmvogel* ('Stormy Petrel') bomber version (Hitler partly got his wish). They also included a new secret aerial weapon, the R4M rocket. Individually, the R4M was an unguided, folding-fin rocket with a 520 g (18 oz) warhead. Twenty-four such rockets were mounted under the wings of Me 262s (12 each side) and were fired in a ripple salvo into the bomber formations. The R4Ms were inaccurate technologies, but if they did hit they had a devastating effect on a bomber airframe. Some Me 262s were also equipped with the hefty BR 21 rockets, actually an aerial adaptation of the 210 mm (8.3 in) Nebelwerfer 42 infantry rocket. Only two of these could be carried on an Me 262, the launch tubes mounted beneath the fuselage.

Chapter 4

Looking back to the combat narrative in our introduction to this book, it is evident that the Me 262 was a shock to the system for Allied fighter and bomber crews. Fighter pilots watched helplessly as the jet roared past them and disappeared towards the horizon; bomber gunners swung their weapons erratically on their mounts in an attempt to get a lead on the fast-moving interceptor. In total, Me 262 pilots claimed to have shot down 542 Allied aircraft by the end of the war. Considering the total production figure for the type – 1,430 aircraft – this is an astonishing kill rate. Only *c.*100 Me 262s were lost in return. But their story takes a familiar path for late-war German innovations. There just weren't enough of them. Problems with maintenance, production, manpower and fuel supply often meant that no more than 200 were operational at any one time. Nor did performance data automatically translate to tactical advantage. They were travelling so fast that the engagement window for firing on enemy bombers was just a few seconds; the fighter pilot quickly had to break off the attack to avoid ramming into the bomber. Moreover, they were not invulnerable – talented Allied fighter pilots could and did defeat them in aerial combat. One particularly successful tactic was to attack the Me 262's airfields, which once discovered, the Allies did unrelentingly. US and British bombers also hammered Me 262-related factories and fuel plants, reducing the inflow of new jets of the fuel on which they depended. All told, the strategic bombing campaign was a force far greater than the Me 262 could stop.

EXPLORING NEW DESIGNS

In the last two years of the war, the Me 262 had plenty of jet-powered or rocket-powered company, secret designs and production models that started to toy around the edges of science fiction. Keeping our focus on jets, Heinkel produced the design for the innovative He 162 *Salamander* in an accelerated development programme at the end of 1944. This aircraft was a single-seat interceptor, powered by a bulbous BMW 109-003E turbojet that literally sat on the top of the fuselage between the wings; the aircraft had twin fins so the jet exhaust vented through the gap. In total some 275 were produced, but the war ended before the aircraft could make an impactful contribution. The aircraft company Henschel followed a similar engine layout to the He 162 in its Hs 132, which was not a fighter but rather intended as a single-seat dive-bomber, armed with a 1,000 kg (2,205 lb) bomb beneath the fuselage and 20 mm (0.79 in) and 30 mm (1.18 in) cannon arrangements. By the end of hostilities in Europe, however, only three prototypes had been completed.

Of all the secret late-war fighters developed by Germany in 1944 and 1945, two of the wildest rides must surely have been the Bachem Ba 349 *Natter* ('Grass Snake') and Messerschmitt Me 163 *Komet*. Both were rocket-powered interceptors. Investigations into the potential of rocket-powered aircraft began well before the war, not least in the hands of aeronautical engineer Dr Alexander Lippisch, the formative figure behind the Me 163. Rockets seemed to promise optimal levels of performance, especially in terms of maximum speed and climb rate. The challenge would be in taming their volatile fuel and potentially explosive characteristics.

The Me 163 came first. It was a strange, squat and stumpy aircraft, with an overall length of 5.69 m (18 ft 8 in), a height of 2.76 m (9 ft 0.5 in) and a wingspan of 9.33 m (30 ft 7.5 in). Two of its immediately noticeable characteristics were its pronounced swept-wing planform and its complete lack of integral undercarriage. On take-off – which by all accounts was a horrid, bucketing experience – the aircraft would run on a wheeled trolley that was jettisoned after take-off; the Me 163 would land on a retractable skid beneath the forward fuselage, combined with a fixed rear tailwheel. Accidents were, needless to say, very common.

Another precarious element of the Me 163 was its fuel source. The aircraft's 1,503 kg (3,307 lb)-thrust HWK 109-509A-2 motor was powered by mixing two chemicals: T-Stoff (80 per cent hydrogen peroxide with stabilizer, and 20 per cent water) and C-Stoff (calcium permanganate or sodium permanganate mixed in water), the latter acting as a catalyst for

Chapter 4

the former. It was critically important to keep these two hostile fuels separate until they were burned, hence the aircraft had two separate and clearly labelled fuel tanks on the top of the fuselage.

The armament arrangement was initially a single pair of 20 mm (0.79 in) cannon, but this was increased in the Me 163B-1a to two 30 mm (1.18 in) MK 108 cannon. Even later, there were experiments in equipping the Me 163 with upward-firing guns and underwing rockets.

The Me 163 was certainly fast. Very fast. It had a maximum speed of 960 km/h (596 mph) and a dizzying initial climb rate of 3,600 m (11,810 ft) per minute. It could reach an altitude of 12,100 m (39,700 ft), far higher than the operational service ceiling of the Allied bombers. The problem, however, was that it sucked up its fuel load with unquenchable thirst – it was only capable of 7.5 minutes of powered flight. The tactical intentions for the Me 163 were, therefore, novel. As the Allied bomber stream approached, the *Komet* would blast off from its airfield and lock itself into a steep 45-degree climb, racing to reach an altitude of about 9,144 m (30,000 ft). The enemy bombers would at this point be far below, at about 6,100–7,620 m (20,000–25,000 ft). The *Komet* would now cut off its engine and trade altitude for speed in several unpowered dive attacks, opening up on the bombers with its cannon as it shot past them. Eventually it would lose enough momentum to warrant breaking off the attack, whereupon it would glide back to its base and land on its retractable skid.

There was a mortal gulf between theory and practice. The *Komet* went into combat service in mid-1944, and from that point until the end of the war only achieved nine kills in the hands of Jagdgeschwader 400 (JG 400), based in Brandis, near Leipzig. But once the initial surprise had worn off, the Allied fighter pilots got the measure of the new threat. The *Komet* was exceptionally manoeuvrable in its dive pattern, but once it had lost much of its forward momentum it was vulnerable to interception during the descent, especially as it approached the airfield, which is where the Allied fighters made many of their kills. The Mustang and

Thunderbolt pilots would also wait until the *Komet* was completely down, then strafe up the static aircraft. The *Komet* was also a real handful to fly competently, so as Germany's stock of experienced pilots diminished it was harder to find men who could both fly the aircraft well and achieve kills at the same time. Plus the *Komet* experienced the problem of all late-war jets and rockets: shortages in fuel resulting from Allied bombing of fuel plants.

The Me 163 design actually made a limited migration to Japan during the war, specifically in the form of a reverse-engineered version called the Mitsubishi J8M *Shusui* ('Autumn Water') or, in Japanese Army service, the Ki-200. In total, seven prototypes were built, the first flying on 7 July 1945. Only as the war in the Pacific was ending, however, was the design finalized, so it made no operational contribution against the high-flying streams of US B-29 Superfortresses. The Japanese built a properly inferior version of the Me 262, the *Nakajima Kikka* ('Tachibana orange blossom'). The prototype of this aircraft was so underpowered that it needed an auxiliary rocket to enable it to take off. Again, the end of the war cut short the development programme.

If it seems risky to have put a human being inside an Me 163, then it was outright madness to have done the same with the Bachem Ba 349 *Natter*. Unlike many of the other types we have studied so far in this chapter, the *Natter* skipped the lengthy development process. In fact, it was designed and produced from 1944 as part of the *Jägernotprogramm* ('Emergency Fighter Programme'), a seat-of-the-pants effort to create defensive interceptors that were cheap and quick to build, but which, optimistically, were still capable of claiming air superiority.

The *Natter* was an oddity on first sight. Constructed largely of laminated wood, it was just 6.1 m (20 ft) long with a stubby wingspan of 3.6 m (12 ft) and an extremely prominent tail fin. Its main powerplant was a Walter 109-509A-2 liquid-fuel rocket, designed to give just 70 seconds of thrust with 1,700 kg (3,748 lb) of power output. In addition, however, it had four 1,200 kg (2,646 lb) thrust Schmidding SG-34 solid-

Chapter 4

fuel booster rockets, two either side of the rear fuselage. These were jettisonable units, to be discarded after imparting ten seconds of thrust.

It might be sensed from this description that the *Natter* did not have a conventional take-off. In fact, it was launched vertically from a metal launch tower, the four booster rockets providing it with ten seconds of climb before they were jettisoned and the main engine took over. Such was the violence of the launch that the flight controls were initially handled by autopilot, as the human pilot would typically black out for some seconds. (The *Natter* was only 2,200 kg /4,850 lb at launch, so there was not much weight to restrain it.) The *Natter* would then make a powerful climb to its combat altitude, flying up and through the bomber formation, attacking it with the weapons load of 28 R4Ms or 24 Föhn 73 mm (2.87 in) unguided rockets, mounted in the nose. The assault made, the pilot would now put the aircraft into a dive before jettisoning the nose cone and at around 1,000 m (3,000 ft) deploy a parachute from the rear of the aircraft that would lower it to the ground. He would also jettison the canopy; the deceleration caused by the aircraft parachute deploying would throw the pilot out of the cockpit, and he would land using his own parachute.

One wonders at the bravery, or fear, of those who manned such aircraft. On the very first manned flight alone, the test pilot, Lothar Sieber, was killed when the aircraft went into an erratic flight trajectory and smashed into the ground; he had probably been unconscious long before this point. Sieber goes down in history, however, as the first person to lift off vertically from the ground under rocket power, although he had little time to appreciate the fact. Such were the adverse physical forces acting on the aircraft from the beginning to the end of its flight that the *Natter* was classified as semi-expendable. The aircraft never had an operational outing – likely more a blessing for the German pilots than the Allied air crews.

The same could probably be said for the Focke-Wulf *Triebflügel* ('Thrust Hunter'), another Luftwaffe attempt at creating an *in extremis* interceptor. It was a hybrid aircraft (I use the term with a hint of puzzlement): a cross between a helicopter, with its vertical take-off and landing characteristics, and a jet aircraft. The *Triebflügel* had no conventional wings but instead had three wing-like blades on a rotating fuselage mount, the blades powered by an angled ramjet engine mounted on each tip. On take-off, the aircraft would sit pointing vertically upwards, resting on four castoring wheels extending out from the tail on extensible struts. The theory was that the ramjets were fired up, causing the rotor to turn and eventually, with the assistance of four auxiliary rockets, lift the aircraft from the ground. The pitch of the blades could be angled to produce level flight. Four cannon in the nose served as the armament. When it returned to earth it would land vertically again, resting on its tail unit.

The on-paper specs for the *Triebflügel* were certainly impressive. It had an estimated speed of 1,000 km/h (621 mph) and an extraordinary service ceiling of 14,000 m (42,920 ft). Thankfully for future pilots, it stayed on the drawing board. It likely would have been lethal to fly, with unforgiving flight characteristics and the distinct possibility of explosive accidents. It never reached prototype stage and remained a secret weapon that stayed on the drawing board.

GERMAN JET BOMBERS

Generally speaking, Germany's development of a bomber fleet was badly mismanaged. Hitler's prioritization of tactical over strategic air power meant that Germany never satisfactorily developed a mass-production heavy bomber comparable to the American B-17 or the British Lancaster. Instead, the Luftwaffe was hobbled by the limitations of its two-engine medium and light bomber types, made principally by Junkers, Dornier and Heinkel. Within this domain, however, from 1943 Germany engineers explored the concept of a jet-powered bomber. Combining jet propulsion and a significant bomb load in one aircraft raised a tantalizing possibility – a bomber aircraft with the speed and performance that could match or exceed those of the enemy fighter defence. This was the concept of the *Schnellbomber* ('fast bomber').

Chapter 4

The front end of an Arado Ar 234, as displayed at the Steven F. Udvar-Hazy Center at the National Air and Space Museum in the USA. The glass cockpit gave the pilot exceptional all-round visibility.

History's first turbojet-powered bomber was the Arado Ar 234. Its origin lay in a 1940 requirement, issued by the German Air Ministry, for a high-speed, high-altitude reconnaissance aircraft. The only company to rise to the challenge was Arado, who on 15 June 1943 flew the first prototype of the Ar 243 *Blitz* ('Lightning'). During the development phase, the Arado engineers played about with the engine configuration in several prototypes, experimenting with different powerplants and with either two or four wing-mounted turbojets. These early aircraft also had no landing gear, using a jettisonable wheeled trolley for take-off and retractable skids for landing. Nevertheless, during trials the aircraft was demonstrated to Hitler personally; the Führer liked what he saw, and the *Schnellbomber* had the green light.

Eventually, prototypes settled into the production Ar 234B. Out went the trolley and skids and in came a conventional nosewheel landing gear. The aircraft was powered by two BMW 003A-1 turbojets, one mounted beneath each wing. The first variant was an unarmed reconnaissance type, the Ar 234B-1, but then came a bomber variant, the Ar 234B-2. Given that the landing gear took up much of the space in the slender, cigar-shaped fuselage, the aircraft's bomb load – up to 2,000 kg (4,409 lb) – was suspended directly from the engine nacelles and from the fuselage centreline.

The Ar 234 is a satisfying aircraft to look at, with aerodynamic sleekness and a glistening sense of the future in its all-glass front end, which gave the pilot excellent visibility. It also had decent performance: even with a full bomb load it could achieve 668 km/h (415 mph) at 6,000 m (19,700 ft). Unladen, it was capable of 735 km/h (459 mph), faster than the Allied fighters. It had a lofty service ceiling of up to 10,000 m (32,810 ft), which meant that when it performed its first combat operations – aerial reconnaissance flights over the Allied beachhead at Normandy in August 1944 – it went largely undetected. It also had almost fighter-like manoeuvrability.

The Ar 234 was a sound design, and it was produced in a number of different mission variants – reconnaissance aircraft, light bomber, pathfinder, long-range bomber. And it was proven in combat. Flying out of bases in western Germany, Ar 234s conducted numerous fast-paced bombing runs against Allied ground forces in Europe, opening with a sortie on Liège on 24 December 1944 during the Ardennes offensive. Its most famous missions were multiple strikes against the Allied-captured Ludendorff Bridge over the Rhine in March 1944 by aircraft of III./KG 76, although these resulted in few hits and significant losses from anti-aircraft fire.

As with many of the aircraft we have discussed, the Ar 234 suffered from late-war issues relating to serviceability, technical problems (the engines in particular were prone to flame-outs and other failures),

Chapter 4

production and fuel supply. Only about 214 were built in total, which included prototypes of a new four-engine Ar 234C night-fighter.

The Ar 234 was a forward-looking design. But it looked positively conventional when compared against two of the other secret jet bombers Germany developed during the late years of the war. When the first unpowered glider prototype of the Horten Ho IX was flown on 1 March 1944, onlookers must have wondered at what they were seeing. The aircraft was essentially a tailless flying wing, with a bulbous fuselage and a long cockpit that gave it a bug-like appearance. It was, however, one of the forebears of advanced post-war stealth aircraft such as the B-2 Spirit and F-117 Nighthawk. It was designed as a single-seat fighter-bomber to meet an ambitious 1943 requirement issued by head of the Luftwaffe, Hermann Göring, namely for an aircraft that could carry 1,000 kg (2,205 lb) of bombs over a distance of 1,000 km (620 miles) with a maximum speed of 1,000 km/h (620 mph). The brains behind the Ho IX VI, the first prototype, were Reimar and Walter Horten, fighter pilots/engineers who had already conducted flying-wing experiments with glider aircraft.

Why the flying wing? The flying wing, as the name suggests, is an aircraft that consists of one largely uninterrupted wingspan, the fuselage blended smoothly into the whole. Such aircraft typically do not have vertical or horizontal stabilizers, which also means that they do not have conventional flight surfaces. Skirting over many technicalities and debates within the field of aeronautics, we can summarize by saying the flying wing offers the ultimate in aerodynamic efficiency by reducing drag to a minimum. Conversely, the design is highly unstable, although if this instability can be mastered it makes the aircraft highly manoeuvrable.

Reimar and Walter co-operated with other Luftwaffe engineers to produce a powered prototype, the Ho IX V2; in February 1945 two Junkers 109-004B-1 turbojets powered this aircraft to a demonstration speed of 960 km/h (597 mph), although the prototype was destroyed on landing after an engine failure. Nevertheless, the German Air Ministry was convinced enough about the design to transfer its development and intended production to Gothaer Waggonfabrik, a rolling-stock manufacturer that during wartime branched out into aircraft production. The aircraft was now renamed the Gotha Go 229.

There were ambitious plans for this strange flying wing. Several more prototypes were built, including night-fighter and fighter-bomber versions, the latter to be armed with two 1,000 kg (2,205 lb) bombs and four 30 mm (1.18 in) MK 108 cannon. But despite its inclusion in the *Jägernotprogramm*, the Go 229 never went beyond prototype stage before the end of hostilities in Europe. Some of the surviving specimens were spirited away by the United States and Britain upon their discovery, for trials and investigation.

It might seem hard to beat the Go 229 in terms of futuristic design, but the Junkers Ju 287 certainly had a go. It was a prototype high-speed heavy bomber born from a design study conducted by engineer Hans Wocke at Junkers in mid-1943. The most outlandish element of this work was not necessarily the configuration of the four Junkers Jumo 109-004B-1 turbojets: two either side of the forward fuselage and two mounted beneath the wings. (A later prototype experimented with fitting six engines.) Rather, it was that Wocke designed the aircraft with *forward-swept* wings, creating an aircraft of almost unparalleled ugliness, but which tests apparently confirmed had significant aerodynamic advantages. Specifically, the layout was meant to improve the lift characteristics of the aircraft when the turbojets were operating at low power. There was some merit in the idea, although the wings faced extra stress from wing-warping effects.

The Ju 287 is notable in the history of German secret aircraft because it embraced crude improvisation to get ahead. Its V1 prototype included the fuselage of a He 177 *Greif* ('Griffin') long-range heavy bomber, the tail unit from a Ju 388 *Störtebeker* multi-role aircraft, the mainwheels from a Ju 352 *Herkules* ('Hercules') transport aircraft and, with something of an appreciative nod towards their enemies, nose wheels from captured

American B-24 Liberator bombers. It had a bombload of up to 4,000 kg (8,818 lb), double that of a Heinkel He 111. Design and development of the Ju 287 was driven hard through 1944 and 1945, but the Junkers factory in Dessau was overrun in April 1945. This terminated the programme in Germany, certainly, although the intrigued Russians transported the prototypes and many of the German engineers back into the Soviet Union to conduct further experiments.

OVER THE HORIZON

Although Nazi Germany did not develop a meaningful heavy bomber programme during the war, beyond limited production of a small range of types, that did not prevent it from sketching out designs for a heavy bomber unlike all others. Back in the late 1930s, as global tensions increased, the Reichsluftfahrtministerium began to consider the outlandish possibility of a bomber with hemispheric range, capable of performing a round-trip combat sortie from Germany to the United States. Considering that the *one-way* distance from Berlin to New York is 6,400 km (3,977 miles), the idea bordered on the realms of fantastical. Indeed it stayed little more than an interesting concept until it was revisited in the early 1940s and evolved by April 1942 into a formal *Amerikabomber* project.

Various engineers and aviation companies explored the concept, many of them focusing on refining versions of existing long-range conventional aircraft. But the Sänger *Silbervogel* ('Silver Bird') design, developed by aerospace engineer Eugen Sänger and mathematician and physicist Irene Bredt, occupied a different category of vision altogether.

In concept, it was nothing short of an intercontinental supersonic bomber. It was shaped like a huge, flat dart with relatively small wing surfaces, utilizing the aeronautical principle of the 'lifting body'. (In such a design, the body of the aircraft produces the majority of the lift, rather than in the wings; to visualize this, think of the design of the American Space Shuttle.) Overall length was estimated to be 27.98 m (91 ft 10 in), but the span was just 15 m (49 ft 2 in). The main powerplant was nothing less than a 109-tonne (100-ton) thrust rocket engine.

To get airborne, the *Silbervogel* was to be fired along a 3-km (2-mile) rail track atop a rocket-powered sled, accelerating the aircraft to a speed of 1,850 km/h (1,149 mph) before it became airborne. Once it was aloft, its main engine would take over for a duration of eight minutes – enough, theoretically, to take it to breathtaking speeds of 22,100 km/h (13,724 mph) and an altitude of 145 km (90 miles), into our planet's thermosphere. By this point, it was effectively a spacecraft. An important part of the engine design included what we now call regenerative cooling, in which some of the aircraft's fuel or oxidizer flows in tubes around the exhaust bell of the engine both to cool the exhaust and to pressurize the fuel.

Once the *Silbervogel* was at altitude, the engine would cut out and the aircraft would slowly begin to descend but then bounce off the denser atmosphere below and essentially skip to the other side of the world using nothing more than atmospherics. As it passed the United States, it would deposit a conventional bomb load or, feasibly, a nuclear weapon before continuing its journey into the Pacific and landing somewhere in Japanese-occupied territory.

The *Silbervogel* didn't come to fruition in World War II, or any other time for that matter. It was simply too futuristic to work. But it feels wrong to say that it did not have an impact. Both US and Soviet aviation agencies, including NASA, utilize some of the principles of the *Silbervogel* in space programmes, especially the principle of regenerative cooling.

MANNED FLYING BOMBS

It is already evident that being a test pilot on a German secret aircraft design was only for stoic personalities. One could argue that excessive risks to pilots and crew in the experimental aircraft were only possible in a nation descending into an apocalyptic defeat, in which life was cheap and victory, however unlikely, could be bought at any price. A most

Chapter 4

extreme expression of this mindset within the Third Reich is the Fiesler Fi 103R – the 'R' stands for the project code name, *Reichenburg*. The underlying idea was nothing short of a suicide glider-bomb, a human volunteer pilot willingly flying a warhead-loaded craft into an enemy target, particularly the ships of an invasion fleet. The idea was taken seriously, with the focus on adapting a prototype pulse-jet aircraft, the Messerschmitt Me 328, or the Fiesler Fi 103 (the V-1 flying bomb), which we will encounter in due course.

The Fi 103R was eventually selected as the best fit for the project. It was little more than the original flying bomb but fitted with control surfaces and a basic cockpit for a human pilot. To give the weapon some range, the idea was that one or two of these aircraft would have been carried beneath a He 111 bomber for launch in proximity to the target.

Technically speaking, the Fi 103R was not a suicide aircraft. The stated procedure was for the pilot to point the aircraft towards the intended objective but then bail out from the cockpit at the last moment, allowing the 850 kg (1,870 lb) warhead to slam home. This was an exercise in gross dishonesty. The pulse jet engine was so close behind the cockpit that any pilot bailing out would almost certainly have slammed into, or been sucked into, the air intake. This was never tested in practice, as although some 175 Fi 103Rs were made and about 70 undaunted individuals were recruited, it was never used; saner heads apparently prevailed.

The same can't be said for Japan. The practice of battlefield suicide reached an elevated cultural status in Imperial Japan during the later years of the war. In aviation terms, this expressed itself in the Yokosuka MXY7 *Ohka* ('Cherry Blossom'). It was a rocket-powered kamikaze aircraft, consisting of a 1,200 kg (2,646 lb) impact-detonated warhead mounted in the nose and powered by three solid-fuel Type 4 Mk 1 Model 20 rockets. A human pilot would man the *Ohka*, and would stay in it from take-off until the moment he slammed into an American ship, hitting at a terminal dive velocity of 927 km/h (576 mph). Just in case he got twitchy at the idea of his imminent death, he was sealed into the cockpit and only had enough fuel for a one-way trip. The aircraft itself had only a short range of about 37 km (23 miles), thus it had to be transported to the target area in the bomb bay of a modified Mitsubishi G4M bomber.

Production of the *Ohka* began in late 1944 and continued until March 1945, during which time 755 were manufactured. They were unleashed in action, particularly against the US invasion fleet around Okinawa in April 1945. In total, seven ships were either damaged or sunk by these terrifying craft, but most of the aircraft either missed their targets or were shot down while still connected to their parent aircraft. They were a tragic exercise in futility.

PIGGYBACK PLANE

One day in February 1944, a Junkers Ju 88 bomber on a test flight out of Peenemünde-West on the Baltic coast smashed into the ground just 3 km (1.8 miles) from the village of Thiessow, blowing apart in an unusually large explosion. With due deference, Luftwaffe authorities held a funeral for the crew shortly after, displaying full military honours.

The rites of passage, however, were a front for another German secret weapon programme, the *Mistel* ('Mistletoe') composite aircraft. It consisted of two aircraft bolted together top to bottom via a trapeze structure: a manned fighter aircraft on top serving as the control aircraft, and a crewless Ju 88 medium bomber below. The bomber had been emptied of people and equipment and instead received a 3,800 kg (8,378 lb) high-explosive anti-tank (HEAT) warhead in the nose. The warhead was an absolute monster, designed to cut through 7 m (23 ft) of steel armour or 18 m (60 ft) of concrete. The operational concept was that the fighter aircraft would guide the bomber/bomb to the target area, point it at the target via a simple gun crosshairs (like many of the weapons featured here, it was primarily intended for anti-ship use), then release it by severing the connection via

Chapter 4

explosive bolts. The Ju 88 would then fly to its point of impact under its own power.

Again, the *Mistel* smacks of desperation and a rising tolerance for waste. But the principle of the 'piggyback' aircraft actually dated back to pre-war British civilian experiments, and to early-war German explorations of different ways to deliver DFS 230 assault gliders. The 1944 designs were an explosive mutation of these plans. There was no fixed composite pairing in the *Mistel*, but the final production and operational arrangement was a Messerschmitt Bf 109G or Focke-Wulf Fw 190 A-8 on top, hitched to a Junkers Ju 88 A-4 below. The visual impression was supremely ponderous, but *c.*250 *Mistel*s were produced and some were actually committed to combat. In the hands of Kampfgeschwader (KG) 101, based at St. Dizier, it made its combat debut on 14 June 1944 against the Allied invasion fleet off Normandy. A single example set out with some local public fanfare at sunset, but on its way was spotted by a Royal Canadian Air Force (RCAF) Mosquito fighter-bomber, piloted by Flight Lieutenant Walter Dinsdale. Dinsdale and his navigator, Flying Officer John Dunn, were at first struck with puzzlement at the vision before them. They evidently overcame this, for they promptly shot it down with cannon fire. Dinsdale later recounted to news reporters:

> *It was a very awkward thing, and it lumbered along like an old hippo at about 150 mph. I recognised it as a Ju 88, but couldn't figure out what the thing on top was. I thought it was one of their glider bombs mounted in a new way. It was on top, mounted between the rudder and the main wing. My first short burst hit the starboard wing and cockpit of the Junkers. I thought I had killed the pilot, but, of course, there was no pilot as the whole thing is controlled from the fighter on top. Carrying on for a few minutes, circling to port with the fire increasing, he then dropped away and crashed behind the German lines. The explosion lit up the countryside for miles around.*[33]

The poor showing for the first *Mistel* operation did not prevent it being used again, on both the Western and the Eastern fronts, with some marginal successes. An attack against Allied shipping off Gold Beach in Normandy on 24 June 1944, for example, inflicted serious damage upon the Royal Navy frigate HMS *Nith*, and possibly damaged the French blockship *Courbet* off Sword Beach in August. Plans to attack the British fleet at Scapa Flow and Soviet factories and electricity-generating plants around Moscow and Gorky were fleshed out, but eventually abandoned owing to changes in tactical circumstances. *Mistels* were launched at bridges built across rivers by the Soviets as they advanced into Germany, but the damage they inflicted was limited and quickly repaired.

The Allies also conducted some secret experiments into the principle of converting aircraft into flying bombs, but with some additional sophistication. Between August and December 1944, the US Eighth Air Force took surplus B-17 and PB4Y bombers, loaded them with explosives and fitted them with a rudimentary cockpit camera plus a radio guidance system. The intention was to have a two-man crew pilot the aircraft to the vicinity of the target, at which point they would bail out and control would pass to a CQ-17 mother ship, relying on the visual information provided by the camera. The US Navy attempted a similar project, Operation *Anvil*, using converted B-24 Liberator bombers operating with Ventura PV-1s as the control aircraft; the parallel USAAF project was called Operation *Aphrodite*. None of these ventures came to anything operationally, although they did have some important human and indeed political consequences. Lieutenant Joseph P. Kennedy, Jr., scion of the great Kennedy dynasty, was killed alongside Lieutenant Wilford J. Wiley while conducting an Operation *Anvil* test; the 9,600 kg (21,170 lb) of Torpex explosive aboard the aircraft detonated prematurely over southern England.

In this chapter, we have far from exhausted the limits of Nazi Germany's secret aircraft experiments. Others worth a brief mention include the Messerschmitt Me 321, a monster transport glider designed

Chapter 4

by Messerschmitt and Junkers in 1940 as a heavy-lift invasion aircraft, intended to transport loads up to the size of a Panzer IV medium tank; the six-engined Me 323 variant capable of carrying 120 fully equipped troops; the Dornier Do 335 *Pfeil* ('Arrow'), a super-streamlined heavy fighter in a twin-prop push-and-pull configuration, capable of 763 km/h (474 mph); and an assortment of early combat helicopters, including the Focke-Angelis Fa 284 with contra-rotating rotors capable of lifting up to 3,000 kg (6,600 lb) loads and the lightweight Focke-Angelis Fa 330 *Bachstelze* ('Wagtail') for use from submarines. In most cases, however, the German experimental aircraft produced were an example of maximum effort resulting in minimal reward.

Chapter 5

Vampires and Bat Bombs – Allied Aerial Innovations

Regarding the air war in World War II, turning our focus upon the Allies produces a significant shift in perspective. As we shall see, the Allied armed forces were not averse to innovation in aerial combat. Their abiding focus, however, was to form an overwhelming armada of standardized aircraft and throw it into the skies. They were invested in improving the quality of that air fleet through new types and ever-improved variants, certainly, but in a way that didn't interfere with tactical concentration or strategic mass.

To give some parity with the preceding chapter, this chapter will open with an assessment of British and American jet aircraft developments. These were far more restrained in scope than the proliferation of German designs. But we will also explore some of the secret Allied technologies that made a perceived or real impact on the air war, not only in terms of aerial combat, but also in the realm of anti-aircraft defence. This will include a limited consideration of the profound contribution of radar, although the technicalities of that subject mean that only an overview will be provided. Nevertheless, assessing these technologies will remind us that the war for the skies

Chapter 5

was as much about technology as it was about the individual skills of pilots and gunners.

ALLIED JETS

The military and civil powers of the United Kingdom have a long, snooty history of condescension towards individual talent. To that point is the great English aviator and engineer Frank Whittle, who during the 1920s began to design an aircraft jet engine, inspired by previous theoretical work on jet turbines by Alan Arnold Griffith. Whittle actually took out a patent for a turbojet engine in January 1930, but his efforts to promote the idea to the RAF met with a dismissive attitude. Incredibly, Whittle's financial situation meant that in January 1935 he was not able to afford the renewal fee for the patent, thus it lapsed. In January 1936, however, he paired up with two innovation-minded investment bankers, Sir Maurice Bonham-Carter and Lancelot Law Whyte, and together they founded the Power Jets Company to realize his vision.

Following successful tests of a Whittle jet engine in April 1937, the British Air Ministry finally showed a grudging interest the following year and provided some investment, albeit on conditions of strict secrecy – commercial promotion was no longer a possibility.[34] The Whittle design, in the form of a 526 kg (1,160 lb) thrust Power Jets W.1A turbojet, found its way into the first British jet aircraft to take to the skies, the Gloster E.28/39. The maiden flight of this aircraft was on 15 May 1941. It was a short and simple design, the reverse-flow gas turbine centrally mounted through the fuselage. Two prototypes were made, the first being lost in an accident. The engines were then uprated to deliver more power; the second prototype featured the 798 kg (1,760 lb) thrust W.2/500 engine, which took the aircraft to a respectable maximum speed of 750 km/h (466 mph).

Although the Gloster E.28/29 was trialled as a jet fighter aircraft, it never received the intended nose-mounted machine-gun armament and remained experimental. But the lure of jet aircraft was now established

The Gloster Meteor began front-line operations in July 1944. Although designed as a fighter, it mainly performed ground-attack and photo-reconnaissance missions during the remainder of the war. Credit: Print Collector/Getty

within the RAF. In 1940 the Air Ministry issued Specification F.9/40, calling for the development of a fighter aircraft using Whittle jet propulsion. (By this stage, other aviation companies were in the jet engine game, including Rover, Metropolitan-Vickers, de Havilland and Rolls-Royce.) The result was the Gloster Meteor, a single-seat interceptor fighter powered by two wing-mounted turbojets. After a series of eight prototypes and an assortment of powerplants, it had its first flight on 5 March 1943 then went into production as the Meteor F.Mk 1. Powered by two 771 kg (1,700 lb) thrust Rolls-Royce Welland engines, the aircraft had a maximum speed of 668 km/h (415 mph) at 3,050 m (10,000 ft) and a service ceiling of 12,190 m (40,000 ft). The main production variant (210 built), the F.Mk III, was equipped with Rolls-Royce Derwent engines, which added another 120 km/h (75 mph) of pace, making it one of the fastest aircraft of the war.

Chapter 5

The Gloster Meteor was an aggressive racehorse, equipped with four nose-mounted 20 mm (0.79 in) Hispano cannon. It began operational sorties in July 1944, flying out of Manston airfield in Kent to intercept V-1 flying bombs; the first kills were made on 4 August. It also deployed to forward airfields in Belgium in 1945, mostly flying low-risk reconnaissance and ground-attack sorties; it was prohibited from penetrating deep into enemy airspace from the fear that the Germans might down one of them and recover its secrets. Such was the integrity of the Meteor's design that the aircraft went on to have a long post-war career with the RAF and in export markets, serving in various capacities until the 1980s and breaking some flight records along the way.

It was not the only British jet interceptor developed during World War II that would establish itself after 1945. Another was the de Havilland Vampire, which first flew in September 1943 after an accelerated 16-month design and development programme. The Vampire would become, at least following the secrecy of wartime conditions, one of the most recognizable early British jets, with its distinctive twin-boom tail and a short fuselage featuring two air intakes that converged on a single jet exhaust pipe venting between the tail booms. It had a maximum speed of 824 km/h (512 mph) and, while it would have been technically interesting to see it in combat against German fighters, it did not enter service with RAF fighter command until the summer of 1946.

The Americans also entered the jet fighter age during World War II. Their first contribution to this emerging arms race was the Bell P-59 Airacomet, a joint development between Bell Aircraft Corporation and General Electric, the latter utilizing information about the Whittle-type turbojets provided by the British. The Airacomet was another single-seat interceptor, this one powered (in the P-59B production variant) by two 907 kg (2,000 lb) thrust General Electric J31-GE-5 turbojets, one set either side of the fuselage beneath the wing roots.

The Airacomet was a serviceable but rather lacklustre aircraft, with performance not impressive enough for the aircraft to achieve operational status. It also had the disadvantage of being overtaken by what was to become one of the great American jets of the early Cold War period, the Lockheed P-80 Shooting Star. Lockheed's work on jet engines and the aircraft to take them began back in the late 1930s but gathered pace in 1943 in the hands of its secretive R&D 'Skunk Works', the Lockheed Advanced Development Projects. A prototype of the P-80 first flew on 8 January 1944 and subsequent improvements produced an aircraft with excellent speed and handling characteristics. The aircraft had low-set wings projecting straight out from the sleek body and a high-profile, high-visibility cockpit. The P-80A, the first production version, was powered by a single fuselage-mounted 1,814 kg (4,000 lb) thrust General Electric J33-A-11, which gave a maximum speed of 933 km/h (580 mph). Armament consisted of six 12.7 mm (0.5 in) calibre machine guns in the nose.

The P-80 has the honour of being the first jet fighter used operationally by the USAAF; a small number of development aircraft were deployed to Italy in May 1945, although the war in Europe was ending at this point. Full production of the aircraft began in December 1945 after the end of the global war, although the P-80 would go on to gain plenty of combat experience in the Korean War (1950–3).

DOWN THE PICKLE BARREL

The scale and effects of strategic bombing form a profound distinction between World War I and its successor. The first of the 20th century's global conflicts merely hinted at the possibilities of long-range aerial destruction, minor airship or fixed-wing aircraft raids whose greatest consequence was more public alarm than physical damage. Strategic bombing in World War II, by contrast, unleashed city-destroying forces on the planet. Millions of homes and hundreds of thousands of factories and installations were destroyed by aerial bombardments. The size and destructive capability of bomber air fleets grew almost inexhaustibly, particularly on the Allied side; from 1943, raids of more than 1,000 bombers at a time became common. In Europe alone, the British and Americans dropped nearly 2.7 million tonnes (2.6 million tons) of bombs, killing anywhere between 300,000 and 600,000 German civilians and leaving millions more wounded or homeless. Over in the Pacific, one single US B-29 firebombing raid – Operation *Meetinghouse* on 9–10 March 1945 – wiped out 41 km^2 (16 square miles) of central Tokyo and killed approximately 100,000 civilians, rendering 1 million homeless. (One of the reasons the Japanese authorities hesitated to surrender after the dropping of the Hiroshima atomic bomb was that they had simply got used to the news of their cities being wiped out.) In World War II, there were increasingly few urban zones where civilians were shielded from the horrors of war.

But for all its destructiveness, aerial bombing was supremely inaccurate. A startling report by British civil servant David Bensusan-Butt in August 1941 charted how only one in three British bombers operating at night got within 8 km (5 miles) of their targets. In fact, bombing inaccuracy was the key reason for the more indiscriminate violence of the Allied Combined Bomber Offensive. The commander-in-chief of RAF Bomber Command, Air Marshal Sir Arthur Harris, from 1942 pioneered 'saturation bombing' (aka 'area bombing' or 'carpet bombing') – basically, put great numbers of bombers into the air, co-ordinate them in huge formations, and flatten an entire urban area rather than go for point targets.

The Americans were fully aware of the inaccuracy of aerial bombing well before they joined the war in 1941 and began R&D into technologies that might introduce more precision into the whole business. Doing so was also regarded as an ethical step, reducing as far as possible civilian casualties proximate to legitimate targets. In 1920, a Dutch engineer working for the US Navy, Carl Lucas van Norden, began work on the next-generation bombsight that would take his name. The result was the Mark XV, although in US Army service it would be the M-7 and, in a refined version from late 1943, the M-9. The wider world would know of it simply as the Norden.

The Norden bombsight was surrounded by high levels of official secrecy during the war years, although in reality most of its technological secrets were in the hands of the enemy from early on. Credit: Allan J. Cronin/CC BY-SA 3.0

A bomb falling from 6,096 m (20,000 ft) takes approximately 37 seconds to reach the ground. A multitude of mathematical and environmental factors affect where it lands, including: the ground speed of the aircraft; wind speed and direction; turbulence; air density and humidity; bomb drag and aerodynamics; release altitude and velocity; ballistic trajectory calculations, and more. Add the conditions of combat, and the challenge was extraordinary. The Norden bombsight aimed to take some of the guesswork out of bomb-aiming. It was a gyroscopically stabilized, automated, electromechanical bombsight. It took inputted information about altitude, airspeed, drift, trail and bomb ballistics and calculated the bombing solution, even, via a mechanical linkage, triggering bomb release automatically when the aircraft reached the position calculated by the sight. The bombardier still had much work to do, but a lot of the heavy lifting was taken by the Norden.

Chapter 5

When used in favourable test conditions, the Norden seemed to deliver on the promise of precision bombing. In tests using a standard measure of bombing accuracy, the circular error probable (CEP; the radius of a circle in which 50 per cent of ordnance lands), the Norden fulfilled its potential with a truly impressive CEP of 23 m (75 ft 6 in) – far smaller than many of the factories that the Americans might want to bomb. In one demonstration in 1939 (before an envious British representative), six bombs were dropped from 3,657 m (12,000 ft) into the outline of a battleship painted on to a range at Fort Benning, Georgia, with no misses. Such was the accuracy of the Norden that it led, famously, to the USAAF claim that its bombardiers could 'drop a bomb into a pickle barrel from 30,000 feet'.

Given its vaunted capabilities, the Norden was demonstratively wrapped in secrecy. The initial production sight, produced for use by the US Navy, was classified as TOP SECRET. In time, as the Norden became more widely issued to Navy and USAAF units, its secrets logged in highly transferrable instruction manuals, its security level was downgraded first to CONFIDENTIAL and later, by 1941, to RESTRICTED. But in practice, the USAAF continued to treat the Norden with almost theatrical levels of secrecy. To quote aviation historian Dan Hart:

Bombardier trainees were sworn under oath to protect the secrets of the bombsight and to give their own life in the process if necessary. In order to keep the Norden bombsight out of enemy hands, if need be, they were told initially to shoot certain parts of the bombsight with their pistol. Later they were trained on setting off an incendiary device that would melt the bombsight into a pool of useless metal. Safe bomb vaults, guarded by security personnel were created for the storage and maintenance of the Norden. The upper portion of the bombsight, called the 'sighthead,' would be kept in the vault until time for a mission and then be escorted under armed guard to the plane. Once back at base the sighthead was removed and escorted under armed guard back to the security vault.[35]

The US authorities even hid the Norden's design from its closest ally, the United Kingdom, despite direct petitions from then British Prime Minister Neville Chamberlain in the late 1930s – such was the concern that an example of the bombsight might fall into curious foreign hands.

In reality, however, many of the Norden's secrets were already out. Certainly its very existence was well known, being referenced in public congressional debates and even featuring in articles in the popular engineering press from the late 1930s, some of which neatly understood most of the device's functions. Furthermore, the Norden gave superb bombing results when delivering ordnance over some blue-sky, uncontested range in the American Midwest or South. It gave far less accurate results, it was soon noted, over war-torn Europe, with its liberal coverings of heavy and low cloud, and the disruptive effects of German air defence. In operational circumstances in 1943, the CEP was 370 m (1,200 ft), with only 16 per cent falling within 300 m (1,000 ft) of the point-of-aim (POA).

This unsettling information brought about important tactical changes in US air operations, pioneered in part by the reformist-minded General Curtis Emerson LeMay. The 'Combat Box' organized American bombers into large and co-ordinated formations, with a particularly competent bombardier in the lead aircraft. When he dropped his bombs, the others followed, creating something of a hybrid between saturation bombing and precision bombing.

So, the Norden was not as good as touted, but it was still an excellent device for the times, hence the flawed attempts at secrecy. Imagine the dismay, therefore, if the American authorities had known the truth. Not only had a Norden employee sold drawings of the device to the Germans in 1938, but in 1940 the Soviet Union managed to get hold of a Norden and handed it to the Germans for further analysis. And despite the firm instructions to Allied air crews about destroying the bombsight, the pressing realities of combat meant that by the end of 1943 the Germans had plenty of examples taken from downed US bombers. Secrecy, as ever, struggled to stay watertight in leaky reality.

OUT OF THE BOX – BAT BOMBS

By this stage, we might be tempted to think that it was only on the Axis side that craziness reigned in secret aircraft design, the Allies being models of sober judgement and rational restraint. It is an important corrective, therefore, to end this chapter with one of the more outlandish Allied contributions to the air war – the bat bomb.

Lest the reader think that we are about to discuss a bat-branded piece of conventional ordnance, do not be diverted – here we are speaking about nothing less than weaponized bats. Bat bombs were the brainchild of Dr Lytle S. Adams, a dental surgeon from Irwin, Pennsylvania. Incensed by the Japanese attack on Pearl Harbor in December 1941, Dr Adams began to consider retaliatory measures. An unlikely idea stirred, driven by the recognition that many Japanese domestic and commercial properties were constructed from easily ignited paper and wood. He took this knowledge and married it with recent experience of witnessing bats in flight. As he explained to the *Bulletin of the National Speleological Society* in an interview in 1948: 'I had just been to Carlsbad Caverns, N. M., and had been tremendously impressed by the bat flight. [...] Couldn't those millions of bats be fitted with incendiary bombs and dropped from planes? What could be more devastating than such a firebomb attack?'[36]

In some ways he was right. Firebombing Japan's tinder-like housing would prove to be absolutely devastating when delivered via the conventional US strategic bombing campaign against Japan in 1944–5. What was unusual about Adams' proposal was the delivery method. The incendiary-laden bats, he believed, would take refuge in the nooks and crannies of Japanese buildings, and when the device exploded, the bat, and the building it was attached to, would be burned to a crisp.

Fearing no ridicule, in January 1942 Dr Adams sent the proposal to the White House for consideration. More remarkably, it received official approval from President Roosevelt and was passed to the Army Chemical Warfare Service (CWS) for exploration, with Dr Adams a leading member of the team. They set about scouring the United States for the right species of bat, one substantial enough to carry a small bomb weighing up to about 28 g (1 oz). They chose the free-tailed bat, and several hundred unfortunate creatures were collected.

The weapon component of the bat bomb was developed by Dr L.F. Fisser, a special investigator for the NDRC. He invented two bat-transportable incendiary devices, one weighing 17 g (0.5 oz) and the other 28 g (1 oz), having burn times of four minutes and six minutes respectively and triggered by a time-delay mechanism to allow the bats to do their flappy work. The devices were attached to skin on the bats' chest.

Perhaps unsurprisingly, it isn't easy to turn bats into guided weapon systems. To keep the bats alive during preparation and deployment stages, they had to be chilled in refrigerators to make them slip into hibernation. They were then dropped in batches of about 180 in cardboard containers that self-opened at about 320 m (1,000 ft), leaving the bats free to fly to their targets. What actually happened in many of the tests was that the hibernating bats did not wake up and simply died in the boxes when they hit the ground. Many of those who did wake up struggled with the unaccustomed weight of a small bomb on their chest, and others wilfully flew away from the simulated Japanese buildings on the test ground and set fire to aircraft hangars and even a general's car.

But the project persisted, and in August 1943 it was transferred from the US Army to the US Navy, who renamed it Project X-Ray, then promptly handed it over to the US Marine Corps. The Marines kept at it, sporadically setting fire to various buildings. Full-scale bomber trials were envisaged, but in late 1944 someone evidently saw sense and cancelled the whole project, which had cost an estimated $2 million (equivalent to about $35 million today).

Admittedly, my tone has not been respectful towards the bat bombs. There is actually a cold logic behind it; Dr Adams certainly had a proposal that was worth reflection. But the sheer unpredictability of the delivery mechanism became evident early on in the project. The enemy of many secret weapons projects is a collective lack of common sense.

Chapter 6

Autumn Winds and Blazing Typhoons – Air Defence

***

The war fought from and between opposing aircraft was but one element of the air conflict in World War II. From the 1930s, the European powers in particular began to wrestle with the future of air defence, the technologies and tactics that might be used to defeat an air attack from the ground. A generalized fear underpinned much of this effort. From the 1920s, there had been some well-publicized apocalyptic predictions about the capabilities of strategic air power in future warfare. In 1931 the future British Prime Minister Stanley Baldwin even dismissed reassurance altogether and said: 'the bomber will always get through'.[37] Defying statements such as this was the gauntlet thrown down to military engineers and scientists.

The foundation of the story of air defence in World War II is, in many ways, the story of radar. This exciting new technology was developed during the second half of the 1930s as a means of early warning against approaching enemy aircraft. It also became a critical adjunct to the process of gun-laying – setting anti-aircraft guns to the correct range, azimuth and elevation to hit their targets, or at least get close. Many countries were in the radar game – principally France,

Germany, the Netherlands, Italy, Japan, the United Kingdom, the United States and the Soviet Union. It was the British, however, who gave radar its first rigorous operational outing. In both the Battle of Britain (July–October 1940) and the Blitz (September 1940–May 1941), radar demonstrated that it was integral to the future of air defence. Germany, the United States and the Soviet Union quickly became fellow pioneers and explorers in the field. The details of the 'radar war', the great struggle of electromagnetic measure and countermeasure, is beyond the scope of this book, but its underpinnings will be recurrent in this chapter.

The technologies and tactics of air defence had, by the final years of the war, reached a scale that few could have foreseen. Back in August 1939, for example, over-confident Nazi potentate Hermann Göring had declared that not a single bomb would ever fall on the Ruhr. By 1944, with German cities pounded to dust in many places by strategic bombing, 1 million personnel were serving German homeland anti-aircraft (AA) defence, which included 9,000 heavy and 30,000 light AA guns, and Göring's confidence had long been buried in the rubble. Finding a sure response to strategic bombing became a desperate preoccupation for both the Germans and the Japanese, but it was also a race into which the Allies threw their intellectual energies.

THE ALLIES – GUNS AND ROCKETS

Secret weapons played a crucial role in air defence, part of the quest to find the decisive AA technologies. The true work of air defence was nevertheless undertaken by forests of gun barrels turned skywards, conventional weapons firing conventional ammunition. The AA guns of World War II were typically divided into light and heavy types. Light anti-aircraft (LAA) weapons were designed to engage low-range, low-altitude aircraft, and were more mobile (towed and vehicle mounted) and, usually, fast-firing to match their fast-moving opponents. They were principally automatic cannon or machine guns, in calibres at or below

40 mm (1.5 in). The heavy anti-aircraft (HAA) systems were the big guns for the big bombers, typically in calibres of 88 mm (3.5 in) and above, the larger shells being able to reach altitudes of more than 9,144 m (30,000 ft). 'Heavy' was the keyword in their descriptor; HAA guns were physically large weapons, typically located in permanent or semi-permanent gun emplacements along common enemy flight paths.

The lively arguments about whether AA fire was effective in World War II much depends on your perspective. On one side of the scales, the sheer challenge of putting a shell, measuring just a few centimetres in diameter, into or right next to an aircraft flying at hundreds of kilometres an hour on a changing flight path perhaps 6 km (3.7 miles) above the Earth, was so great that literally thousands of shells had to be fired for each kill. (Although it is often overlooked that AA fire serves a range of tactical purposes, such as disrupting bomb runs.) On the other side, we should recognize that AA guns accounted for about 50 per cent of all the aircraft brought down in World War II. But regardless of whether the wartime engineers took the glass half full or glass half empty position, it was clear that the kill ratios could be improved. For the British in the late 1930s, they turned to consider rockets.

Partly this was to do with economics. Britain simply didn't have enough AA guns at this time. Rockets, in contrast to artillery pieces with their expensive unitary cartridges, were fairly cheap to produce and could be fired from the most rudimentary launchers. They could also work across a broad range of altitudes, based on simple adjustments to propellant or fuel loads.

To maintain secrecy, the British authorities would eventually refer to rockets as 'unrotated projectiles' (UPs), although it doesn't seem too much of a leap of imagination to work out that rockets are being discussed. The work was led from 1935 by the Research Department, Woolwich Arsenal. By 1939 they had produced two rocket types, officially 508 mm (2 in) and 76.2 mm (3 in) diameter weapons powered by a cordite-based solid fuel.

Chapter 6

Despite intensive investment in aerodynamics R&D, there was no getting away from the fact that the rockets of the day were unguided and therefore, like a particularly expensive firework, inherently inaccurate. Thus the ongoing research was cancelled in the summer of 1939. The outbreak of war just months later, however, rekindled the experiments and produced some operational types.

The first applications of the rockets were for the Royal Navy, who at this time was facing the threat of German dive-bombers attacking UK coastal shipping. The Apparatus Air Defence Type L belonged to the category of 'Parachute and Cable Device' (PAC). The underlying principle of the PAC was that a rocket, when fired up into the air, would draw with it or deploy from it a long steel cable. The dangling cable would, theoretically, either entangle itself around the wings or fuselage of an enemy aircraft, cutting through airframes or interfering with engines or control surfaces, or would cause aircraft to deviate from their intended course, like fish avoiding a fishing net. The Type L consisted of a 58 mm (2 in) rocket supporting a canister containing a 183 m (600 ft) length of cable. On each end of the cable was a parachute device, one parachute larger than the other. Alongside the smaller parachute was a light explosive mine. When the rocket reached an altitude of 305 m (1,000 ft), the cable-parachute device was ejected and unfurled. The unequal drag imparted by the large parachute vs the smaller one would drag the mine on to the aircraft's wing, blowing it off. Another PAC variant, the Type J, instead had the cable drawn up behind the rocket from a cable spool mounted on the deck.

With the rocket launcher mounted on a ship, it was hoped that the cable would provide an ensnaring barrier to any attacking aircraft. They were fiddly contraptions, however. PAC-type devices were sound in principle, but they included a lot of moving parts and components. This not only complicated their production but also made their set-up and use time-consuming. As a simplified option, therefore, the British researchers produced several pure rocket weapons. To raise the possibility

A spectacular barrage of rockets from British Z-batteries light up the skies over London as they attempt to counter German night raiders in March 1944. Credit: Popperfoto/Getty

of at least one direct hit, various 76.2 mm (3 in) multi-rocket launchers were developed, each given a reassuringly irreverent title to reflect the appearance of the launcher unit, including 'Pig Trough', 'Pillar Box' and 'Radiator'. As well as the ship-mounted rockets, the British Army also started developing types for land use, principally to defend static positions. The first of these was the Projector, 3-inch Mk 1, built by G.A. Harvey of Greenwich – a simple rail-fired rocket weapon, aimed visually by the operator.

Chapter 6

For British mainland air defence, the 3-inch rocket (UP-3) was used as the weapon of choice for the 'Z-batteries'. An individual Z-battery consisted of 64 twin-rocket launchers, which meant that 128 rockets could be unleashed in a single salvo. Later variants in the series modified the number of rockets mounted per rail and the mobile configuration. The Projector, Rocket, 3-inch No.4 Mk 1 and 2, for example, had a wheeled launcher unit that could ripple-fire 36 projectiles. Z-batteries also fired PAC weaponry, specifically the Type K, which again used the double-parachute cable configuration and mine device we saw earlier. Given that more than 100 of these weapons could be launched in a single salvo to an altitude of 5,791 m (19,000 ft), the impediment to low-flying enemy aircraft must have been considerable.

And yet, although the Z-batteries made their first kills in 1941, and indeed proved quite effective at disrupting bomber attacks, their kill ratios were low. There were some intrinsic limitations. Given that their targets were continually changing bearing, altitude and speed, it was difficult to find the right moment to commit to launching hundreds of undirected rockets, and there was huge wastage. Falling rocket casings posed a considerable danger to local populations below. They also became associated with one of the most tragic disasters on the British home front. On 3 March 1943, the unfamiliar sound of a Z-battery firing in Victoria Park in London caused a surge of people down the stairs in Bethnal Green underground station, resulting in a pile-up of human bodies that killed 173 people.

GERMANY – FROM GUNS TO GUIDED MISSILES

From the late 1930s, the bulk of German investment in air defence went on interceptors, radar, conventional AA guns and associated gun-laying technologies. German AA crews and support services became adept at generating thick and accurate clouds of flak above their towns, cities and industrial plants. Later in the war, however, when it became clear that even tens of thousands of guns were not sufficient to stop the strategic bombing offensive, German researchers began to investigate new generations of rocket weaponry. By this stage of the war, there was nothing to lose.

The first of the German rocket weapons was the Henschel Hs 297 *Föhn* (a word referencing a warm autumn wind), developed in 1943 and fielded in 1944–5. The individual rocket was a 73 mm (2.87 in) weapon weighing 2.74 kg (6 lb 1 oz) and carrying a 280 g (10 oz) warhead mixing RDX and TNT. It was strictly a short-range weapon, with a vertical altitude of 1,200 m (3,900 ft), hence was primarily intended for use against Allied fighter-bombers making low-level attacks. The rocket, however, was spin stabilized by angled vents to improve accuracy. Thirty-five rockets could be launched in a salvo from the launcher, the 73 mm *Föhn-Gerät*, although in Volkssturm civil defence hands it was the *Volkssturm-Flugabwehr-Raketenwerfer* ('Volkssturm Anti-Aircraft Rocket Launcher'). The firing effect was visually impressive and genuinely dangerous to enemy aircraft, but the threat was reduced by the fact that all the rockets had impact fuses – only a direct hit on the aircraft would have an effect, thus there was a lot of wasted energy going down range.

Compared to the *Föhn*, the *Taifun* ('Typhoon') was an altogether bigger beast. It was in development from the end of 1944 at the infamous Heeresversuchsanstalt Peenemünde (HVP; 'Peenemünde Army Research Centre'), the epicentre of so many German secret weapons programmes, and went into production between January and May 1945. The *Taifun* was a 1.93 m (6 ft 4 in)-long, spin-stabilized unguided rocket, with a flight ceiling of 15,000 m (49,200 ft) – this was a weapon designed to hit the highest-flying Allied bombers. It could roar up to this altitude at a velocity of more than 1,000 m (3,000 ft) per second, driven by liquid-fuel propellant. Again, the rocket had a contact fuse, although a secondary timer fuse ensured that live rockets did not drop back down to earth.

Only about 600 of the *Taifun* were made in total, so its impact on the war effort was forgettable. Ironically, its most important contribution to historical weapon development was that it went on to influence the design

Chapter 6

of the 76 mm HEAA Rocket T220 – aka 'Loki' – a successful American sounding rocket of the post-war era. (Sounding rockets are used to carry experimental equipment on sub-orbital flights.)

Another German rocket experiment essentially gave birth to what today we call Man-Portable Air-Defence Systems (MANPADS). This was the *Fliegerfaust* ('Flight Fist'). In appearance, the *Fliegerfaust* looks like some sort of drainage contraption. In the *Fliegerfaust* B variant, it featured nine parallel 20 mm (0.79 in)-diameter tubes arranged in a circular configuration and fitted with two grips, the rear grip incorporating a shoulder rest. (The *Fliegerfaust* A had only four barrels.) Each tube held a small rocket, an adaptation of a 20 mm (0.79 in) aircraft cannon shell. All nine rockets were fired electrically by squeezing the rear trigger. Even here the designers showed their meticulous nature, in that five of the weapons tubes were fired immediately from alternate tubes and the other four were launched 1/10th of a second later from the remaining tubes; this meant that the flight of each rocket was not disturbed by the blast of the rocket next to it. Angled vents in the bottom of each tube also imparted spin stabilization to the rocket to improve accuracy.

The *Fliegerfaust* was another short-range air defence weapon, effective over distances of about 2,000 m (6,561 ft). It took some talent to use on the part of the operator, as it was aimed by a basic visual sight, so the shooter would have to calculate angle and lead on the basis of visual judgement. Another option, particularly for defence of airfields, was a German version of the PAC weapon, the RSK 1000. Developed by Rheinmetall-Borsig, and also known as the *Kurzzeitsperre* ('Short-Range Defence'), the RSK 1000 system had heavy launch tubes emplaced around the defended site. Each launch tube held multiple 21 cm (8.3 in) rockets, each attached to a generous 1,000 m (3,280 ft) of sharp steel ribbon, plus a parachute pack connected to the ribbon. When the need arose, a number of rockets would be launched; at the end of the cable run-out, the rocket would explode and detach the parachute, which would then lower the cable slowly back down to earth. Firing multiple rockets at once, therefore, could generate a lethal steel web over the airspace.

There are several recorded instances of Allied aircraft being destroyed or significantly damaged by the RSK 1000, but isolated incidents aren't a ringing endorsement of an air defence system. Unguided rockets and PAC weapons certainly put on a pyrotechnic show, but their poor accuracy always hampered their relevance. This is why the German researchers also homed in on a new form of secret weaponry – guided surface-to-air missiles (SAMs).

GUIDED SAMS

We often associate guided weapons with the computerization of the post-war era, but some of the groundwork was completed during World War II. German SAM research was mostly conducted at the HVP, set in the remote north of Germany on the Baltic coast. This infamous centre of weapons research is eternally associated with the design and development of the V-2 ballistic missile, and the misery of slave labour that fed the station's activities, but it was also the place in which the science of missile guidance was advanced. The horrors of Nazi ideology and the best of modern engineering ran side by side at Peenemünde.

Guided SAMs dangled the promise of that ultimate 1:1 missile-to-kill ratio, and thus SAM programmes became more aggressively pursued in Germany from 1943. The first was the Henschel Hs 297, first developed in 1941 by Henschel engineer Herbert Wagner, but given official authorization in 1943, when it was relabelled the Hs 117 *Schmetterling* ('Butterfly'). The Hs 117 stood 4.2 m (13 ft 9 in) high and ran on a BMW 109-558 liquid-fuelled rocket engine that gave 57 seconds of thrust. During that time, it would hit 860 km/h (535 mph) – sufficient to catch most fighters of the day – out to an operational range of 32 km (20 miles) and a maximum altitude of 9,000 m (29,527 ft). Guidance to the target came via radio control from a ground operator, who kept the aircraft in an optical sight and steered the missile towards it. Detonation of the

Chapter 6

A Henschel Hs 117 Schmetterling, the panels stripped from its wings, as displayed at Deutsches Technikmuseum, Berlin. The Hs 117 was one of the early attempts at creating an effective guided SAM. Credit: André Gerwing/CC BY-SA 4.0

25 kg (55 lb) warhead was performed by radio command; plans to develop and install a proximity fuse were not realized.[38]

The *Schmetterling* reached prototype stage by January 1945, at which point the whole project was cancelled. But by this time other options were on the table, not least the *Wasserfall Ferngelenkte FlaRakete* ('Waterfall Remote-controlled Anti-Aircraft Rocket'), a far more sophisticated piece of kit. Unlike the *Schmetterling*, the *Wasserfall* was up and running before war's end; it was test fired in February 1944. It was under development from 1942 as a palladium against Allied long-range bombers. It was a big rocket: 7.85 m (25 ft 9 in) in height, weighing 3,700 kg (8,200 lb). In acknowledgement of its origins in Peenemünde, its carried more than a passing resemblance to the V-2 ballistic missile, albeit with cruciform wings on the midpoint. Maximum range was 25 km (16 miles) and it got there fast – its liquid fuel engine, developed by Dr Walter Thiel, blasted it to a truly supersonic speed of 2,772 km/h (1,772 mph). The tip of the spear was (in its final form) a 306 kg (674 lb) liquid explosive, developed to maximize the area of blast effect within an enemy bomber formation.

The true selling point of the *Wasserfall*, however, was its guidance system. For daytime interceptions, the missile was radio guided in azimuth and elevation by a ground operator, who maintained line-of-sight with the enemy aircraft. (The control inputs at first moved four graphite rudders set in the flow of the rocket exhaust, but as the missile speed increased these were replaced by four air rudders mounted on the tail.[39]) In the blackness of night, a different system was required, the *Rheinland* radar-control system. The radar component of the missile picked up the approaching bomber and relayed this signal via the transponder of the missile to a direction-finder set, and the interchange between these components set missile azimuth and elevation. The data was fed into a comparator computer, compared to the data from the radar, and corrections made. When launched, the missile was gathered into a radar beam by a control transmitter. The missile rode this beam towards the target, but eventually the missile's own infrared homing system would take over, guiding the missile to its destination based on the heat-signature of the engines. An infrared proximity fuze was also fitted to detonate the warhead within 10 m (32 ft) of the aircraft.[40]

This was truly a next-generation missile and guidance system. Development and test firings continued throughout 1944 and into 1945, but they ceased in February 1945 when Peenemünde, hit repeatedly by Allied bombings and facing the advance of the Russians, was abandoned. What could have been? Albert Speer, the Reichsministerium für Rüstung und Kriegsproduktion ('Reich Minister of Armaments and War Production'), after the war reflected that:

Chapter 6

> *To this day, I am convinced that substantial deployment of Wasserfall from the spring of 1944 onward, together with an uncompromising use of the jet fighters as air defense interceptors, would have essentially stalled the Allied strategic bombing offensive against our industry. We would have well been able to do that – after all, we managed to manufacture 900 V-2 rockets per month at a later time when resources were already much more limited.*[41]

There were yet more experimental SAM designs being tested in 1944–5. The *Enzian* ('Gentian') E.1 designed by Dr Hermann Wurster of Messerschmitt in 1944 was an outlier, being something of a rocket conversion of the Me 163 rocket interceptor aircraft. Wurster sought to produce a pilotless version of the aircraft, one that could be launched and guided to the target before detonating a massive half-tonne warhead, hopefully killing several bombers at once. The aircraft's powerplant was replaced by four Schmidding 109-553s boosters plus a Walter RI-10B sustainer motor. The four solid-fuel boosers were fixed externally, together generating 7,000 kg (15,000 lb) of thrust to give the missile powerful initial acceleration, while the liquid-fuelled Walter motor gave it a constant speed of about 1,046 km/h (650 mph). Maximum range was 25 km (15.5 miles) under radio guidance.

The *Enzian* project thrashed about trying to find the right formula for the weapon, which suffered many technical issues. So many, in fact, that the project was cancelled in January 1945. Also cancelled shortly after was another SAM R&D project, called *Rheinocter* ('Rhine Maiden') *R*, the development of which had been under contract with Rheinmetall-Borsig A.G. of Berlin-Marienfelde since November 1942. The *Rheinocter* weapons were huge rockets 5.9 m (19 ft 4 in) long. The slender body was a two-stage rocket. The lower booster stage, fitted with four large wooden fins, generated 75,000 kg (165,000 lb) of thrust for 0.6 seconds, still enough time to accelerate the missile to speeds of near Mach 1. (Launch was via a steel rail or an adapted 8.8 cm/3.5 in Flak gun carriage.) When it burned out at around 300 m (1,000 ft), the booster unit detached and the main stage rocket took over for ten seconds of thrust. This stage was stabilized/directed in flight by four canard-type steering surfaces around the nose and six swept-back fins on the body. Guidance was via radio command; red flares attached to the tail unit gave the operator a visual point of reference as he guided the missile to the target.

As with many of the German SAM projects, experimentation seemed to trap the *Rheinocter* project in a cycle of R&D before its final cancellation in February 1945. There were many test firings, but no operational launches. The cancellation was signed by SS-Obergruppenführer und General der Waffen-SS Hans Kammler, whom Hitler had appointed commander of Nazi missile projects in January 1945. It was he – a despicably cruel Nazi – who took the scythe to the other SAM projects, in a hurried effort to rationalize Germany's technical focus.

IN THE PROXIMITY

The Allies, and especially the Americans, also pursued some important research into SAM systems. The American interest was stoked in 1944 by the trauma of meeting the first kamikaze air attacks, undeviating assaults that required filling the sky with bullets and cannon shells as the only countermeasure. Two ship-based short-range SAMs were designed: the 'Missile, Surface-to-Air, Lark', built by the Consolidated-Vultee Aircraft Corporation, and the KAN Little Joe by the Naval Air Material Unit. Both were radio-guided, line-of-sight weapons. In fact, the latter was a simpler missile designed temporarily to fill the gap that the more advanced Lark would, hopefully, occupy.

Neither ultimately reached operational status during the war, but while Little Joe was cancelled in 1946, Lark went on to put a notch in the post of military engineering – it was, in January 1950, the first US SAM to intercept a moving air target.

In World War II, SAMs were important from the view of pure science, but inconsequential in terms of the war effort. The same cannot be said

Chapter 6

for the next object of our attention. This was a device that, arguably, was *the* most important secret weapon after the atomic bomb. It soaked up more than $1 billion of R&D investment (about $15 billion today) and involved the development and production input of more than 100 factories. It was also the mechanism that changed the entire framework of air defence. This was the proximity fuse.

The bulk of AA shells fired during World War II were fitted with either contact fuzes that detonated the warhead on impact or, more common in HAA, time-delay fuses that exploded the shell at a pre-set altitude, based on the seconds that elapsed from firing. Neither was terribly efficient. The time-delay fuses at least didn't rely on a direct impact, but the final explosion still had to be within metres of the enemy aircraft to produce a destructive effect. And, as we have seen, that was hard to achieve. All manner of fuse-setting procedures and technologies were applied to speed and refine the process, but getting the shell to detonate at just the right moment in time and space involved as much luck as judgement.

The proximity fuse was the elusive holy grail of AA technology. A proximity fuse self-detonates when it detects it is in the vicinity of the target, removing the need to calculate altitude (except in as much as it related to gun lead) and the complexities of on-the-ground fuse setting. The problem was that at the beginning of the war, most combatants had the vision of the proximity fuse, but the technical challenges of realizing it were simply enormous.

A scientist could take one of several angles to create a proximity fuse. It could be activated by the magnetic field of the target; this was fine for ships (as we will see later), but the magnetic field of aircraft was too low to be a viable option in air defence. Another option was to use a photoelectric sensor in the fuse. Here the shell detonated when the fuse sensed significant changes in external light conditions, such as when it passed into the shadow cast beneath an aircraft with the Sun above it.

We saw the German attempts to utilize photoelectric fuses in the previous chapter, and their limitations. Interestingly, the Japanese developed what appears to have been a successful photoelectric fuse, the Type 3, but applied it to air-dropped ordnance rather than AA shells. A US Naval intelligence report from September 1945 explained the basic functioning of the device and suggests its potential impact, had the war not ended when it did:

DESCRIPTION AND OPERATION OF JAPANESE TYPE 3 PHOTOELECTRIC FUSE

This report concerns the Japanese Type 3 fuse, which was used operationally on 250- and 800-kilogram aircraft bombs to cause detonation of bombs 18 to 45 feet above the earth. This fuse functions in daylight or darkness.

Operation depends on transmitting from the fuse a beam of pulsing light, which is reflected back to the fuse and activates a photoelectric cell, which, in connection with an electric circuit, causes detonation at a desired height.

The fact that this fuse is sensitive only to light pulsing within a certain frequency range and may drop for up to 30 seconds before arming makes it a formidable weapon to counter and a valuable device for exploitation in military applications—if it is as reliable as claimed by Japanese naval officers.

This fuse required the development of two new vacuum tubes and appears to represent an example of an original and appreciable accomplishment by Japanese engineers.[42]

The Type 3 illustrates that the photoelectric fuse had a future, it just wasn't a future to be realized fully in World War II.

What was really needed was a radar-based proximity fuse. Such a fuse would trigger detonation via the reflected radar signals coming from an aircraft. Given that by the end of the 1930s, operational radar was already detecting aircraft, developing a proximity fuse based on this technology seemed a tantalizing possibility. In Britain during the late 1930s, scientists and engineers asked the question: Could a proximity fuse be created by mounting a radar receiver in the shell nose, this activated by picking up the radar signals from the ground transmitter? The answer proved to be 'no'. The reflected signal from the aircraft was so weak that the receiver would require a signal amplifier bigger than the shell warhead could contain. The only real solution would be to install both the transmitter and the receiver into a unitary fuse.

The technical problems involved here were of the moonshot variety. They included:

- Miniaturizing the components, including glass-bodied vacuum-tube electronic valves, sufficient to fit inside an artillery shell only a few inches across, already packed with explosives and other mechanisms.
- Making those components resilient enough to survive the acceleration from being static to a velocity of about 792 m/sec (2,600 ft/sec) within the length of a gun barrel. This created forces of about 20,000-g, plus the shell would be spinning at about 500 rpm, so enormous centrifugal forces would be exerted in addition to the accelerative forces.[43]
- Develop the association battery technologies to power the device during its flight.
- Ensure the fuse remained inert and unthreatening to handle at all times until it was a safe distance from the muzzle of the gun.
- Finally, ensure that the fuse was suitable for mass production for a variety of different Allied artillery pieces.

Undaunted, the British led the way in the late 1930s, even developing some prototypes, but by 1940 the scale of the technical challenges plus the drains of existing war production meant the programme was stalled. Thus it was transferred to the United States in the autumn of 1940 as part of the 'Tizard Mission', or officially, the British Technical and Scientific Mission. This interaction was led by polymathic inventor Sir Henry Tizard, one of the leading lights behind the development of wartime radar, as head of the Aeronautical Research Committee. The purpose of the mission was to exchange and rationalize secret scientific information with the United States, including developments such as centimetric radar and the possibility of an atomic bomb. Progress on the proximity fuse was shared, and thereafter the bulk of the work passed to the US Navy, who had more capacity to do the project justice.

The US authorities immediately understood the importance of the proximity fuse. Between 1940 and 1943, the United States poured vast resources into related R&D, the project headed by Section T of the National Defense Research Committee (NDRC). Section T was led by Merle Tuve, a geophysicist at the Carnegie Institution of Washington, and a pioneer in radar and, later, atomic energy. The work scaled up profoundly, bringing in the talents of companies such as Eastman Kodak, Exide, National Carbon Co., Sylvania and the Radio Corp. of America (RCA). A new lab was established, the Applied Physics Laboratory (APL) at Johns Hopkins University in Baltimore. Project secrecy was maintained fanatically from the outset. The device was given the name 'VT' fuse, the abbreviation standing for 'variable timing' to obscure its concept and technology. The VT fuse would remain one of the great secret weapons of World War II, its internal workings hidden from the Axis powers for the rest of the conflict.

The VT design, as installed in a 127 mm (5 in) AA shell (the standard US Navy HAA weapon) was the miniaturized culmination of genius and effort. A radar transmitter and receiver unit were installed in the tip of the fuse. Their power source was a battery, but before the shell was fired the battery's electrolyte fluid was held in a glass ampule, separate from the battery's stack of carbon and zinc plates. This design was a crucial safety feature, as it meant that the battery was inert until it was on its way to the target. The acceleration of firing broke the ampule, releasing the electrolyte, and the centrifugal forces drove the acid around the plates, generating a 140-volt charge within three seconds of propellant ignition, by which time the shell was safely distant from the muzzle. The battery now activated the transmitter/receiver components. When the intensity of the return signal from the enemy aircraft reached a designated strength, which was calibrated to correspond with the blast radius of the shell (about 65 m/213 ft), the receiver activated a thyratron trigger (a gas-filled tube serving as an electrical switch). The trigger released an electrical charge from a capacitor; this charge initiated a detonator which in turn set off the main explosive charge.

The VT fuse had shown impressive results under test conditions, and it went into accelerating production from the summer of 1942. As other weapons in this book have shown, test conditions are one thing; combat conditions are quite another. But the VT fuse was a game-changer from the outset. It was first used in combat on 5 January 1943, when a 127 mm (5 in) shell fitted with a VT Mk 32 fuse, fired from the US cruiser USS *Helena*, destroyed a Japanese Aichi D3A 'Val' dive-bomber with spectacular efficiency. Thereafter the VT kill rates escalated. The VT fuse didn't care whether it was day or night, whether the target was a fast-moving fighter or a steady bomber. All the gunners needed to do was put the shell in the general vicinity and let the VT fuse do its work. By the end of 1943, only 25 per cent of US naval AA shells had been fitted with VT fuses, but they accounted for more than 50 per cent of the kills. The VT fuse became an invaluable tool in the fight against Japanese kamikaze aircraft in 1944–5, and in a version for US Army AA guns with VT-fused shells killed more than 1,000 German aircraft during the same period.[44]

The VT shells were also the great counterweight to the German V-1 flying-bomb campaign. After prolonged persuasion, the Americans provided the British with VT fuses. Thus equipped, British coastal AA batteries blunted the efficacy of the V-1 onslaught; on one day alone, of 97 V-1s launched against Britain, only four managed to make impact in London; the guns downed 65 of them (the rest were accounted for by fighters and balloons, and three landed in open country).[45]

Away from the arena of air defence, however, there was another, and terrible, innovation spun out from the VT fuse. In land warfare, VT shells could be set to deliver airburst effects over enemy troops, detonating about 9–15 m (30–50 ft) above ground rather than striking the earth. To this day, airburst munitions are deeply feared by infantry. They render frontal cover irrelevant, as they impart force and fragments down as well as forwards, like a great aerial shotgun blasting the earth. This feature also improved their effectiveness in complex terrain such as forests, and against troops on the reverse sides of hills, as was demonstrated during the Ardennes campaign and the Battle of Hürtgen Forest in 1944–5.

Perhaps the greatest compliment to this battle-winning technology came from Lieutenant General George S. Patton, not a man given to easy praise. He wrote to Major General Levin H. Campbell Jr., the chief of Army Ordnance, and told him that 'The funny fuze [the VT fuse] won the Battle of the Bulge for us. I think that when all the armies get this shell we will have to devise some new method of warfare.' Many others echoed his sentiments, here Vice Admiral George F. Hussey, Jr.: 'If a secret weapon is defined as a truly effective weapon on which absolute secrecy has been maintained, then the Navy's VT, or proximity fuze, was one of the outstanding secret weapons of the war. It is not only an amazing anti-aircraft device, but has proved equally effective in land warfare.'[46] Given the often ambivalent outcomes of secret weapons, this is high praise indeed.

Chapter 7

From Flying Bombs to Superguns – German Vengeance Weapons and Guided Missiles

Hitler's technical horizon [...] was restricted to the traditional weapons of the army and the navy. In these areas he had continued to learn and increase his knowledge [...] but he had little feeling for such new developments as radar, the construction of an atom bomb, jet fighters and rockets [...] very often [...] Hitler would lecture his military advisers on the technical know-how he had just acquired [from them]. He loved to present such pieces of information with a casual air, as if the knowledge were his own [...] Hitler's decisions led to a multiplicity of parallel projects. They also led to more and more complicated problems of supply. One of his worst failings was that he did not understand the necessity for supplying the armies with sufficient spare parts [...] From 1944 [...] his programs became totally unrealistic. Our efforts to push these through in the factories were self-defeating.[47]

ALBERT SPEER

Chapter 7

This insider's quotation, from none other than Hitler's own wartime armaments minister, tells us much about Hitler's relationship to weapons development. For the arms manufacturers and R&D bodies, Hitler was that most frustrating of individuals, someone with absolute power but an amateur's knowledge. His decision about a weapons programme was the Third Reich's equivalent of the thumbs up or thumbs down in the Roman gladiatorial arena, the decision often made not on the basis of sage advice, but more on gut instincts and time-sensitive moods. Worse still, Hitler's vacillating appetites for weapons programmes created a mess of efforts, projects with overlaps, redundancies, over- or under-investment, dead ends and equally futile open ends.

Hitler's drives and instincts about weapon development were also tied to the tightening psychological cords regarding the progress of the war. His mounting fury at reversed fortunes from late 1942 meant that he began scouting for secret solutions, weapons of terror and destruction that made flesh his desire to bring the world down in flames. This chapter will study secret weapons in the context of ordnance and missiles. We shall meet the usual catalogue of solutions, the fast and the furious, the comical and the dreadful, the non-starters and the trend-setters. But in this context, there are few better places to start than Hitler's so-called *Vergeltungswaffen* – 'vengeance weapons'.

V-WEAPONS

The V-weapons were a sub-category of what Joseph Goebbels, the Nazi propaganda minister, referred to as *Wunderwaffe*, or 'wonder weapons'. He and his department began using the term more frequently in public statements and speeches from late 1942 and early 1943. It was essentially a one-word promissory note to the German public, saying, 'Don't worry, the war might appear to be going badly, but we have decisive, albeit secret, new weapons waiting in the wings. Once unleashed, our enemies will crumble.' It is no coincidence that on 18 February 1943, shortly after the German defeat at Stalingrad, he also asked an electrified audience at the Berlin Sportpalast: 'Do you want total war [*Totaler Krieg*]? If necessary, do you want a war more total and radical than anything that we can even imagine today?' Goebbels was, in his own malevolent way, promising to unleash hell, and the V-weapons would be part of that.

The 'vengeance' component of the 'V-weapons' heading related to the desire to strike back at the Allied heartlands in retaliation for the strategic bombing campaign. The fury was, naturally, directed at Britain but also, from June 1944, the western territories reclaimed by the Allies. Since the Allies had increasing air superiority, and the Luftwaffe's strategic bombing capability was negligible, other solutions had to be found.

The first of the V-weapons, at least in numerical terms, was the V-1 flying bomb. Its original concept, which had been mooted as far back as 1935, was a protean form of the modern cruise missile. A pilotless aircraft carrying a massive warhead could, potentially, provide a cheap and effective solution to delivering heavy strikes against distant enemy targets, without the associated risk to air crew. Fast speed and small size would increase the chances of the weapon getting through to the target. Apart from some limited tests in 1941, the idea stayed mostly theoretical until 1942, when the changing circumstances of the war turned it into a secret project under Luftwaffe authority; the programme's cover name was *Flakzielgerät* 76 (FZG 76; 'AA Target 76'), which was also the name given to the aircraft prototype. The aircraft also had the code name *Kirschkern* ('Cherry Stone'). By June 1942 the aircraft's title had changed to the Fiesler Fi 103, the official designation given by the Reich Aviation Ministry (RLM), and a year later it also became the V-1. This last name, above all others, is the one that stuck.

Unlike the many more complex secret weapons programmes of the Third Reich, the FZG 76 was oriented from the outset towards low cost and simple technology. It was an expendable weapon, after all. It consisted of a pilotless aircraft with a steel fuselage 7.3 m (23.9 ft) long, shaped rather like a huge aircraft drop fuel tank, with two right-angled wooden wings and two small elevators at the rear. Mounted

Chapter 7

high above the rear of the fuselage was the powerplant, an Argus As 109-014 pulsejet.

The pulsejet design was a triumph of simplicity. It was little more than a tube for igniting a fuel-air mixture. At the front of the engine was a spring-controlled flap grid, which could open and close the airflow. When launched, the airflow pushed open the flap, at which point the fuel system pumped atomized diesel into the ignition chamber. A spark plug then ignited the fuel–air mixture. The resulting explosion momentarily closed the front flap and also provided a 'pulse' of force to power the aircraft in flight. When the pressure dropped, the flap opened again and the cycle was repeated, at a rate of about 42 pulses per second. The rasping engine had an immediately identifiable noise, hence the later Allied nickname 'buzz bomb', but it worked, plus it could run on cheap low-octane fuel.

Operational range of the V-1 was 250 km (160 miles) and it could maintain speeds of 640 km/h (400 mph) at 600–900 m (2,000–3,000 ft) – as with today's cruise missiles, it was a low-flying weapon, to evade detection and defences. It was unguided: a set of gyroscopes provided the input to control yaw and pitch; azimuth was directed by a magnetic compass; altitude was checked by an aneroid barometer. Range to target functioned via a small vane anemometer mounted on the nose. The propeller spun in the airflow, and once it had made a pre-set number of revolutions, a counter connected to the propeller triggered a mechanism that locked all control surfaces and deployed spoilers beneath the tailplane, causing the aircraft to go into a steep dive into the ground. The V-1 had a substantial warhead – 850 kg (1,870 lb) of Amatol – with various fuse options: contact, short-delay (to allow more penetration before detonation) and two-hour time delay.

Launching the V-1 required some infrastructure. Most V-1s were ground-launched from 49 m (160 ft)-long inclined catapult ramps, from which they were thrown by a steam-catapult mechanism known as a *Dampferzeuger* ('Steam Generator'). The catapult generated a launch speed of 320 km/h (200 mph), sufficient to get the V-1 into the air and stabilized under the power of its own motor. From July 1944, the Luftwaffe also began operational launches of V-1s from beneath specially adapted He 111 H-2 bombers. The aircraft would make a low approach towards the target – an effort to evade radar detection – then climb quickly to an altitude of 450 m (1,476 ft) to launch the missile and then turn for home. Although there would be far fewer air-launches of V-1s, in many ways they were simpler to operate and more flexible than the ground-launch structures, which the Allies termed 'ski jumps'. On the flip side, air launches proved to be less accurate than ground launches and had a far higher percentage of mechanical or operational failures.

The first powered flight test of a Fi 103 was conducted in December 1942, and by October the following year the weapons were in mass production. A unit, Flakregiment 155 (W), was formed to operate them and 96 launch sites were constructed in occupied northern France and the Netherlands, aimed at Britain. Air-launched variants would be deployed by III./KG 3.

Cross-Channel attacks began on 13 June 1944 and they would run until March 1945. It was an extraordinary campaign for the British – a disorientating, robotic onslaught against London primarily, but also taking in cities such as Portsmouth, Southampton, Manchester and Gloucester. The initial onslaught was rapid-fire, with 2,452 fired against England in June 1944 alone. By the end of the war and the V-1 campaign, some 100,000 houses were destroyed or significantly damaged and 6,184 people were killed with 17,981 seriously injured.

If they got through to their targets, the destruction the V-1s caused was substantial. But it became an increasingly big 'if'. The V-1 was not an accurate weapon, and many landed harmlessly in open countryside. The British became increasingly competent at destroying them, either through immense batteries of coastal anti-aircraft guns, now benefiting from proximity-fused shells or by fighter interception. A total of 8,892 V-1s were ground-launched and about 1,600 were air-launched against

Chapter 7

England. Some 7,488 crossed the English Channel, but 3,957 were destroyed in mid-air.[48] Furthermore, from July 1944 bomber forces and tactical aircraft allocated to Operation *Crossbow* – the overarching Allied defence against the V-weapons programmes – found and bombed many of the V-1 sites. By January 1945, the Luftwaffe was compelled to relinquish its launch sites in France but maintained operations from the Netherlands and western Germany until the end of the war.

The V-1 campaign augured a new era in remote warfare. It caused destruction and death, certainly, but not sufficient to turn back Germany's increasingly inevitable defeat. A window into the German appreciation of the V-1 campaign comes from an enlightening study prepared by the German Air Historical Branch (8th Abteilung) in late September 1944, which clearly celebrates the victories of the new weapon, but also the heavy drag of operating them:

> *Among the special weapons we may also expect certain innovations, recent use of the Fi 103 gives rise to hopes of success [...] During the 11 weeks of V-weapon attacks on London, considerable disruption and damage has been caused, and pressure exercised on the morale of the population. Substantial elements of the British defences have been pinned down over the target and along the path of the missiles. To a certain extent, operational units of the Allied air forces have also been used to attack the launching sites, the production centres and vehicles on which they were transported to the launching sites.*
>
> *Nevertheless, although comparatively few missiles were shot down, the Fi 103 cannot on the whole be said to have seriously damaged the enemy defence potential. [...]*
>
> *The production of the Fi 103s necessitated certain plants and materials which should have been used in the production of other war weapons. Furthermore each V-weapon had to be fitted out with complicated steerage and compass equipment which were lost once the weapon had been fired. The transportation of the weapons and*

the manning of the launching sites required large forces. On the other hand the use of lower octane petrol was counter-balanced by the bottleneck in the German fuel production industry, and these weapons also represented a saving in flying and ground staff personnel.

The military situation does not justify the increase in the range to 400 kms planned for 1945 and which is to be achieved by reducing the explosive charge to 500 kgs. Only at one point in the Reich West of Duisburg is the distance to Greater London 400 kms, everywhere else it is far greater. The firing of Fi 103s from aircraft may prove initially successful, but it is entirely dependent on the weather conditions and is also very vulnerable to enemy attack.[49]

The contextual realities of operating the *Wunderwaffe* would also impact upon a weapon that would, in due course, change the nature of global security and space exploration.

V-2 BALLISTIC MISSILE

Extended-range firepower – well beyond the range of conventional heavy artillery – was an important sideline interest of the re-emerging German armaments industry during the 1920s and 1930s. In the coming war, there would be a rich target selection at distant ranges – cities, border fortresses, production facilities, protected headquarters, military depots, logistical hubs. Aerial bombing, of course, provided strategic reach, but it was clear that the future bomber fleets would have to fight their way through contested air spaces. German weapon designers thus began looking at other, potentially unstoppable, options. The V-2 ballistic missile grew out of this vision.

To get around the artillery prohibitions of the Versailles Treaty, Germany launched a major programme of R&D into long-range rocket weaponry. At first, this was conducted at the Artillery Research Station at Kummersdorf, but in 1937 it was transferred to the new Peenemünde Army Research Centre in the Baltic. Overall command of the research

Chapter 7

lay in the hands of Colonel Ing. h. c. Walter Dornberger, but engaged from the outset was one Wernher von Braun, a scientist and aerospace engineer who would leave a bright ballistic trail across the face of modern history.

Von Braun and others worked on a series of rocket types, all given the 'A-' suffix. A-1 to A-3 were liquid-fuelled, of increasing size, power, altitude and range. As well as a powerplant experience, they also gave von Braun the testbeds for refining improved systems of gyroscopic control. The prototypes and associated tests were a mix of breakthroughs and frequent, explosive failures, but progress was sufficient to maintain investment and interest. It also led in 1942 to the A-4 rocket, more famously known in its 1944 relabelling, the V-2.

The first successful flight test of this immense rocket took place on 3 October 1942. Its performance was beyond anything anyone had ever seen before. It flew to an altitude of 96.5 km (60 miles) – the very boundary between the Earth's atmosphere and space – and crossed 201 km (125 miles) in just 296 seconds. At full speed, it topped 5,310 km/h (3,300 mph); there would be no air defence system in the world that could stop this. Hitler immediately saw the potential and on 22 November 1942, he gave the order to mass produce what was history's first operational ballistic missile.

The V-2 was a completely different animal to the V-1. It stood 14 m (46 ft) high, most of that height taken by a smooth, tapering body, but with four large tail fins fitted with rudders and four graphite vanes in the jet stream for further directional control. (At this time, Peenemünde had a supersonic wind tunnel designed by wind tunnel specialist Rudolf Hermann, thus the aerodynamics of the A-2 were honed to perfection.) The top end of the missile housed 910 kg (2,002 lb) of Amatol. The rocket's power came from the combustible results of mixing liquid oxygen (the oxidizer) with a 75 per cent alcohol/water mixture fuel. Note that the motor only ran for about 65 seconds before cut-off, leaving the missile to complete the rest of its flight purely on a ballistic free-fall trajectory.

German engineers and support crew swarm around a V-2 rocket during tests. This photograph gives an impression of the missile's size, much of the inner space taken up by its liquid fuel. Credit: Universal History Archive/Getty

Chapter 7

Range was about 330 km (205 miles). Guidance signals to the control surfaces came from an analogue computer responding to information coming from an accelerometer and a system of gyroscopes, and sometimes a radio control mechanism for engine cut-off.

Being a vertically launched rocket, the V-2 did not need the 'ski jump' of the V-1. After Allied Operation *Crossbow* air raids in 1944 destroyed purpose-built launch bunkers near the Channel coast, the V-2s were thereafter deployed from mobile launchers, another seminal innovation. The missile was collected from a railhead and loaded on to a *Vidalwagen*, a 14 m (46 ft)-long A-frame trailer towed by a truck or similar light vehicle. This took the missile to the firing troop transfer point, where it was transferred to a *Meillerwagen* trailer to take it to the firing point; the powered trailer also functioned as an erector to place the missile on its firing stand, and it could act as a service gantry. Although these trailers were accompanied by a veritable fleet of support vehicles (each V-2 battery included a total of 32 vehicles), their mobility prior to launch made them extremely hard to hunt by Allied ground-attack forces.

V-2 operational units were formed in late 1943 and the first attack on Britain came on 8 September 1944, when a V-2 ploughed into a residential area of Chiswick, London. In total, 1,115 were fired on England, each impact arriving in complete silence (the rocket was travelling faster than the speed of sound) and leaving a broad and deep area of total destruction. It was a terrorizing weapon, undetectable and undefeatable once airborne. A total of 1,115 were fired at England. The Belgian port of Antwerp, a coastal hub for Allied logistics, came off worse, with 1,351 strikes by war's end. In one dire incident, on 16 December 1944 a V-2 fired from Hellendoorn in the Netherlands struck Antwerp's Cinema Rex, which was packed with civilians and Allied servicemen, killing 597 of them in one cratering blast. Only the Allied victory and reclaiming of Europe brought the attacks to an end.

The V-2 showed a glimpse of future, hemispheric warfare, and both the rocket and Wernher von Braun would go on to have a development role in the post-war US space programme. It was a costly and labour-intensive weapon system, however, with each rocket taking about 20,000 man hours to produce. It is also notorious for the ghastly conditions endured by some 60,000 slave labourers who passed into the Mittelbau-Dora concentration camp, north of Nordhausen, near Germany's southern Harz Mountains. The camp provided expendable labour to the Mittelwerk underground V-2 production plant; about 10,000 people would lose their lives there, worked to death. In Germany, secret weapons often developed at a grave human cost.

In the final two years of the war, the researchers at Peenemünde explored many other derivatives and redesigns for the A-4/V-2, playing around with guidance, rocket motors, fuel types, and other configurations. One of the most ambitious proposals was the A-10 *America-Rakete* ('America Rocket'), a prodigious rocket 25.8 m (84 ft 8 in) high, consisting of an A-10 lower stage rocket but with an A-4 or A-9 (an extended-range version of the A-4 equipped with wings to sustain flight) as the nose section. This was basically a two-stage Intercontinental Ballistic Missile (ICBM), one with a conceptual range of 5,000 km (3,107 miles). Thankfully, it never saw its way off the drawing board, but the manifestation of such missiles would throw long shadows over world security from the late 1950s.

THE V-3 MULTI-CHAMBERED GUN

Germany's missile V-weapons were not war-winning, but they had operational impact and changed the direction of military technology. Nothing technologically redeeming can be said of the third vengeance weapon, the V-3 multi-chamber cannon, aka the *Hochdruckpumpe* ('High Pressure Pump'). The core design ran as follows. A standard artillery gun has a single chamber at the rear, the shell fired by the gas pressure from the propellant gas behind it. What if, instead, an extended barrel had multiple chambers and propellant charges arranged along its length, each firing just as the shell passed it? This way, the shell would undergo

Chapter 7

a continual acceleration, reaching super-high velocities that delivered extreme ranges.

The idea of the multi-chamber gun was not new by any means when the Germans began investigating it again in 1941. In fact, there had been attempts to design and make such a weapon in the United States and later France since the 1860s, without success or benefit. In 1942, August Cönders, chief engineer at Röchling Eisen- und Stahlwerke, was inspired by a French patent to have another crack at the multi-chamber gun design.

Cönders was a respected individual. He had developed an impressive fortress-penetrating shell called the 21 cm (8.3 in) Röchling Granate 42 Bde, which became another secret weapon in the German arsenal. It was a fin-stabilized, sub-calibre round made from hardened chrome-vanadium steel. The small cross-section but high density gave it the ability to punch through up to 4 m (13 ft) of reinforced concrete. The downside was that it had poor accuracy over its maximum range of 11 km (6.8 miles), so despite some limited combat use in 1942–3, the shell failed to make an impact (so to speak). But Cönders saw that developing a new supergun – one that could strike the UK from across the Channel and southern North Sea – could change that. His proposal to create a new V-weapon went up the chain of command and was eventually approved by Hitler in 1943.

Cönders set to work. The gun would have a 50 m (164 ft) barrel with up to 28 side chambers. His ambition was to accelerate a shell to about 1,524 m/sec (5,000 ft/sec) – considerably faster than a rifle bullet – which could give a range of about 290 km (180 miles). So Cönders, working largely unilaterally within the German armaments industry, began to develop working models and, eventually, a full-size 150 mm (5.9 in) gun. But this process brought a stack of failures and headaches: repeated burst barrels, poor ballistics, struggles to synchronize chamber firings, inaccuracy, limited range. Eventually, engineers from the Reichsforschungsrat ('Reich Research Council') were sent in to help, and things began to improve. Furthermore, during 1943 work commenced on constructing an ambitious 50-gun underground battery for the superguns at Marquise-Mimoyecques near Calais. (The barrel was so long that it was incapable of supporting its own weight, thus had to be constructed with external support along its length, such as an earthen bank or using an inclined railway track.)

It was all wasted effort. The gun never achieved a range of more than 88.5 km (50 miles) and the battery installation in France was smashed in July 1944 by an RAF air raid using 5,443 kg (12,000 lb) 'Tallboy' bombs (more about those soon). Two shorter versions were nevertheless produced and used in combat, one set on a railway track to fire at US forces during the Ardennes battle in December 1944, the other pounding away at Luxembourg between December 1944 and February 1945 from a concrete slab laid up a hillside in a ravine at Lampaden, south-east of Trier. Neither achieved anything like war-changing impact, and they eventually became curiosities discovered by advancing Allied troops, much like UN weapon inspectors would ponder Saddam Hussein's derelict 'Project Babylon' supergun in the early 1990s.

Before we leave superguns, we should observe another German proposal, one made by engineer Otto Muck. Muck was a man who threw ideas around liberally – some say he held more than 2,000 patents (the author has been unable to confirm that) – although he is more famous for his post-war theories about the fate of the mythical city of Atlantis. In May 1943, Muck had the idea of a supergun that fired a shell at extraordinary velocities and ranges through electromagnetic acceleration, meaning the gun had no propellant, no flash. The idea did not find reality, largely because of multiple impracticalities (a 100,000 kW power supply, for instance), but today the prospects of warships being fitted with electromagnetic railguns is a very real possibility for the future.

AIR-TO-SURFACE GUIDED BOMBS

The chronic inaccuracy of air-dropped 'dumb' bombs has already been explained. It was a problem all combatants negotiated from various angles, but one potential solution was the guided bomb, the weapon that could be steered, or steer itself, right on to the target. Hitting the pickle barrel might, plausibly, be taken literally.

However imperfect the early efforts, World War II was the birthplace of what we today call precision-guided munitions (PGMs), and the German researchers were at the vanguard. Three technologies made the emergence of PGMs possible. Radar offered means of target detection and tracking, but also homing functions, while radio could facilitate remote control or act as a datalink. To radar and radio, we can add television. In the history of television, the first primitive transmission of live images occurred in 1909. By 1940, the technology was still crude, but it had progressed sufficiently for weapons engineers to experiment with TV guidance. By placing a TV camera in the nose of a bomb and beaming the pictures back live to a receiving station, an operator could execute a form of line-of-sight guidance, but beyond his own visual position.

During World War II, the Germans put their full weight behind PGMs, with dozens of different concepts, prototypes and experimental models. Here we will take those that managed to make it into the operational domain.

One of the leading designs was the Henschel Hs 293, which entered development in July 1940. The core weapon was a modified SC 500 500 kg (1,100 lb) general-purpose bomb; the modifications involved removing the tail fins to make space for control features and adding aileron-fitted wings to the bomb body, giving the whole contraption the properties of a glide bomb. Suspended beneath the bomb was a rocket unit (usually a Walter HWK 109-507 engine), which provided ten seconds of thrust both to extend the range of the weapon and to enable the deploying aircraft to release it from a lower altitude. The device was radio guided using the 18-channel Kehl-Straßburg radio control link system. The tail of the bomb held the Funkgerät 230 (FuG 230) Straßburg receiver, while aboard the command aircraft was a Funkgerät 203 (FuG 203) Kehl transmitter, from which the operator could send control signals.

The mode of deployment was as follows. A carrier aircraft (usually a Dornier Do 217 or a Focke-Wulf Fw 200) would transport the missile to within its operational range of the target, which was 5 km (3 miles). The weapon was released in the direction of the target at an altitude of about 4,000 m (13,123 ft). The rocket unit ignited, providing thrust, then cut out after ten seconds. A flare unit would also ignite at the rear. The Hs 293 was now an unpowered glide bomb, whistling through the air at up to 900 km/h (560 mph). The operator would use the flare signature to guide the weapon visually to target; he had to maintain line-of-sight throughout.

Most of the *c.*12,000 Hs 293 bombs built were of the format just described, but variants abounded. There were wire-guided versions, TV-guided versions, ones designed to explode underwater, even one with a magnetic fuse to detonate itself when flying through an enemy bomber formation (although the main intended target was enemy shipping). There was also an Hs 294 spin-off, this given front-end streamlining so it performed like a torpedo when it entered water; explosive bolts would blow off the wings, tail and propulsion unit the moment it submerged. This variant never went into production.

First blood to the German PGMs was drawn in August 1943, when Hs missiles were at the heart of a concerted attack on Allied shipping in the Bay of Biscay. On 25 August, the glide bombs struck and damaged the sloop HMS *Bideford*. Two days later, they sank the sloop HMS *Egret*, killing 194 crew, and struck and damaged the Canadian *Tribal*-class destroyer HMCS *Athabaskan*. (*Egret* was the first ship ever sunk by a guided aerial missile.) Many other ships were sunk or damaged by Hs 293 bombs around the Mediterranean over the remainder of 1943. The worst incident was that of HMT (His Majesty's Transport) *Rohna*, destroyed by a single Hs 293 off the coast of Algeria on 25 November 1943. Packed with crew and passengers, the stricken ship took 1,138 men (the bulk US servicemen) to their graves in unforgiving choppy seas.

Chapter 7

The Fritz-X guided bomb prefigured modern precision-guided munitions. Had they been available in larger numbers and from earlier in the war, they might have changed the balance of theatre naval power. Credit: Sanjay Acharya/CC BY-SA 4.0

The ship-killing guided bombs led to significant changes in Allied maritime air defence tactics and naval deployments. But as the Allies grew to understand the weapon, they became increasingly successful in developing and deploying electronic countermeasures (ECM) to jam the control signals, the British with the Type 650 transmitter and the Americans with the XCJ transmitter. The Hs 293 became less effective in the maritime context, hence in 1944 it was repurposed for attacking inland targets, particularly bridges in the Western Europe campaign from June 1944.

The Hs 293 was a high-explosive blast bomb, most effective against relatively soft-skinned vessels. Its close cousin, the Fritz-X, however, was a pure-bred warship killer, designed specifically to punch into the largest armoured vessels. Its development began in 1939 and tracked alongside that of the Hs 293, not least because both used the same Kehl-Straßburg radio control technology. But its designer, Dr Max Kramer at the Deutsche Versuchanstalt für Luftfahrt (DVL; 'German Research Institute for

Aviation') in Berlin-Adlershof. The destructive component was the armour-piercing PC 1400 bomb, a heavy 1,400 kg (3,080 lb) device fitted with a chromium-vanadium or manganese-silicon steel-penetrating nose cap. The tail was heavily modified, a 12-sided frame enclosing four stocky fins. Two of these fins had solenoid-activated spoilers; the guidance receiver unit in the tail transferred control instructions to the spoilers, the resulting distribution of drag giving directional control. The forward body of the bomb had four short fixed wings arranged in a cruciform pattern, and the whole design, which included gyroscopic stabilization, was very aerodynamic. It was controlled in exactly the same way as the Hs 293, via radio controls from an operator who maintained line of sight.

The Fritz-X went through several prototypes. The X-1 variant developed by the Ruhrstahl company eventually went into production in 1943, with Rheinmetall-Borsig. (Note that the Fritz-X appeared under several names, including Ruhrstahl X-1, SD 1400, PC 1400 X-1 and the FX-1400. 'Fritz-X' was the favoured name, both for the Germans and the Allies.) It first saw action on 12 July 1943, launched at Allied shipping in Augusta harbour, Sicily, albeit without confirmed hits. That would change on 9 September, when the battleship *Roma*, flagship of the Italian fleet, and her sister ship *Italia* were both struck by Fritz-X bombs, released by six Do 217K-2s from III./KG 100, the Germans intent on preventing the ships transferring to Allied control following the Italian armistice. *Roma*, hit twice by these brutal weapons, was sunk with 1,393 men lost; *Italia* suffered serious damage. Fritz-X would kill again. In September 1943 off Salerno, ships sunk or severely damaged included the battleship HMS *Warspite*, the light cruiser USS *Savannah*, the light cruiser HMS *Uganda* and several merchant ships.

Fritz-X demonstrate the vulnerability of ships to guided weapons. Yet the Allies improved their ECM technologies and procedures, sufficient to blunt many attacks, albeit not all. Growing Allied air superiority in the Mediterranean and elsewhere also made life very uncomfortable for the control aircraft – a Do 217 or He 111 transporting a heavy bomb, or

Chapter 7

loitering in a combat zone, made a soft target for fighters. Finally, as always, there was the production war, which Germany was progressively losing. The intention had been to manufacture 750 *Fritz-X* per month, every month, but by the war's end only 1,386 had been made.[50]

One final German ASM worth mentioning is the Blohm und Voss Bv 246, known as the *Hagelkorn* ('Hailstone'). Although this weapon went into series production in December 1943, and some 1,000 were made, it never saw combat operations. Which is just as well from the Allied perspective, because it had potential. Its designer, Dr Richard Vogt, was an aircraft designer rather than an ordnance expert. His Bv 246 was another glide bomb, but this had long and thin high-mounted wings; total wingspan was 6.4 m (21 ft). It had such excellent glide properties that if released from an altitude of about 7,000 m (23,000 ft) it could carry its 435 kg (1,000 lb) warhead to a distance of 161 km (100 miles). This meant that the carrier aircraft could stay at a safe distance from any air defences around the target.

The development of the V-1 flying-bomb meant the Bv 246 suddenly lost a role. Although the first versions of the weapon were unguided (necessitated by the loss of line-of-sight at distance), however, in 1945 there were experiments fitting it with the *Radieschen* ('Radish') passive radiation seeker. In this form, it was one of the earliest concepts of an anti-radar missile, self-guiding to enemy radar transmitters. The Germans pursued innovation to the end.

Chapter 8

Tallboys and Disney Bombs – Allied Ordnance and Missiles

***

Although the German PGMs have acquired more historical profile than similar Allied weapons, this does not mean that the Allies were slack in this area. The British were, admittedly, not leaders, focusing as they did more on heavy and specialist bombs (see page 160), but the United States certainly took steps into the age of precision warfare.

FINDING THE TARGET
The Americans' first significant output in this field was the Vertical Bomb-1 (VB-1). What sounds like a statement of the obvious was actually a standard 454 kg (1,000 lb) general-purpose AN-M65 bomb fitted with a radio-controlled four-fin tail unit, to give adjustment in the vertical axis. It was also known as the AZON bomb, the acronym standing for 'AZimuth ONly', a reference to the sole dimension of control. As with the German guided bombs, the AZON was joystick controlled by the bombardier in the aircraft; he followed the weapon's progress via observing a smoke flare burning on the tail unit.

The AZON was a simple improvement over a standard bomb, but an improvement nonetheless. It was used to make attacks on point

Chapter 8

Here we see the BC-1156 control lever joystick control unit for the US AZON bomb. The bombardier would keep visual contact with the falling bomb and adjust its descent direction to the target. Credit: Steven Fine/CC BY-SA 2.0

targets – mostly bridges, but also an oil refinery and ammunition dumps – in the second half of 1944. It led to an improved version, the RAZON, which added 'Range' to the spectrum of control, although this did not see service until the Korean War. More importantly, perhaps, it also set the conceptual framework for post-war PGM conversion packages, such as the US Joint Direct Attack Munition (JDAM), a tail-unit GPS guidance system that has turned large stocks of dumb bombs into weapons of the most exceptional accuracy.

The US Navy was not to be left out of the PGM action. Its contribution was the ASM-N-2 Bat, in no way to be confused with the ludicrous bat bombs to which we gave critical evaluation previously. The Bat took the same munition as used in the AZON but wrapped around it an advanced radar-guided glide bomb, resembling a small aircraft. This device could reach targets up to 32 km (20 miles) away, released from beneath the wings of aircraft such as the PB4Y-2 Privateer patrol bomber. This time, there was no squinting down sights and toggling joysticks. It was what we would today call a 'fire and forget' missile, using active radar homing. It contained a transceiver, a piece of kit that combined the functions of transmitter and receiver. So, despatched in the general direction of a target, it would then hunt that target itself. The Bats proved themselves in combat, principally in the Pacific and Far East. They were used to good effect destroying Japanese bridges in Burma and one even hit and damaged the Japanese escort ship *Aguni* from the absolute limit of its combat range.

The US engineers and scientists were evidently intrigued by the potential of glide bombs. A very late-war development was the US Navy's experimental CTV-N-2 Gorgon IIC, which had some passing similarities to the V-1 in layout, with a top-mounted pulsejet and an intended operational range of 130 km (80 miles). Unlike the unguided V-1, however, the Gorgon had a high-mounted wing, vertical and ventral tail stabilizers and front canards, plus it also used active radar homing, a field in which the Americans became the leaders. Although intended for use in ship-to-shore bombardments in the expected assault on Japan, the Gorgon saw no wartime service and instead played its role as a post-war experimental drone and, when the experiments were done, a target aircraft.

The Bat and Gorgon were just two of the glide-bomb experiments. There was also another series of American air-launched glide bombs that began with the GB-1, designed between 1941 and 1943. The GB-1 took an M34 910 kg (2,000 lb) bomb and strapped it to an unpowered glider with a twin-tail layout. This weapon had a bulbous, cheap and ungainly look, which awarded it the nickname 'Grapefruit Bomb'. The weapon had no guidance system but had a gyroscopically stabilized autopilot and was released GDO (general direction of...), with a range of 32 km (20 miles).

For a few days in May 1943, GB-1s were thrown at targets in Germany during USAAF bombing raids. They had some redeeming qualities, such as causing German AA batteries to fire on them, believing that they were enemy aircraft, but they were also wildly inaccurate, so had little subsequent use. Yet they spawned many experimental guided variants before war's end, including ones controlled by heat-seeking, radio command guidance, semi-active and active radar guidance, and television guidance, all of which informed post-war weaponry.

Chapter 8

THE BRITISH CONTRIBUTION – BIG BOMBS, BOUNCING BOMBS

Dotted throughout the history of World War II, the names of certain individuals stand out for their associations with secret weapons and maverick ingenuity. Britain's counterpoint to, say, Germany's Wernher von Braun, is surely Barnes Wallis.

Born on 26 September 1887 in Ripley, Derbyshire, Wallis's love of engineering and his appetite for invention both manifested early. He launched his career, aged 17 and pushing against the will of his parents (they wanted him to attend university), working as an apprentice at Thames Engineering Works in London, moving soon after to J. Samuel White shipbuilder on the Isle of Wight, then in 1913 to the prestigious Vickers-Armstrong company. Here he was trained in the arts and knowledge of airship and aircraft engineering; he also completed a degree in engineering in 1922, through an external study programme via the University of London.

Wallis showed precocious talent for invention and lateral thinking. He became a leading airship designer, heading the creation of the *R80* and *R100* (the latter sister ship of the famous, and ill-fated, *R101*). In the 1930s he left an enduring legacy on aircraft development by inventing the geodetic design of fuselage and wing structures, which provided the super-robust framework for the Wellington bomber and some other prewar British aircraft. Once war was joined in 1939, however, Wallis demonstrated an aptitude for ordnance design.

Wallis was a firm believer in the potential of strategic bombing to wreck the means of Germany's warmaking. He gave deep thought to how to take the war to Germany's industrial heartland, the Ruhr, not least to attacking the three great dams that gave the region megawatts of hydroelectric power, plus copious water for manufacturing processes. These were the Möhne, Eder and Sorpe dams. Wallis wrote an influential paper, 'A note on a method of attacking the Axis Powers', which he distributed in March 1941. It was emphatic about the rewards for attacking the dams, plus coal fields and oil storage tanks: 'If their destruction or paralysis can be accomplished THEY OFFER A MEANS OF RENDERING THE ENEMY UTTERLY INCAPABLE OF CONTINUING TO PROSECUTE THE WAR.' In the same paper, he described his thinking behind a massive 'earthquake' bomb that could unleash unequalled destructive effects. In a subsequent paper in April 1942, he offered a new weapon to solve the dam problem – a 'Spherical Bomb – Surface Torpedo'. Both of these projects would receive official endorsement and, in tight secrecy, Wallis began working to perfect his designs.

The chronology needs some clarification here. Wallis's first on-paper design was for a monstrous 10,200 kg (22,400 lb) bomb. Such ordnance, he proposed, would be dropped from a high altitude, so it had plenty of time to gather pace. On impact, the bomb's weight and velocity, plus its sharp pointed nose, would combine forces to punch it up to 41 m (135 ft) below the surface; when it detonated there, it would produce a rippling earthquake effect in the surrounding terrain, which Wallis estimated would affect a radius of 11.7 hectares (29 acres). Targets such as dams and factories would be destroyed by the displacement of the very earth on which they sat.

It was a grand idea but was immediately arrested by the fact that there was no bomber in the RAF capable of transporting such a weapon. Undaunted, Wallis duly designed one – the six-engine 'Victory Bomber'. This aircraft was projected to attain exceptional speed, altitude and lift performance, but the whole project, including the bomb, was cancelled in May 1941 by the Air Ministry, who couldn't justify the expansive diversion of resources. There was a war on, after all.

Wallis's 1942 proposal for a 'Spherical Bomb – Surface Torpedo' found more receptive ears, however. Based on his water-tank tests, the concept was of a bomb that could be dropped on to water from a specially adapted low-flying bomber. The bomb would skip across the water, going *over* sub-surface or surface obstacles such as torpedo nets, then striking

Chapter 8

the target and coming to a stop. At that point it would sink below the surface and be detonated at a set depth by a hydrostatic pistol; the weapon was a curiously packaged combination of surface-skipping torpedo, mine and depth charge. The shockwave and the 'bubble pulse' effect generated by the underwater explosion would cause great damage to ship hulls and – Wallis's primary targets – German dams.

Wallis and his team – Wallis was definitely *not* the only big brain on the project – performed an endless variety of tests throughout 1942 to convince RAF authorities of the practical viability of the 'bouncing bomb'. These included test drops of scale models plus the destruction of a disused dam at Nant-y-Gro, near Rhayader, Wales, on 24 July 1942, obliterated by 127 kg (279 lb) of explosive. By February 1943, the project had received the green light. Two variants were under development: the spherical 'Highball' for use against German ships (the Allies particularly had *Tirpitz* in mind) and the larger drum-shaped 'Upkeep' for use against the dams.

The R&D process for the two bouncing bombs is, in its details, a fascinating wrestle with the principles of engineering and physics. Numerous dramatic drop tests were conducted in the process, many of them captured for posterity on film, available to watch online. (These were the days before the Health and Safety Executive; when watching the video footage, note the sometimes ludicrous proximity of observers to the unpredictable bounce-line of the device.) There are also many surviving reports of the trials, such as this excerpt dated 24 June 1943, regarding tests conducted at Reculver, Kent:

> *There is a considerable variation in the range of bombs dropped under the same conditions (cf U 13 and U 16). The line error is not large. It was noticed that when the track of the bomb was across the waves the line error was small and the axis of the cylinder remained horizontal, whereas when the track was along the waves the line error was greater and at the end of the run the axis of the cylinder*

might be at 30° or 45° to the horizontal. It was to be expected that if the bomb did not hit a target beforehand it would continue to travel forward after it sank. Analysis of the photographic record taken of the drop with the live bomb, shows that it actually moved back 90 feet before detonation, indicating that the axis of rotation had precessed more than 90°. No estimate could be obtained of the position as regard line.

Bombs should not be dropped from heights of less than 50 feet, as at lesser heights the splash from the first impact with the water strikes the aircraft and may cause damage. [...]

In order to determine whether the 'Torpex' filling would be detonated by the shock at impact with the water, a live filled bomb, without detonators, was dropped from about 500 feet. It did not detonate.

The complete explosive train was tested by dropping a live filled and fully armed bomb (U 26) in the open sea. It detonated satisfactorily at a depth calculated to be 33 feet. The plume first appeared 4 seconds after the bomb was last seen on the surface. [...] It reached a maximum height of 760 feet. While rising the plume was roughly cylindrical and had a mean diameter of about 200 feet.[51]

The final design of both weapons eventually emerged, and the aircraft was created to deliver it – a Lancaster Special B Mk III, a standard Lancaster heavily modified by Avro chief designer Roy Chadwick.

Upkeep was 1.52 m (60 in) long and 1.27 m (50 in) in diameter, a 4,200 kg (9,250 lb) drum containing 2,990 kg (6,600 lb) of Torpex explosive. In use, the bomb was held beneath the bomber's forward fuselage by a pair of swinging triangular mounting brackets. A crucial part of the bomb's performance came from imparting backspin to it; the reverse spin meant that the bomb skipped from the surface of the water rather than sank, and also that when it descended down the face of the dam it 'clung' to the surface rather than bounce off. The 500 rpm spin, which began ten minutes out from the target, was delivered by a hydraulic motor with a belt-drive connection to the bomb.

Testing revealed that the optimal performance of Upkeep was dependent upon very low-level release – just 18 m (60 ft) above the water – and at 373 km/h (232 mph) precisely. The altitude, or lack of it, was a tall order for even the best pilots. The squadron chosen for the dam attacks, No. 617 Squadron – aka 'The Dambusters' – practised ultra-low-level flying until it became second nature, not least because the entire approach to the target would be made at treetop height, quite literally. To aid precision in the final attack, however, Benjamin Lockspeiser, director of scientific research at the Ministry of Aircraft Production, developed a height reference system: two angled spotlights shone down beneath the aircraft, and when the beams intersected that meant the aircraft was at the correct drop height. Release distance calculations were performed by a simple Y-shaped wooden contraption; the bombardier would place the rear of the device against his eye, and it was time to drop the bomb when the two forward points corresponded with designated features of the dam.

Upkeep was the product of one man's vision, an entire team's innovation, and hundreds of test hours. The proof of all the effort, the true test of Wallis's self-belief, came with Operation *Chastise* on the night of 16–17 May 1943. Nineteen Lancasters of 617 Squadron, led by 24-year-old Wing Commander Guy Gibson, threaded their way across occupied Europe, often flying at about 10 m (33 ft) from the ground, to assault all three of the Ruhr dams. In the attack, the aircraft were bitterly resisted by German air defences, and by the end of the raid eight of the 19 aircraft were lost. Many of the Upkeep bombs missed or overshot their targets, but a consequential few worked as planned. While the Sorpe dam remained relatively unscathed, both the Möhne and the Eder were breached, sending avalanches of water through the valley below.

Chastise appeared a resounding success, a triumph of air-crew bravery and ordnance engineering. Yet history would qualify any rejoicing. Both dams were repaired in a matter of weeks rather than the expected years, and the Ruhr's industrial productivity was little affected. On the human level, 1,650 people were drowned or otherwise killed in the flooding; 1,026 were foreign POWs and forced labourers. 617 Squadron nevertheless adopted an apposite motto: *Après moi le déluge* ('After me the flood').

Upkeep would never again be used during the war. The smaller Highball variant was taken into production, but had its thunder stolen by Wallis's big bombs, to which we shall turn again shortly, and never saw action. Other nations, allies and enemies, took note of the bouncing bomb principle and tried to develop home-grown varieties. The Germans retrieved an Upkeep from a Lancaster that crashed during Operation *Chastise* and attempted some reverse engineering. Their efforts were thwarted because they never factored backspin into the design; this was a critical secret the British maintained. They also developed an intriguing *Kurt* rocket-assisted skip bomb. The front end of this device looked somewhat like the Highball bomb (although the Germans had no captured examples), but to the 386 kg (850 lb) warhead was fitted a rocket unit to deliver powered acceleration. When the weapon hit the water, the rocket unit fell away, leaving the bomb to skip on its way; range across water was 457 m (500 yd) and the bomb was fitted with a hydrostatic pistol. In tests the *Kurt* was dropped by twin-engined Me 410 *Hornisse* ('Hornet') heavy fighters and single-engined Fw 190 fighters, but as a late-war entry the weapon never saw production or service, not least on account of the progressive loss of German authority in the air.

Finally, the United States also produced a Highball copy, under the code name 'Baseball'. Testing this weapon bought tragedy, as the US scientists decided to drop it at just 7.6 m (25 ft), in order to maximize cross-water range. An A-26C Invader attempted this in the ocean off Eglin Air Force Base in Florida; the bomb bounced off the water and smashed the aircraft's tail clean off. The aircraft immediately nose-dived into the water, killing all three crew instantly.[52]

TALLBOY AND GRAND SLAM

His bouncing-bomb vision satisfied, Wallis could turn back to his interest in massive air-dropped penetrator bombs. It was now 1944, and there was a target-rich environment in occupied Europe. Hardened objectives ripe for heavy ordnance included U-boat pens (some of these had reinforced concrete roofs 7 m/23 ft thick), underground storage bunkers, V-weapon sites and railway tunnels. There was also that most tempting of naval prizes, the German battleship *Tirpitz*, operating out of sheltered fjords in Norway.

The first of Wallis's big bombs was 'Tallboy'. This was scaled down from his original 1942 plans, but it was still a beast. It measured 6.4 m (21 ft) in length and weighed 5,430 kg (12,000 lb), the outer body cast in a single piece of high-tensile steel with a hardened and perfectly ogival nose piece to aid penetration. Special attention was paid to the bomb's aerodynamics so it could achieve optimal terminal velocity; impact speed was about 1,210 km/h (750 mph), just shy of the sound barrier, when dropped from 5,500 m (18,000 ft). To improve stability, its four large fins were canted slightly to impart spin during the fall. On impact, the Tallboy could penetrate about 4.9 m (16 ft) of concrete, and when its 2,358 kg (5,200 lb) of Torpex filling detonated the resulting crater might measure 24 m (80 ft) deep and 30.4 m (100 ft) across. It would be deployed by specially modified Lancasters of No. 9 Squadron and No. 617 Squadron.

The 'Grand Slam' bomb was basically a Tallboy but taken to extremes of size; indeed in the design stages the weapon was originally called 'Tallboy Large'. This was the '10-ton bomb' Wallis originally envisaged. It weighed a staggering 10,000 kg (22,000 lb) and measured 8.08 m (26 ft 6 in) from tip to tail. On impact it could penetrate 6 m (20 ft) of concrete, or 40 m (130 ft) of earth. With 4,300 kg (9,300 lb) of Torpex on board, the weapon unleashed astonishing devastation. The Lancaster B.Mk 1 (Special) designed to carry it was a major overhaul of the standard bomber, stripping out everything that wasn't required, strengthening the undercarriage, uprating the engines. Still, when carrying the Grand Slam,

Ordnance ground crew handle a Grand Slam bomb carefully using a crane at an airbase in Lincolnshire. Note the smooth aerodynamic profile of the bomb, to maximize terminal velocity. Credit: Ian Dunster/UK government/public domain

which hung low and heavy underneath the aircraft, the bomber had almost no manoeuvrability.

Both Tallboys and Grand Slams were extensively used in combat in 1944 and 1945. Tallboy's first outing on 8/9 June 1944 set the scene, absolutely demolishing the Saumur rail tunnel in France, despite its being many metres beneath a hillside. Tallboys were used repeatedly throughout 1944, smashing U-boat pens and dock facilities. The greatest of its kills, however, came on 12 November 1944, when three Tallboys finally wrecked and capsized the *Tirpitz* at its anchorage near Tromsø, during Operation *Catechism*. (*Tirpitz* had previously been attacked twice by Tallboy-equipped Lancasters, being significantly damaged during Operation *Paravane* on 15 September 1944.)

The Grand Slams delivered their seismic effects in 1945. Alongside 11 Tallboys, two Grand Slams helped bring down the important Bielefeld viaduct on 14 March, after which the bombs were used against a number of railway bridges and viaducts, most of the targets being destroyed. They were also used to hit U-boat pens in Bremen and Hamburg, punching through the ferro-concrete overhead cover of both, and also smashed coastal gun batteries on the islands of Heligoland and Düne in the Heligoland Bight on 19 April.

Wallis's big bombs were not always as decisive as we might imagine. Accurate direct hits were difficult to achieve on point targets, and sometimes detonation would occur immediately on impact rather than after deep penetration. Nevertheless, their hurricane-like blast and cavernous cratering brought operational results, and even to this day many modern armies retain outsized bombs for special purposes.

Of the three British armed services, it was not only the Royal Air Force that took secret air-dropped ordnance into action. The Royal Navy was also active in R&D related to deep-penetration bombs, but it took a quite different route to that pursed by Wallis and others. Commander (later Captain) Edward Terrell was another of the UK's energetic inventors, part of a specialist RN team investigating enemy weapon development. He developed a new type of plastic armour and while working at the Directorate of Miscellaneous Weapons Development he contributed to the development of the Hedgehog and Squid anti-submarine weapons (see Chapter 10). From September 1943, however, he also began working on what would become, officially, the 4,500 lb Concrete Piercing/Rocket Assisted Bomb. In popular parlance it was known as the 'Disney Bomb'.

While the RAF used mass and freefall velocity as penetrative forces, Terrell looked towards assisted speed. As its title expressed, the weapon was only 2,041 kg (4,500 lb) in weight; it was 5.03 m (16 ft 6 in) long, 380 mm (15 in) in body diameter and carried a warhead of 230 kg (200 lb) of Shellite, a mere sliver of the high-explosive capacity of a Tallboy or Grand Slam. The crucial component was a tail section that contained 19 rocket motors from the 3-inch Rocket

Projectile weapon. The bomb was dropped over its target at an altitude of 6,095 m (20,000 ft) and at about 1,524 m (5,000 ft) altitude a time-delay or barometric switch would fire the rockets, accelerating the missile to a supersonic speed of 1,590 km/h (990 mph). Driven at this pace, the armour-piercing casing would cut through, potentially, more than 4 m (13 ft) of concrete, the base fuse detonating the warhead once it was firmly buried in the target.

Terrell's development of the Disney Bomb had to push against some considerable opposition from various quarters, but its development was eventually embraced in early 1944 and test drops were made in the spring of that year. The weapon actually became a joint development with the USAAF – hence the name Disney Bombs – who were looking for their own deep-penetration weapon but without the cumbersome weights and measures of the British big bombs.

The Disney Bombs were first dropped in anger by B-17 Flying Fortresses of the 92nd Bombardment Group over German E-boat and midget submarine pens at IJmuiden in the Netherlands on 10 February 1945. Intelligence indicated that hits and penetration had been achieved. Further raids were made against fortified targets in Germany in March and April, although results were often disappointing, as much for operational reasons as for weapon performance. Secret weapons still had to cope with the vagaries of war.

THE GRAND PANJANDRUM

The big bombs and bouncing bombs were born in response to specific tactical and target challenges. In their case, the effort produced viable and valuable weapon systems. But, as ever, sometimes the hard work of engineers and scientists went off the beaten track. We end this chapter on ordnance with just such an example.

In the mid-18th century, the actor Charles Macklin made the professionally relevant claim that he could read any paragraph once and thereafter he could recite it from memory verbatim. This was tested with

Chapter 8

a paragraph of nonsense verse by Samuel Foote, which was quoted in the 1820 novel *Harry and Lucy* by Maria Edgeworth (note, in tone and content it is very much text of its time):

> *So she went into the garden to cut a cabbage leaf, to make an apple pie; and at the same time a great she-bear coming up the street, pops its head into the shop. 'What! no soap?' So he died, and she very imprudently married the barber; and there were present the Picninnies, and the Joblillies, and the Garyulies, and the grand Panjandrum himself, with the little round button at top; and they all fell to playing the game of catch as catch can, till the gunpowder ran out at the heels of their boots.*

Little did the theatrical and literary types realize that their work would inform, at least in naming, one of the most preposterous weapons developments of World War II, the Great (rather than Grand) Panjandrum, or just Panjandrum.

The weapon was part of a portfolio of Allied experiments from 1943 exploring methods of breaching German coastal defences. Its concept came from an officer working with the Combined Operations headquarters but was developed by the Royal Navy's Directorate of Miscellaneous Weapon Development. In overall architecture, the Panjandrum has been likened to a giant explosive double Catherine wheel firework. It consisted of two large and wide outer wheels (3.2 m/10 ft diameter) connected by a fixed central drum axle that also contained a 1.8-tonne (2-ton) explosive warhead. Multiple angled rockets were fixed around the circumference of each wheel. The intention was that when the rockets were ignited, they would turn the wheels through the force of torque (as, indeed, a Catherine wheel is spun around its axis when fixed to a post), driving the whole fiery contraption from an amphibious landing craft, up the landing beach and into the fortification walls or strongpoints. At this point the wheels would shatter, and the explosive charge would drop neatly against the foot of the obstacle. When it detonated, it would blast through whatever was preventing the Allied soldiers from pushing their way off the beach.

Theory would meet non-compliant reality in the most spectacular fashion. Brian J. Ford, in his work *Secret Weapons: Death Rays, Doodlebugs and Churchill's Golden Goose* has unpacked the misplaced, or rather ignored, science around the Great Panjandrum, pointing out that: 'If the number of the rockets was too low, the device would not be able to overcome the rolling resistance of the sandy beach. However, if the number and power of the rockets were substantially increased, then wheel-spin could set in. There was no means, as it were, of slipping the clutch as the giant wheels slowly gained forward velocity.'[53] Ford also explains the fact that while the rotation of wheel meant that at any one time about half of the rockets would be driving the great device forwards, the other half would in essence be trying to push it back.

The scientific principles of the Great Panjandrum were not promising at the outset. A variety of potential redesign solutions were obstinately ignored (such as mounting the rockets on a separate wheeled trolley that carried the warhead), and the boffins pushed on regardless. The test site for the outlandish weapon was chosen – the beach at the picturesque seaside resort of Westward Ho! near Bideford, Devon. Given its popularity as a place of recreation, the beach tests completely undid all the secrecy surrounding the project, as hundreds of curious onlookers milled around to see it in action. They certainly witnessed a spectacle. From September 1943, the development team performed numerous tests, launching the Panjandrum from a landing craft in the surf, often filming the trials. (Again, readers are able to watch some of these tests online.) The results were a sequence of impressive failures. Sometimes the great wheel didn't make it to the beach, other times it did so but simply toppled over. Sometimes it ran relatively true, other times it wandered off in absent-minded fury. Rockets occasionally detached themselves, fizzing around the Devon sands in lethally erratic patterns.

Chapter 8

All manner of remedies were sought to the problems – more rockets, a third wheel, the attachment of steering cables between the wheel and the launch boat. Nothing seemed to help. Furthermore, officialdom was increasingly unimpressed. During a January 1944 trial in front of several VIPs and photographers, the Great Panjandrum outdid itself, lurching at the guests and forcing them to take cover, jettisoning its rockets and finally laying on its side and burning itself out. Enough was enough. The project was terminated soon after. As the great American actor W.C. Fields once remarked: 'If at first you don't succeed, try, try again – then quit; no use being a fool about it.' That phrase also had relevance in the field of secret weapons.

Chapter 9

Limpets and Pigs – The Small-Boat War

***

The phrase 'secret weapons' can have a misguiding clinical tone. It evokes the white lab coats and geeky inventiveness of James Bond's beloved Q-branch, where weapons are high tech in both design and application. In reality, people get their hands dirty designing, developing and, especially, deploying secret weapons.

Nowhere is this more the case than in the use of secret miniature submarines in World War II. Their design was ingenious, their technology was advanced, but their operation was absolutely grim on a human level. The products of the scientists and engineers were only converted into working propositions when brave individuals took them into the most hostile physical arenas, and suffered accordingly.

LIMPET MINES

Before we get to submarines, we pause to consider one of the most important secret tools of the underwater war – limpet mines. Although we most often identify the efforts of MI(R) with land warfare, it also made some significant contributions to naval weaponry. Specifically, in the late 1930s Major Millis Rowland Jefferis, a brilliant military engineer

Chapter 9

working for MD1, began work on a new type of anti-ship weapon. He studied methods by which powerful bombs could be attached discreetly to the hulls of ships, using powerful magnets. He liaised with Robert Stuart Macrae, the editor of the magazine *Armchair Science*, who would go on to become one of MD1's most creative engineers; he happened to be the inventor of the Sticky Bomb explained in Chapter 2, and he subsequently became Jefferis's second-in-command. Macrae would soon be working full-time on development of the magnetic mine. One of his faithful collaborators was Cecil Vandepeer Clarke, an engineer and inventor who by his own admission liked to blow things up.

There were many technical obstacles to overcome, not least sourcing magnets that were powerful enough to hold a heavy explosive charge and its casing to the hull of a ship, which was likely to be covered with various marine accretions. They eventually used incredibly powerful magnets made by General Electric Company in New York, for use in research laboratories. Macrae and his team also had to produce an underwater time-delay mechanism. They experimented with an aniseed ball sweet, which was found to dissolve in water at a usefully predictable rate.

The final output was the Mk 1 Limpet Mine. It was designed for human deployment, the intention being for special forces divers, surface swimmers or canoeists to approach the enemy vessel covertly, place the charge on the ship's hull, then retreat to a safe distance before the charge detonated via a timer mechanism. The standard design consisted of a 2 kg (4.5 lb) high-explosive charge in a boxy waterproof plastic case. In the OSS catalogue – the Americans also adopted the limpet mine – the writers explain that the explosive case could also be delivered empty, for the user to fit a custom charge, or it could be 'requisitioned ready loaded with Torpex'. The explosive box was framed by six powerful horseshoe magnets (three on each side), to attach it to the ship's hull, placing it at least 1.5 m (5 ft) below the waterline. By being beneath the surface, the mine could amplify the blast effects of its relatively small charge by utilizing the incompressibility of water. The blast of the mine could tear a hole about 7.6 m (25 ft) square in the side of a ship; often multiple mines would be placed. The best location was over the ship's boilers, as the inrush of water into the boiler space would kill the ship's propulsion, plus cause secondary explosions. Each end of the explosive casing was threaded to take a time-delay fuse and a detonator. The delay before detonation could be varied considerably, from just a few hours to more than eight days. The temporal options provided tactical flexibility. For example, the operator could place the limpet mine while the enemy ship was in dock, but time it to detonate when the ship was offshore and in deep waters.

More than 2.5 million limpet mines were produced. Notably, about 1 million of that total went to the Soviet Union for use against German coastal shipping around the Baltic, and against smaller enemy craft along the Soviet Union's mighty rivers. Several improved variants – Mk II, III and IV – were produced and there were some offshoots. The OSS catalogue, for example, shows a limpet-type device affectionately called the 'Pin-Up Girl'. The device had a non-magnetic method of attachment, it being fixed to the side of the ship via a cartridge-powered pinning device that literally fired a heavy steel pin into the plates of the ship's hull. While we are thinking of magnetic mines, we should also note the Allied 'Clam' anti-vehicle magnetic mine that worked on similar principles, although the later German application of Zimmerit anti-magnetic-mine coating to its armoured vehicles limited the applications of these weapons.

The naval limpet mines were used by several Allied naval special forces teams, including the Royal Marines Boom Patrol Detachment (RMBPD), the Norwegian Independent Company, the Australian Services Reconnaissance Department, and the Z Special Unit (a joint Allied force operating in East Asia). The most famous action of the latter was Operation *Jaywick*, conducted on the night of 26 September 1943. A mixed Australian and British commando team clothed themselves as Malay fisherman and took a motorized fishing boat close to Keppel harbour in Japanese-occupied Singapore. Under cover of darkness, members of the team infiltrated the harbour using collapsible canoes and placed limpet mines on Japanese ships. When the mines exploded the following day, seven Japanese vessels were either sunk or seriously damaged. Another renowned covert operation using limpet mines was Operation *Frankton* on 7–12 December 1942, in which a small RMBPD penetrated the German-occupied French port of Bordeaux in six folding kayaks and placed limpet mines that subsequently sank two merchant ships and damaged four others. The raid, however, came at a cost – of the 13 men deployed, six were captured and executed and two died from hypothermia; remember my opening comments. The raid was immortalized in the 1955 Technicolor war film *The Cockleshell Heroes*.

But the Allies weren't the only ones to master the art of limpet-mine operations. The Italians were fellow pioneers in naval special forces with their Decima Flottiglia MAS (Decima Flottiglia Motoscafi Armati Siluranti; '10th Torpedo-Armed Motorboat Flotilla'), a force of marines and combat frogmen in action between 1941 and 1943. The underwater soldiers of '*La Decima*' had several types of Italian-made limpet mines to play with: explosive charges ranging from about 10 kg (22 lb) to more than 100 kg (220 lb). They could also deploy them using another of the great secret weapons of World War II – the human torpedo.

ITALIAN INNOVATION

On the night of 18/19 December 1941, the Italian submarine *Scirè* stopped 2 km (1.3 miles) off the British-controlled harbour of Alexandria, one of the great logistical hubs for Allied operations in the Mediterranean and North Africa. The submarine deployed three diminutive underwater vessels and their crews. The craft were officially titled Siluro a Lunga Corsa ('Long-Running Torpedo'), but to the men using them they were better known by their blunt nickname – *Maiale* ('Pig'). The objective was to steer these vessels deftly into Alexandria, where there crews would mine and destroy British warships in one of the most famous covert naval actions of World War II.

A modern reconstruction of the Siluro a Lunga Corsa. The ring of serrations around the forward body indicate the enormous warhead. Credit: Robert Orlando/CC BY-SA 4.0

The underwater torpedo concept was as uncomfortable as it was audacious. It had been pioneered by the Italians in the last two years of World War I. At this time, the Italian Navy was striving to find solutions to emasculate the powerful fleet of the Austro-Hungarian Navy. (When World War I began, Italy was on the side of Germany and Austria-Hungary as part of the Triple Alliance, but in April 1915 it negotiated the Pact of London that resulted, in May 1915, in the country swapping sides and declaring war on Austria-Hungary.) The hub of the Austro-Hungarian Navy was its home port at Pula in Croatia, where it based 16 battleships, including four *Tegetthoff*-class dreadnoughts. Because of submarine and surface vessel threats, however, these mighty vessels generally stayed at safe anchor, protected by anti-submarine and anti-torpedo nets. Soon, creative Italian minds were looking for non-conventional ways to breach these defences and attack the ships beyond.

The early, secret inventions had an improvisatory aura about them. The *Grillo* ('Grasshopper'), for example, was an electric-powered,

Chapter 9

shallow-draft punt vessel that featured chain tracks running around the two sides of the hull. The idea was that the small vessel would approach the battleships under cover of darkness and use its tracks to climb over the top of the defensive nets, rather like a tank grinding over a wall. They were also known as *Barchino Saltatore* ('Jumping Punts'). Manned by four crew, each *Grillo* was armed with two 450 mm (17.7 in) torpedoes, these mounted on davits to swing the weapons into the water at the moment of attack.[54]

The *Grilli* were ingenious, but their surface approach made them vulnerable to being spotted. Such was proved the case in two unsuccessful attacks on Pula in April and May 1918, which resulted in the light vessels taking heavy fire and having to be scuttled by their crews. There had to be another way.

Indeed there was, and it was pioneered by the collective efforts of Major Raffaele Rossetti of the Corps of Naval Engineers and Second Lieutenant Raffaele Paolucci, who served in the Medical Corps but also had the inventor's mindset. Both initially worked independently on ideas to solve the Pula challenge. Since 1915, Rossetti had focused on the idea of taking a B57 600 mm (23.6 in) torpedo and modifying its design and powerplant so that two frogmen in diving suits could sit astride it and 'ride' it directly to the target. The device – what we today would call a Swimmer Delivery Vehicle (SDV) – was named the *Mignatto* ('Leech'). Paolucci, meanwhile, was looking into the possibility of fitting a limpet mine with flotation bags, these taking the weight off the mine and allowing a diver to swim along while towing it, eventually placing it against the hull of the target ship. His plan proved unworkable in testing, but he heard about Rossetti's work and the two men teamed up, productively so.

Rossetti and Paolucci took their work with utmost seriousness, not least because they would be the crew of the first attack – they were, in essence, packing their own parachutes. The *Mignatto* went through subsequent modifications, not least by removing the plan to sit on the torpedo; now the two frogmen would simply hold on to it using handles fitted on the body. It was a powerful weapon, though, fitted with two 170 kg (375 lb) magnetic limpet mines fitted on the nose.

On 1 November 1918, Rossetti and Paolucci made their attack on Pula using the weapon they had so painstakingly designed. It was deployed near to the harbour via a succession of surface craft, then the two men guided it across the netting defences and in among the Austro-Hungarian ships and their complacent crews. After about four-and-a-half hours of stoically riding the torpedo, they deposited one of the limpet mines against the hull of none other than the Austro-Hungarian flagship, lead vessel of the *Tegetthoff* class, SMS *Viribus Unitis*. (Strictly speaking, the ship was now called *Jugoslavija*, as the day before it had been transferred to the navy of the State of Slovenes, Croats and Serbs.) The timers were set for two hours. During the exfiltration, however, both men were discovered and captured. With dire irony, they were held aboard the very ship they had just mined. Thus they personally experienced the success of their own mission when the mine went off at 0620, sinking the battleship and killing about 400 of its crew (after some debate, Rossetti and Paolucci were permitted to escape the sinking ship). The abandoned *Mignatto* and its second warhead had come to rest undetected against a freighter in the harbour; that ship too was destroyed when the mine detonated.

The raid on Pula was a proof of concept. It demonstrated how a small, cheap, covert SDV was capable of sinking a huge, expensive and powerful surface vessel. The Italians doubled down on the concept during the 1930s, and from 1935 two naval engineer divers, captains Teseo Tesei and Elios Toschi, developed the Siluro a Lunga Corsa (SLC; 'Long-Running Torpedo').[55] Much had changed since the *Mignatto*. Measuring 7.3 m (24 ft) long and powered by a 1.2 kW (1.6 hp) electric motor, the SLC had successfully reinstated the riding design, the two-man crew sitting astride the torpedo in tandem. Although they remained exposed to the open sea, and wore full diving suits, a wave break at the front gave

Chapter 9

them a token shield, plus they had more advanced controls, including a magnetic compass, a depth gauge, a clock and a bubble level for longitudinal trim control. Maximum speed was 5.6 km/h (3.4 mph) and range was 28 km (17 miles). The nose of the vessel was a 300 kg (660 lb) warhead, which was designed to detach and could be locked on to the hull of a warship through a variety of means, or simply dropped beneath the vessel. The SLC was a clever design, but its ungainly appearance and the awkwardness of its operation meant it acquired the unflattering *Maiale* nickname.

The SLC was promising. From 1940, when Italy entered World War II, it also had a conflict in which it could be tested. SLCs were adopted by the Decima Flottiglia MAS, who conducted their first, and unsuccessful, actions using them in 1940. But on the night of 18/19 December 1941, *La Decima* crews delivered their game-changing attack in Alexandria. The three SLCs, once deployed, made their way to the British anchorage, evading outer defences by slipping in when the British opened a boom to admit three destroyers. They then negotiated the torpedo nets and found the battleships HMS *Valiant* and HMS *Queen Elizabeth*, prestige vessels in the Royal Navy. In the case of the *Valiant*, the Italian divers found it impossible to attach the explosive charge to the keel, so instead dropped the bomb on to the sea bed 1.5 m (5 ft) directly beneath the hull. The crew attacking the *Queen Elizabeth* managed to attach their warhead successfully to their target; the third warhead was dropped beneath the tanker *Sagona*. Between 0547 and 0554, the three mighty warheads erupted in Alexandria harbour, seriously damaging the battleships, plus *Sagona* and the destroyer *Jervis*, which had been oiling alongside *Sagona* at the time of the explosion.

Six of the Italian crewman were captured during the attack on Alexandria, but the operation had been an astounding success. *La Decima* notched up further victories. Operating covertly from the oil tanker *Olterra*, which was at that time interned in a neutral Spanish port, SLCs attacked Allied merchant ships in Gibraltar in May and August 1943, sinking or damaging a total of six Allied vessels before the oil tanker ruse was discovered.

BRITISH MODELS

On 18 January 1942, Prime Minister Winston Churchill wrote a memorandum to the British Chiefs of Staff. He was clearly in impatient mood: 'Please report what is being done to emulate the exploits of the Italians in Alexandria harbour and similar methods of this kind. At the beginning of the war Colonel Jeffries had a number of bright ideas on this subject, which received very little encouragement. Is there any reason why we should be incapable of the same scientific aggressive action the Italians have shown? One would have thought we should have been in the lead. Please state the exact position.'[56]

The exact position was, from April that year, the accelerated development of the first British human torpedo, the Chariot Mk I. The design team was headed by Commander Geoffrey Sladen and Lieutenant Commander William Richmond 'Tiny' Fell of the Royal Navy's Submarine Service. Built by Stothert & Pitt, a crane maker based in Bath, Somerset, the Chariot Mk I was actually a near-literal copy of the Italian SLC, with the same capabilities and a 270 kg (600 lb) Torpex warhead.

The British were keen to put the Chariots to use. The first attempted mission was an ambitious action in late October 1942 against the supreme German battleship *Bismarck*, which at that time was anchored at Trondheimsfjord in Norway. The operation proved to be abortive, a combination of mechanical failure, bad weather and accident preventing the two Chariots from making their attack. On 2/3 January 1943, however, five Chariots had a go at Italian shipping in Palermo harbour, sinking the *Capitani Romani*-class cruiser *Ulpio Traiano* and damaging the troop ship *Viminale*, although of the eight Chariots that departed for Operation *Principal (iii)*, none returned. Multiple Chariot missions followed throughout 1943, focusing their efforts in the Mediterranean and around Norway. There were few successes, the missions bedevilled by all manner of adversity and bad luck. But the Chariots soon found a new lease of life with different operational parameters and an upgraded variant of the Chariot.

Design of the Chariot Mk II had begun back in 1942, and the first operational models appeared around the spring of 1943, with full production commencing in early 1944. The key change was that the two-man crew now sat in back-to-back positions inside the torpedo's hull, shielded by an optional detachable Perspex hood. (The crew were still submerged in water, however, and conducted operations while wearing rebreathing apparatus, so as not to release air bubbles that could be detected on the surface.) The dimensions of the Mk II were extended – it was 9.3 m (30 ft 6 in) in length, 0.76 m (2 ft 6 in) in diameter and 1 m (3 ft 3 in) in height – but it was sleeker in the water, creating less disturbance. Furthermore, it now carried a 540 kg (1,200 lb) warhead.

Although the Mk II had beefed-up explosive force, one of the major applications for the craft was conducting covert beach reconnaissance, handled by the Combined Operations Pilotage Parties (COPP). Beach reconnaissance was a critical prelude to any amphibious operation. Those conducting such missions were tasked with gathering a long list of hydrographic and tactical information, including beach gradient, beach substrate, tidal range, underwater obstacles, the flow of currents, exits from the beach, and enemy emplacements (above and below water). Survey accuracy dramatically improved the planning, preparation and assault phases of a coastal landing, but it also had to be performed under the guns and eyes of a watchful enemy. The Chariots provided a potentially useful means to gather information from a more resilient platform than simply sending in a diver. Chariots were used for beach reconnaissance operations off Sicily in 1943, as part of the intelligence gathering in preparation for the Operation *Husky* landings in July 1943, and were also applied to spy on German coastal positions around Norway. In 1944, the COPP teams were kept lively surveying the beaches of Normandy prior to Operation *Neptune* landings of 6 June 1944.

Periodically, however, the Chariots were put to more combative use. On 21/22 June 1944, Operation *QWZ* saw a joint British-Italian force of naval commandos use Chariots to attack the Italian cruisers *Bolzano* and *Gorizia* in La Spezia harbour; the two vessels had been seized by the Germans following the Italian armistice on 8 September 1943. (Note that some personnel from *La Decima* had now formed a new naval unit, the *Mariassalto*, to fight on the Allied side.) In a characteristically challenging action, *Bolzano* was sunk. Over the other side of the world, in Phuket harbour, Thailand, on 28–29 October 1944, even more impressive gains were taken when two Mk II Chariots, deploying from the submarine HMS *Trenchant*, mined and sank two Japanese vessels, including the sizeable troopship *Sumatra Maru*.

The Chariots were just one element in a thick catalogue of British midget submarines developed during World War II. SOE's Station IX brought forth the Welman midget submarine, another contribution from its engineer John Robert Vernon Dolphin, who had also designed a folding special operations motorbike called the Welbike. The Welman was a fully enclosed one-man craft, just 6 m (19.6 ft) long and driven by an electric motor to a maximum speed of 3 knots (5.5 km/h; 3.4 mph) over a surfaced range of 67 km (42 miles). The business end of the craft was a detachable 540 kg (1,188 lb) charge of Torpex at the nose.

As was typical of the miniature submarines of the day, the Welman needed the steadiest psychology behind the controls, since the single, lonely user sat in a claustrophobic, hot and airless steel world, staring into dull waters through the tiny armoured glass of what amounted to a conning tower. Some 100 examples were produced between February and October 1943, but they were mechanically unreliable and tactically unwieldy. A single disastrous operation against German shipping in Bergen, Norway, in November 1943 consigned them to

Chapter 9

stores and trials. Interestingly, however, the fact that the Germans captured an example during the Bergen operation possibly contributed to their own midget submarine programme (see page 186).

By far the most famous, and influential, of the British midget submarines were the X-Craft. The X-Craft were another effort to create a diminutive special operations vessel for operations against enemy ships at anchor. A Royal Navy team led by Commanders C.H. Varley and T.I.S. Bell began developing concepts and prototypes from 1939. *X-3*, the first of the operational X-class submarines (aka the X-Craft), was launched in March 1942 and, following trials, was commissioned in November. It was joined by the *X-4* prototype plus six production X-Craft (*X-5* sub-class) manufactured by Vickers from December 1942. In 1944 they would be joined by six of the upgraded *X-20* sub-class.

The X-Craft were four-man midget submarines, the crew consisting of a captain, a second lieutenant, a diver and an engine room artificer. They were crammed inside a vessel 15.5 m (51 ft) long with a beam of 1.75 m (5 ft 9 in) and a displacement of about 30.5 tonnes (30 tons). Powered by a Gardner 4LK 4-cylinder marine diesel engine (actually a development of a London bus engine) generating 31.3 kW (42 hp) the X-craft could maintain 6 knots (11 km/h; 6.8 mph) at the surface and, switching to its electric motor, 5 knots (9.3 km/h; 5.7 mph) submerged. Maximum dive depth was 91.5 m (300 ft) and range was 132 km (82 miles). For combat missions, the X-Craft had two detachable amatol charges, each weighing 2,000 kg (4,400 lb).

We should pause for a moment to reflect on the experience of manning such vessels. The interior environment was predictable ghastly, somewhat akin to miniaturizing a sewerage plant, cramming people into it, then submerging it and sending it into combat. One of its former crew, Geoff Galway, has written about his experiences aboard the X-Craft. Here he gives a grim account of using the 'Wet and Dry' compartment, which was designed to allow the diver to leave and enter the craft smoothly when placing limpet mines:

The wet and dry lockout was a repulsive place, as we had of course to use it as an escape hatch on the divers' routine exit and entry when the X-craft was submerged. The lockout contained the head [toilet], a baby Blake WC of the kind most yachtsmen know quite well.

On leaving the submerged X-craft, the diver or COPP swimmer flooded the inner cylinder which had the same axis and therefore the same centres of gravity and buoyancy as the inner chamber, the water flowing through the WC bowl and discharge tank of the head.

The swimmer or diver operated the wet and dry lockout sitting on the WC pan. A few old friends and used sheets of paper floated up round him in his specially designed COPP Siebe-Gorman diving suit and heavy submarine underwear, before he operated the pressure equalising valve and climbed out.

I found the business of using the head in X-craft so disgusting that I worked out a technique of crouching on the casing à la française, hanging on to the ensign staff. Some found this too acrobatic and some chaps never opened their bowels during their time at sea in X-craft, a most unhealthy state of affairs if an exercise or operation involved living aboard for several days.[57]

Remarkably, considering the atmospheric horrors, the X-Craft crews performed some heroic feats with their vessels. The signal triumph of the X-Craft came on 22 September 1943, with Operation *Source*. Six X-Craft were towed to their launch points off northern Norway, then under their own power headed towards the German anchorage at Kåfjord, Nordkapp. There were the three mightiest surface vessels of the Kriegsmarine: *Tirpitz*, *Scharnhorst* and *Lützow*. The transit to the objective seemed to augur operational disaster – two of the vessels were lost to accident or other misfortune. Another submarine, *X-10*, had to abandon the attack owing to mechanical failure. The remaining vessels, however, managed between them to place their charges under *Tirpitz*.

Ultimately, none of the X-Craft returned from Operation *Source*, the crews either killed or captured, and the Germans in possession of another fascinating piece of marine technology. But *Tirpitz* was almost wrecked when the explosive charges went off, leaving her effectively out of action until May 1944. The humbled ship would eventually be destroyed by British air attack.

Operation *Source* was proof positive of the midget submarine concept. The X-Craft were used in another Norwegian offensive operation, attacking the Laksevåg floating dock on 15 April 1944. Confusion led to the primary target being relatively unscathed, while the unfortunate merchant ship *Bärenfels* was sunk. X-Craft were used intensively for reconnaissance and beach survey work in preparation for the Operation *Overlord* landings. Furthermore, the British also built a slightly larger variant of the X-Craft, the XE-class submarines, specifically for operations in the Far East. Two of their operations – *Sabre* and *Foil* – both conducted on 31 July 1945, involved manually cutting underwater Japanese telecommunications cables off Saigon and Hong Kong respectively, forcing the Japanese to return to wireless communications that the Allies could intercept. For all their operational unpredictability, the British miniature submarines ultimately proved their worth.

GERMAN MINIATURES

The Italians pioneered human torpedo/midget submarine warfare. The British took up the baton and refined this branch of secret warfare. Axis efforts to join this sidebar arms race, however, were diverse and erratic. There had been an early effort, the Versuchs-U-Boot V 80, an experimental design launched in April 1940. It was a four-man testbed for the Walter hydrogen peroxide-based turbine propulsion system, with a range of 93 km (58 miles) at 28 knots (52 km/h; 32 mph). Although it was never commissioned, and was scuttled at the end of the war, it nevertheless provided some insights that went into the design of the Type XVII submarine.

By 1943, however, not only were the Germans emphatically losing the conventional submarine war but their investment in miniature submarines was thin. Too late in the game, therefore, the Germans suddenly sought to develop their own breeds of secret midget submarine. The operational focus of these craft was not only to take on the big surface vessels in their harbours, but also to combat Allied amphibious forces at the point of invasion.

And they went for it. The Nazi war machine's instinct for over-proliferation of specialist types is evident in this late-war effort. Here we summarize the main craft that emerged:

Biber ('Beaver') – A one-man vessel displacing 5.7 tonnes (5.6 tons) and armed with two G7e (TIIIc) torpedoes or two Torpedomine Typ B (TMB). A total of 324 of these vessels were built.

Delphin ('Dolphin') – A prototype two-man fast-attack midget submarine, given a powerful engine and hydrodynamic shape that would have enabled it to keep pace with Allied coastal shipping.

Marder ('Pine Marten') – A curious vessel consisting of a one-man torpedo 8.3 m (27 ft 3 in) long. The single crewman sat under a transparent polymer canopy, with a G7e torpedo slung underneath as its primary weapon. The *Marder*'s nose was a flooding tank rather than a warhead, which enabled the craft to dive to a depth of 25 m (82 ft). An offshoot of the *Marder* was the *Hai* (Shark), which was longer, faster and had more endurance, but never went beyond prototype stage.

Neger ('Moor') – The *Neger* was another dual-torpedo design, this one with an overall length of 7.6m (24 ft 11 in). Range was 89 km (55 miles) at 4 knots (7.4 km/h; 4.6 mph). One alarming failure of the *Neger* was that the operator was sometimes unable to release the running torpedo once the attack run began. For this and a host of other reasons, the *Neger* had an appalling 80 per cent mortality rate for its crew.

Type XXVIIA *Hecht* ('Pike') – Another two-man type, the *Hecht* was an electrically powered vessel inspired by the German capture of the

X-Craft in Norway. Armament was either a G7e torpedo or an explosive charge in the nose; the nose section could also be adapted to carry a diver.

Type XXVIB *Seehund* ('Seal') – The *Seehund* was the most prolific and successful of the German miniature submarine types, with 285 produced in 1944–5. It was a two-man craft with a displacement of 17 tonnes (16.7 tons) submerged, a maximum surfaced speed of 7 knots (13 km/h; 8.1 mph) and 6 knots (11 km/h; 6.9 mph) submerged via a 19 kW (25 hp) AEG electric motor and an impressive surface range of 500 km (310 miles). Armament was two G7e(TIIIc) torpedoes, underslung.

Molch ('Newt') – The *Molch* was a further one-man type, similar to the *Biber* craft with its two underslung torpedoes or mines, but manufactured by AG Weser, Bremen, instead of the *Biber*'s builder, Flender Werke, Lübeck. Some 400 were produced.

Schwertwal ('Sword Whale'/'Orca') – This two-crew vessel reached only prototype stage in 1945. Using a powerful Walther turbine, the vessel had a designed top speed of 20 knots and was armed with two torpedoes.

This parade of midget craft were far from idle in the last years of the war, as Hitler's strategic desperation progressively took the brakes off secret weapons missions. The vessels were operated by German naval special forces units, including the K-Flottille of the Lehrkommando sabotage branch and the K-Verband (full title Kleinkampfverbände der Kriegsmarine, 'Small Battle Units'). The *Seehunden*, for example, conducted some 142 missions between January and May 1945; these ranged from direct attacks on Allied coastal shipping to resupply operations for German garrisons besieged on the French coast. A 40-strong *Neger* flotilla, operating from its base in Favrol Woods west of Honfleur, launched multiple aggressive actions against the British invasion fleet off Normandy in July and August 1944 with significant results – three minesweepers and two British destroyers sunk and one Polish cruiser damaged.

The *Biber* vessels were also active. On 30 August 1944, 20 *Biber* craft struck out from Fecamp against the Allied Normandy bridgehead, claiming two ships destroyed, although no losses were recorded by the Allies. Thereafter the *Biber* redeployed to the Waal/Maas estuary for operations against Allied shipping around the Netherlands, and sank the cargo ship *Alan A Dale* on 23 December. *Molch* and *Biber* vessels collectively sank seven small enemy vessels between January and April 1945, in a total of 102 sorties. The missions included an ambitious multi-vessel assault against the road bridge across the River Waal at Nijmegen on the night of 12 January 1945, a large first wave attempting to blow gaps through defensive netting, and a smaller second force bringing the main charges. The attack, like many others, was carved up by defensive firepower as soon as the Allies got wind of what was happening. Indeed, in January–April 1945, 70 *Biber* and *Molch* vessels were destroyed. Losses of midget submarines remained grossly unequal compared to the amount of damage done. (As proof, consider that 324 *Biber* were constructed.) As in the air, the Allies gained total supremacy on the waves around the coasts of western Europe. Only in the Baltic and Arctic waters did the Kriegsmarine still hold some sway.

DESPERATE MEASURES

Japan was another devotee of the midget submarine and saw the potential early on. The country entered the war in December 1941 equipped with the Type A *Ko-hyoteki*, a two-man vessel displacing 47 tonnes (46 tons) submerged, measuring 23.9 m (78 ft 5 in) and armed with two 450 mm (17.7 in) torpedoes. These minor craft actually fired some of the opening shots of the Pacific War, with five Type As participating in the Pearl Harbor attack. Compared to the aerial onslaught playing out above, their contribution at Pearl Harbor was limited. All the vessels were lost, either to enemy fire or deliberate scuttling. There is the possibility that torpedoes from one of the submarines might have hit the USS *West Virginia* and/or the USS *Oklahoma*, but the evidence is unclear.

Chapter 9

What isn't debatable was that some 101 Type As were completed and many went on to attack US and Allied shipping operating around the multitude of contested Pacific islands, plus made further forays into Allied anchorages. On 31 May 1942, for example, three Type As infiltrated Sydney harbour in an attempt to sink capital vessels. One submarine became entangled in an anti-torpedo net and the crew, showing the same absolute resistance to defeat or capture as their land army, destroyed themselves and their boat with demolition charges. Another craft was crippled by depth charges and, again, the crew took their own lives. The final Type A managed to launch its torpedoes and damaged the depot ship HMAS *Kuttabul*, killing 21 Allied sailors before slipping out to open sea, where it apparently sank, taking its crew with it. A similar attack in Diego Suarez harbour, Madagascar, on 29 May 1942, was also roughly handled by the Allies, but the torpedoes nevertheless damaged the British *Revenge*-class battleship HMS *Ramilies* and sank the oil tanker *British Loyalty*. In November of the same year, Type As made several forays against US supply ships running to and from Guadalcanal, and scored hits on merchant vessels.

While the Japanese midget submarines certainly put some warheads on target, by the final years of the war the immense scale of the US Navy meant that the Pacific naval war became pathetically one-sided. Fatalistic panic, therefore, produced innovations without any regard to their human operators. The Japanese Navy sank into suicidal fantasies, one output of which was the *Kairyu* ('Sea Dragon') midget submarine. The *Kairyu* was a two-man craft, measuring 17 m (56 ft) long and with a beam of 1.3 m (4 ft 3 in). One of the primary strengths of the *Kairyu* was its range. With its 64 kW (86 hp) diesel engine running, it could travel an impressive 830 km (516 miles) at 5.4 knots (10 km/h; 6 mph) while surfaced; its 60 kW (80 hp) electric engine gave it a submerged range of 70 km (43 miles) at 3 knots (5.5 km/h; 3.4 mph). Armament was two 450 mm (18 in) torpedoes and a single 600 kg (1,320 lb) explosive charge in the nose. While the torpedoes were a weapon with stand-off range, the warhead was definitely not – the intention was that, having unleashed their torpedoes, the crew would pilot the submarine straight into an enemy ship, whereupon an impact fuse in the nose would destroy both the vessel and its operators, the last view of the midget submarine's crew being the grime of a ship's hull.

The *Kairyu* was a true last-ditch weapon, designed as a defence in the event of the expected US assault on the Japanese home islands. It is unclear how many were produced; somewhere around 200 seems likely. But the war ended before they could be put to use; had they been deployed, it is likely they would have shared the fate of many midgets submarines: smashed to pieces by gunfire and depth charges, before they could even embrace underwater immolation.

EXPLOSIVE BOATS

Some German midget submarine missions were conducted in tandem with another of the Kriegsmarine's innovations – or desperations, depending on your perspective – the *Linsen* boats.

The *Linsen* boats belong to a category of German craft known as *Sprengboote*, or 'explosive boats': fast craft packed with explosive and guided to their targets remotely. Germany conducted several experiments with the idea between 1909 and 1911, and from 1915, 17 operational examples of a *Fernlenkboot* ('remote-control boat') were developed and deployed on the Flanders coast. Packed with 700 kg (1,540 lb) of explosives, they were steered to the target via a 25 km (16 mile)- or later 43 km (27 mile)-long control cable spooled out from a coastal ground station; wireless transmissions from an overhead observer aircraft provided the instructions on guidance.

The *Fernlenkboot* were awkward to handle, vulnerable to sea conditions, and hard to get on target – these were primitive days in the history of remote guidance. But the principle carried enough theoretical merit to be revived in World War II. In 1941, the HWA covertly authorized the production of explosive boats based on the spruce-built Leichtes Sturmboot 39 ('Light

Assault Boat 39'). This vessel was a low-profile motorboat, driven to a maximum speed of 26 knots (48 km/h; 30 mph) by an outboard motor, and used to transport up to six personnel quickly across rivers, lakes and other inland or coastal waterways. In their explosive format, the boats went into service with the Küstenjäger ('Coastal Infantry'), a specialist sub-unit of the Regt Brandenburg zbV 800, an Abwehr commando formation. In April 1944, the boats were given an operational outing off Italy, when the Küstenjäger used them alongside *Neger* midget submarines against the Allied fleet. The light craft found themselves bucketing in the rough seas, and the attack was ineffective. Shortly after, the Brandenburgers were ordered to transfer their boats to the K-Verband and the overall control of the Oberkommando der Marine.[58] Under new management, the explosive boats were redeveloped by Oberleutnant zur See F.H. Wendel, who was head of the K-Verband Design and Testing Bureau. He changed the core vessel to a heavier and more robust motorboat, with an overall length of 5.75 m (18.8 ft) and powered by a 3.6-litre Ford 95 hp Otto motor V-8. Top speed was 31 knots (57 km/h; 36mph) and range was 148 km (92 miles). This *Sprengboote*, laden down with 300 kg (660 lb) then 480 kg (1,056 lb) of explosive in containers at the stern, was known as the *Linse*.

The *Linsen* of World War II had a distinct twist on the guidance mechanism. Initial guidance was via its one-man crew. As the target hove into view, this man turned on red and green identification lights on the stern, then would heroically throw himself overboard. At this point, control was handed to the crew of a nearby three-man command boat, who steered the attack boat to the target using ultra-shortwave radio guidance from a 7 m-band Blaupunkt transmitter, although wire-guided methods were also developed. (The command boat's crew responsibilities also included remembering to pick up the man overboard.) The lights provided a visual frame of reference and the boat would be guided straight into the hull of the enemy vessel. This impact would smash the bow, resulting in the rear section of the boat sinking; the explosives were detonated either by a 2.5- or 7-second timer delay, once they were beneath the target ship's hull.

Both technical ingenuity and wild improvisation had gone into the *Linsen* craft, and more than 1,200 were produced. Not altogether unexpectedly, though, in action the boats proved to be a clumsy and largely ineffective attempt to redress the imbalance in naval superiority. They were used operationally on several occasions, including against the Normandy landing fleet, against Allied shipping around Antwerp harbour in Belgium, and around the Italian Riviera (the stretch of coast from the French border in the west and crossing Italian Liguria). But successes were always limited, the greater profits of such attack usually going to the conventional E-boats they often accompanied.

The Italian Riviera provides an illustrative theatre. From September 1944, this 289 km (180 mile)-long stretch of coastline was guarded by an Allied fleet known as Flank Force. Despite its power (it included a battleship, five cruisers, more than 12 destroyers, and many other craft),[59] Flank Force came under incessant attack from the special forces of the K-Verbände. They brought with them many of the secret weapons we have already outlined, including the *Marder*, *Molch* and *Linsen*, plus the two-man SMA assault boat, fitted with small-calibre stern torpedo tubes. The contributions from the *Linsen* could be heroic but feeble. On 18 October 1944, for example, a total of 48 *Linsen* massed in German-controlled San Remo, joining other forces in preparation for a major attack. The small boats were gathered together in the town market place, hidden under tarpaulins. However, on 20 October the French destroyer *Forbin* began an offshore bombardment of the town, and one of its 130 mm (5 in) shells struck the *Linsen*, destroying all 48 in a single blast.[60] On 8–9 January 1945, five *Linsen* attacked the destroyer *Le Fortuné*; the destroyer went undamaged, but its gunfire sank two of the attackers. Just a week later, ten *Linsen* sank in bad weather after a fruitless search for targets.

The example of the *Linsen* illustrates how the Holy Grail of secret weapons – destruction of a high-value target by a low-value weapon – was particularly elusive when technology met reality. Nevertheless,

Chapter 9

several other nations tried and tested the explosive boats concept and scored some kills in the process. The Italians developed two explosive-boat types, the Motoscafo da Turismo (MT) and the Motoscafo da Turismo Modificato (MTM). The guidance system on these craft was nothing more than the crewman aiming the craft at the target, jamming the rudder at a range of c.100–200 m (328–656 ft) from the point of impact, then leaping overboard. Impressively, on occasions it worked. On 26 March 1941, six MT/MTM vessels attacked Allied vessels at anchor in Suda Bay, Crete, damaging the Norwegian tanker *Pericles* and the British cruiser HMS *York*, the latter so badly that it had to be grounded to prevent it from sinking. An impotent beast, *York* was then hit by subsequent German air attacks and had to be scuttled. Jumping ahead to 16 April 1945, an MTM boat plus an MTSM motor torpedo boat serving with the Marina Nazionale Repubblicana (the navy of the Italian Social Republic, the puppet state in German-occupied Italy) attacked the French destroyer *Trombe* off the coast of Liguria, damaging the vessel beyond repair. Explosive motorboats might have been something of a poor-man's secret weapon, but it was clear they needed to be taken seriously.

Before leaving the subject of small attack craft, we should again look towards Japan, and the *Shinyo* ('Ocean Shaker') suicide craft. These were surface-riding equivalents of the *Kairyu* suicide submarine. Specifically, they were either a Type 1 (one-man crew) or Type 5 (two-man crew) motorboat capable of speeds of 26 knots (48 km/h; 30 mph) or 30 knots (56 km/h; 35 mph) respectively, with a 270 kg (600 lb) explosive charge in the nose plus two 120 mm (4.7 in) RO-SA anti-ship rockets on the sides. The crews belonged to the Japanese Special Attack Units – military personnel dedicated to suicide tactics in the final two years of the war. As a sad mark of how far Japan had fallen, the average age of the crews of the *Shinyo* was just 17.

Some 6,197 *Shinyo* had been produced by war's end, and unlike the *Kairyu* they did see action. More than 1,500 were deployed against US operations around the Philippines and Okinawa in 1945, where they managed to either sink or damage a small but appreciable number of landing craft, cargo ships and destroyers.

But if one thought Japanese naval suicide secret weapons couldn't get any more rudimentary, think again. Another death-driven band of the Japanese Special Attack Units were the *Fukuryu* ('Crouching Dragons'). Some 4,000 volunteers for this service were gathered in the naval base at Yokosuka just prior to the end of the war. Their patriotic mission, and their training, was focused on converting them into suicide frogmen. Each diver was to be equipped with a special self-contained diving suit fully enclosing the body, including a heavy diving helmet; 9 kg (20 lb) of lead weights would keep the buoyant diver down on the seabed. Air supply was provided by two 3.5 litre (0.92 gallon) bottles of oxygen at 150 bar (2,200 psi).

The tactic was to place the divers, organized in six-man squads, under the water at Allied landing grounds. There they would remain, hidden in the littoral gloom at the ideal depth of 15 m (50 ft), for up to ten hours, shuffling around at a pace of 1.6 km/h (1 mph). They were even provided with liquid food packs to sustain their energy. But not sustain their lives. Each man was to be equipped with a specially adapted Type 5 attack mine, constructed from a 5 m (16 ft) bamboo pole with a contact-fused charge of 15 kg (33 lb) of explosives on the other end. The mines would be placed under the water ready for divers, staggered at 20 m (65 ft 7 in) intervals. The divers would communicate with each other by tapping pieces of metal together. Having selected their targets, each diver would simply collect a mine and ram it against the hull of a ship, he being just feet away from the blast. The successful completion of an attack would be the diver's own annihilation.

As it happened, the *Fukuryu* were spared death, at least from their intended means. None of the Type 5 mines were ready by the time Emperor Hirohito announced the Japanese surrender on 15 August 1945. So the high hopes of the *Fukuryu* programme's commander Captain K.

Chapter 9

Shintani, namely that the suicide divers would be as successful as the Japanese kamikaze air campaign, were never tested.

The *Fukuryu* illustrate the fact that a secret weapon need not be a sophisticated one. In this case, the innovation was in the application of human beings as guidance systems, bending all manner of ethical considerations to meet the perceived crisis.

What we might term the 'small-boat war' during World War II involved a range of secret marine weapons. Their technical secrets often did not remain privileged information for very long once they became operational, not least because the high rate of failure meant examples often fell into enemy hands, for leisurely study and even restoration and testing. This produced something of a chain effect – genealogies of underwater vehicles jumping from nation to nation. Tactically, the small-boat war was one of profound secrecy. Maritime special forces frogmen, sailors and submariners performed acts of the most extraordinary bravery and discomfort, often in the face of near-certain death from enemy fire or from the adversity of their operating environment. New technologies did not do away with the need for a very deep-seated courage.

Chapter 10

Hedgehogs and Electroboats – The Submarine War

As technologically and psychologically impressive as the miniature submarine operations were, a far greater subterranean battle was running its destructive course between 1939 and 1945. This was the fight by and against conventional submarines. At its heart, it was a war of secrets and secret technologies.

World War II was a truly global conflict. Its outcomes therefore depended heavily upon mastery of the sea lanes, not only to maintain inexhaustible military logistics far from home, sometimes in entirely different hemispheres, but also to supply domestic populations, a situation particularly acute in the case of the UK. Naval forces were also the only scalable delivery mechanism for the major invasions conducted by the Western Allies from 1942 onwards.

Although the big-gun ships still cut the waves, they were ageing heroes. The war signalled the end to the era of the battleship. Instead, the submarine and the aircraft carrier took centre stage. This chapter will largely focus upon the secret weapons and the secret war of the

Chapter 10

former. The submarine war was not only a titanic struggle of men above and below the waves, but it was also a fast-running arms race in advanced technology and adaptive tactics. The tactical and often strategic advantage was wrested bloodily from one side to the other as new weapons and devices were deployed, or countermeasures to the same were developed. The naval scientists and engineers, therefore, had to develop and field technologies that had the most profound impact on the war effort.

Given the high stakes, secrecy was paramount and pervasive. The details of each new weapon would be jealously concealed until that inevitable moment when the enemy deduced or discovered its capabilities and adjusted accordingly. Much of this battle of minds and mechanisms was conducted in domains that are outside the strict remit of our study here, but which remain consequentially central. The prime example is the naval code-breaking struggle between the Allies and the Axis, most famously expressed in the Anglo-American efforts to decrypt the Enigma and Lorenz ciphers used by the German U-boat fleet. Each technology described here was one node in a vast, frantically flashing switchboard of components and signals, some containing the promise of final victory.

THE THREAT

By June 1940, Britain famously, resolutely, stood alone in Europe against a German-occupied continent just the distance of a Channel crossing from British shores. As an island bastion, Britain was acutely dependent upon the free flow of merchant shipping to and from its ports. The steep growth of the UK's population in the 19th century and the first half of the 20th century meant that there were many more mouths to feed and many more consumers to supply. Compounding this issue, there had also been a reduction in agricultural land available for domestic production. Prior to the war, therefore, food imports rose to 50 per cent of the total British food supply. According to a retrospective UK report from the Ministry of Food in 1946, prior to 1939 imports accounted for 50 per cent of meat, more than 90 per cent of fats, 80 per cent of sugars, 90 per cent of cereals and 90 per cent of flour. In addition, the island had to bring in bulk cargo loads of animal feed, about 4.54–5.44 million tonnes (5–6 million tons) per animal. Broadening our focus to raw materials, while the UK was self-reliant in important commodities such as coal, it was highly dependent on imports for iron ore and timber; in 1939, for example, the UK had stocks of iron ore that amounted to no more than 12 weeks of peacetime production. Britain was – indeed remains – a nation fed and stocked via the sea.

Germany knew this and saw an opportunity. Britain knew this and saw a terrible danger, one that they had already experienced. During World War I, Germany's intermittent policy of unrestricted submarine warfare had been eye-opening, not least when the scale of impact was measured against the relatively small size of Germany's fleet of submarines – just 28 when the war broke out in 1914. The most predatory and intense phase of the German submarine campaign was between February 1917 and November 1918 – in one month alone, April 1917, the U-boats sank 873,800 tonnes (860,334 tons) of Allied shipping. The Kaiserliche Marine (Imperial Navy) wrapped a chokehold around John Bull's neck.

Shipping losses in the Atlantic led Britain to implement one of the most consequential maritime tactical innovations of both world wars – the convoy system. Convoys play a significant part in the story of this chapter, so they are worth understanding. Logic might suggest that when crossing an ocean as vast as the Atlantic, it is better to send merchant ships singly – the chances of a predatory U-boat or surface raider spotting a single vessel in the rolling, grey emptiness are minimal. That is indeed true for one boat, but not for many boats. If you increase the frequency of single-ship passages dramatically, then there is actually a high statistical likelihood that the U-boat commander would encounter a lone ship or two sooner or later, simply by hanging around the busy sea lanes. Furthermore, the lone ship would almost certainly have no military escort, a reality dictated by blunt economics and by the numerical imbalance between the size of the merchant fleet and the scarcity of escort vessels.

Chapter 10

The convoy system addressed both of these problems. A convoy consisted of multiple merchant vessels making the passage together. Convoy size varied tremendously when viewed across the two world wars: the first convoy in World War I had 12 ships, whereas the largest in World War II had 167 vessels. From the statistical risk point of view, the probability of the enemy making several sightings from 50 ships sailing independently was much higher than sighting 50 ships sailing in a convoy, despite the fact that the convoy covered a much larger area. Furthermore, while it was not deemed feasible to provide an escort for a single ship, it was definitely worth assigning destroyers, frigates and corvettes (later escort carriers) to 50 ships. Although not everyone bought into the convoy theory at first (the United States proved to be famously resistant until reality taught them otherwise), the introduction of the escorted convoy system brought an immediate and profound reduction in losses.

World War I ended in 1918 and with it the submarine war in the Atlantic. There was no turning back the clock, however. In much naval thinking, it was still a world of big-gun battleships, ocean-cutting heavy cruisers, fleet-footed destroyers and frigates. Even Germany remained wedded to the ideal of a powerful surface navy, going on to develop a world-beating range of pocket battleships and heavy cruisers, plus the great *Bismarck* and *Tirpitz* battleships. The Royal Navy remained one of the world's most powerful navies, being the guardian of Britain's coastal, off-shore and oceanic sea lanes. But the submarine war between 1914 and 1918 hinted that a gun-centric surface fleet was no longer enough to ensure naval dominance. Submarines – small, economical, lethal – were changing the tactical dynamic.

In the interwar years, therefore, all the former combatants began to invest in submarine fleets and technologies, to greater or lesser extents. But Germany sought to take a lead in Europe. In was in the 1920s and 1930s that development of some of World War II's most influential secret weapons began.

The Versailles Treaty prohibited Germany from owning or developing submarines. The interwar Reichsmarine deftly evaded this restriction by pursuing submarine R&D through a front company established in the Netherlands by the Krupp concern, with manufacturing facilities in Finland and Spain (in Spain, Germany also pursued covert development of torpedo technologies). Thus by the time Hitler slammed his fist on the table and rejected the Versailles Treaty, Germany had already produced three submarine prototypes, ranging from a small coastal type to a large ocean-going vessel. From 1935, under the authority of the new Kriegsmarine, Germany accelerated its submarine production.

By 1939, Admiral Karl Dönitz – the Befehlshaber der Unterseeboote (BdU; 'Commander of the U-boats') – had a fleet of 69 operational submarines – fewer than he wanted but enough to do some damage. The principal submarine types were the Type VIIB and Type VIIC. Having a handle on the specifications of the Type VIIC will give a useful framework for various developments below. It had an overall length of 67.1 m (220 ft 2 in) at the waterline, an overall beam of 6.2 m (20 ft 4 in) and displaced 871 tonnes (857 long tons) submerged. It was powered on the surface by two supercharged six-cylinder four-stroke diesel engines delivering up to 2,400 kW (3,200 hp) giving maximum surfaced speed of 17.7 knots (32.8 km/h; 20.4 mph). When submerged, two Brown, Boveri & Cie (BBC) GG UB 720/8 double-acting electric motors took over, generating 560 kW (750 hp) and a speed of 7.6 knots (14.1 km/h; 8.7 mph). Range was 15,700 km (9,800 miles) at 10 knots (19 km/h; 12 mph). The craft had an operational dive depth of 230 m (750 ft), although its crush depth went down to 250–295 m (820–968 ft). Armament consisted of five 533 mm (21 in) torpedo tubes (four bow, one stern), with 14 torpedoes or 26 TMA or 39 TMB sea mines, plus a single 88 mm (3.5 in) SK C/35 naval gun on the deck for surface engagements. The sub also collected a variety of machine-gun and cannon deck armaments for AA defence. Total crew complement was somewhere in the region of 44–52 officers and ratings. With its

Chapter 10

Type VIIs and other submarines, the U-boat arm of the Kriegsmarine began its six-year war in September 1939.

The British had not been slacking either. In terms of a submarine programme, in fact, they were not far behind the Germans. In 1939, the Royal Navy had a total of 57 submarines, although they were spread more thinly around Britain's globe-wrapping empire. The Anglo equivalents of the Type VII were the S-class and T-class subs designed during the late 1920s and through the 1930s, the former for operations in home waters or the Mediterranean Sea, the latter for long-distance imperial deployments overseas. But given their historical experience, the British had also begun to invest in advanced technology designed to find and kill submarines. From a technological point of view, the secret war against the U-boats began well before fighting started.

Winston Churchill famously said, in the second volume of his memoirs of World War II, 'The only thing that ever really frightened me during the war was the U-boat peril.' Here is not the place to give a full-blown account of the submarine war in the Atlantic and elsewhere, but an overview provides a sense of what was at stake. Hitler placed a prohibition upon unrestricted submarine warfare at the beginning of the war, and the U-boats quickly made their presence felt on the Royal Navy. On 17 September 1939, *U-29* torpedoed and sank the aircraft carrier HMS *Courageous*, and on 14 October HMS *Royal Oak* was destroyed while at anchor in Scapa Flow in Orkney, Scotland, by *U-47*. Both incidents were unnerving body blows to British naval prestige, but far worse was to come. In June 1940, France fell to the Wehrmacht war machine. The Kriegsmarine was now able to establish U-boat bases on the French Atlantic coast. These facilities, the expansion of the U-boat fleet, and the gradual introduction of U-boats with longer ranges enabled Dönitz's hunters to range deep into the Atlantic to interdict convoys. Furthermore, from late 1939, War Order No. 154 lifted all restrictions on U-boat targets. The gloves were off.

The efficiency and impact of the U-boat campaign were improved profoundly by the introduction of 'wolf pack' tactics, in which multiple U-boats were vectored on to a single convoy via radio communications to deliver a brutal co-ordinated attack, often repeated over several merciless days and nights. The Kriegsmarine also used long-range Focke-Wulf Fw 200 *Condor* aircraft, operating from French and Norwegian airfields, to locate and shadow convoys, while transmitting their position to naval planners. The Allies, meanwhile, countered with beefed-up escorts and improved escort ships and tactics, augmented by the introduction of new anti-submarine technologies, discussed below. The other crucial dimension was the signals war – the effort of both sides to intercept and decipher coded naval transmission – an intellectual battle fought with as much vigour as the shooting war.

The submarine war was one of peaks and troughs for both sides. Ironing out the complexities, for much (not all) of the period 1940–3 the Germans were in the ascendant, if only reflected by the volume of ship sinkings. In 1940, a total of 563 Allied ships were hit by submarine attack, resulting in sinking, damage or capture. In 1941, that figure was 501, but in 1942 it leapt to an extraordinary 1,322, declining to 582 in 1943, 243 in 1944 and just 98 in 1945. Given that the war in Europe lasted for just five months in 1945, it is clear that the U-boats remained a threat until the end, but in 1942 it seemed plausible that the U-boats might starve Britain into submission. Within, and suggested by, these figures, there were two specific 'happy times' for the U-boat crews, blocks of months in which the Allies appeared to have little answer to the U-boats' free-roaming tactics. The first was in July–October 1940, when the Germans exploited a gap in Allied defensive technologies by switching to night-time surface attacks, which resulted in 1,351,519 tonnes (1,489,795 tons) of merchant shipping sunk. The second was in January–August 1942, when the United States entered the war and the U-boats took advantage of its inexperience, killing 609 ships totalling 2.8 million tonnes (3.1 million tons), against a loss of only 22 U-boats.

Chapter 10

But when the pendulum swung back in favour of the Allies, it swung back hard. The annual figures for U-boat sinkings present an escalating and ultimately devastating picture:

1939 – 9
1940 – 24
1941 – 35
1942 – 87 (most of these were in the second half of the year)
1943 – 244
1944 – 249
1945 – 120

By the end of the war, 70 per cent of all U-boat crews were dead, the highest loss rate for any branch of service in the Wehrmacht. The Allied triumph was the product of multiple breakthroughs coming together in one devastating package. These advantages not only included improvements in naval weaponry and escort tactics, but also the introduction of long-range anti-submarine aircraft, themselves equipped with advanced detection technologies and devastating weaponry. By the end, there was nowhere for the submarines to hide.

DETECTION AND DESTRUCTION

By the end of World War I, there were several means by which one could kill a submarine. If it was surfaced and spotted (and remember, it was more common for submarines to attack from the surface than it was for them to attack submerged), you could hit back with gunfire, by ramming, or by a torpedo from another submarine. If the submarine was submerged, it might hit one of your moored mines or you could pound it with depth charges.

The first depth charge was a British invention. This was the Type D, born in 1916 as a bludgeoning response to the U-boat onslaught. The weapon was little more than a large drum filled with explosives, fitted with a hydrostatic pistol to detonate the charge at a pre-set depth. Depth charges were deployed simply by rolling them off the side or stern of the ship, or by firing them outwards from a launching device, ideally over the known position of the submarine but more likely based on an often inaccurate estimate. When the depth charge exploded, the intention was to get the blast close enough so that the overpressure would crush or fracture the submarine's hull, destroying it or forcing it to the surface.

The Type D evolved, by 1939, into the Mk VII. It was a real beast. At its peak development, it had a sinking velocity of 5.1 m/sec (16.8 ft/sec) and a maximum detonation depth – reflecting the improved dive performance of the German submarines – of 270 m (900 ft). By the end of 1942, its massive 130 kg (290 lb) charge of Torpex or Minol could split a submarine's hull catastrophically if it exploded within 8 m (26 ft) and drive it to the surface at a distance of 16 m (52 ft).

That sounds like a decisive weapon, particularly as depth charges were deployed in multiples across staggered depth brackets. The problem, however, was simply identifying the location of the submarine in an ocean that was both deep and vast.

During World War I, work began on technologies that could detect submarines using sound. The underlying principle was similar to the way that bats locate insects using echolocation – emitting an outward sound and locating the prey through the directional sound waves reflecting back off it. Early naval applications of this idea were explored just prior to World War I in the United Kingdom and the United States, mainly for detecting natural underwater hazards. From 1916, however, the Brits angled the investigations towards anti-submarine warfare, and the result was ASDIC.

Contrary to popular belief, the ASDIC acronym does not stand for 'Anti-Submarine Detection Investigation Committee' – this non-existent organization was actually invented as a cover title by the Royal Navy in 1939. Rather, it stood for the wilfully eccentric 'Anti-Submarine Divisionics'. Regardless of names, the technology as it had evolved by 1938 was

Chapter 10

exciting. In outline, it consisted of a sound transmitter-receiver device mounted in a metal dome on the frontal hull of the ship below the waterline. The pulse sound produced by the transmitter – that haunting 'ping' so beloved by the directors of tense submarine movies, so hated by actual submarine crews – was produced by passing an electric current through a quartz plate. The sound was focused and directional; while searching for the submarine, the ASDIC operator would swing the device in a 45-degree arc either side of the ship's course. If the high-frequency beam struck a submarine, it reflected back with a distinctive 'beep' signature and was picked up by the receiver, the information gleaned being presented on an electronic display manned by the operator. The angle of detection and the length of time between transmission, detection and return provided the submarine's range and bearing. The operator tried to lock on to the submarine, keeping it in the auditory spotlight while feeding information up the ship's bridge to guide the depth-charge attack.

ASDIC, later known as 'sonar' by the United States (a name soon adopted by everyone), became one of the most important Allied anti-submarine tools of World War II. It made a submerged submarine an identifiable target rather than an inferred presence. It could also be used in a passive mode to listen out for the sounds of U-boat activity, e.g. spinning propellers, working machinery, even crew noises; these were moments when the U-boat crews were advised to maintain absolute, breathless silence. But it was far from perfect. It gave poor readings in bad weather (in the Atlantic, that was most of the time), and an astute submarine commander would dive below the upper churn of the waves, which acted as a sound reflector for the ASDIC transmissions. It was prone to false detections; a passing whale, a school of fish, or even strong sea currents might be taken as an enemy submarine by an inexperienced operator. The system also lost contact as the detection range closed to within a range of about 300 m (984 ft) and as the submarine passed beneath the ship's hull, hence the last stage of a depth-charge attack was always performed blind.

And of course, the submarine commander was never compliant. He could dive deep and go quiet, or make lots of speed and frothing wake to confuse the signals. During the war, the U-boats also acquired assorted anti-sonar technologies. They could, for example, release a BOLD canister, a metal tin that contained calcium hydride, which when mixed with sea water released large amounts of gas. The canister did this intermittently over *c.*25 minutes, effectively impersonating a U-boat making submerged manoeuvres. An alternative was the *Siegmund* device, which let off a series of explosions to confuse the ASDIC operator. The struggle between ASDIC/sonar, therefore, was not one-sided, however optimistic the Allies had been before the war. (Some had seen ASDIC as essentially the end of the combat submarine.)

In the first year of the war, both sides of the submarine war were essentially feeling each other out, getting a sense of their tactics and technologies. The U-boat commanders were soon cognizant of ASDIC, which gave itself away in the most audible fashion, and began applying their countermeasures. The U-boat fleet was also dealing with a problem of its own, in what is known as *Die Torpedokrise,* the 'Torpedo Crisis'. During the 1920s, Germany had established its secret torpedo development programme in Spain, and during the 1930s it retained close guard over its torpedo designs. At the onset of war, two main types of torpedo were in use: the G7a and the G7e. Both had the same external dimensions: 533.4 mm (21 in) in diameter, 7.16 m (23 ft 6 in) in length, and had a warhead of 280 kg (617 lb) of TNT/HND/AL (a mixture of hexanitrophenylamine, trinitrotoluene and aluminium). The difference was that the G7a was steam-powered using a wet-heater design, while the G7e was electrically powered, its counter-rotating pair of propellers removing almost all trace of wake. Hence the G7e was better suited to daylight attacks, while the G7a, which marked its course with a stream of fine bubbles, was a preferred night-attack torpedo. Both torpedoes were straight-running and unguided, kept on course by an internal gyroscope.

Chapter 10

Die Torpedokrise was the product of several severe defects in torpedo design, resulting in misses and failed detonations. For example, it is a little reported fact that when *U-47*, captained by the legendary Günther Prien, sank *Royal Oak*, six of the seven torpedoes fired failed to explode. Indeed, in the early months of 1940 it was reckoned that 25–30 per cent of all torpedoes were malfunctioning.[61] Pushing through much institutional stubbornness, the engineers identified the problems. German torpedoes used two types of detonating pistol. A contact pistol triggered the warhead when the torpedo struck the hull of the ship. The magnetic pistol was activated by the change in magnetic field as the torpedo passed beneath the enemy vessel. It was discovered that both systems were faulty, but as one of Germany's secret weapons the magnetic pistol draws our attention.

The German magnetic detonator, much like magnetic sea mines, was a significant step forward in naval weaponry, as the weapon didn't actually need to strike the target physically to destroy it. Once the British gained intelligence on the threat, however, they developed a countermeasure. It was called 'degaussing', in which the magnetic field of an entire vessel was dramatically reduced by running a large electric cable around the ship's hull. The Germans responded in turn by increasing the sensitivity of the magnetic detonator, but this adaptation produced problems of its own, not least that the torpedo might detonate simply by responding to the Earth's own magnetic field. So the torpedo was stuck either not detonating at all or detonating prematurely. Another element of *Die Torpedokrise* was a fault in the depth-keeping mechanism of the early torpedoes, causing them to run either too low or ineffectively on the surface.

Short-cutting a very technical discussion, the problems with the German torpedoes were eventually resolved, improving their performance and lethality, but it took until the end of 1942. During that time, however, the Kriegsmarine researchers pioneered some new, highly secret directions in torpedo design.

They broke new ground with the design and introduction of the G7e(TIII Fat II) and the G7e(TIII Lut II) torpedoes. Both of these incorporated what is called programme steering. Rather than running on a straight line until they ran out of power, these torpedoes performed course alterations, zigzagging left and right at preset intervals. The tactical use was to fire the torpedo into a dense convoy, the weapon jinking among the ships until, hopefully, it struck one. It was an ingenious design, albeit one that depended to a certain degree on random luck to hit its target.

The next step forward was far more ambitious – the attempt to get the torpedo to guide itself precisely to the target. The first German effort in this regard was the G7es(TIV) *Falke* ('Hawk'), introduced into service in March 1943. The *Falke* had an acoustic homing mechanism. Acoustic sensors on the torpedo, connected to a steering mechanism, activated after the torpedo had travelled 400 m (437 yd) in a straight line from the launch submarine. The sensors picked up the sounds of the screws of an enemy ship and used them to guide the torpedo directly to the source. Upon reaching the target vessel, the torpedo would therefore attack the stern, blowing off the rudder, propulsion mechanism and even the entire rear end of the ship.

The *Falke* was significant. It meant that a U-boat could fire torpedoes effectively from a fully submerged position and without visual contact with the enemy; the submarine's own hydrophones could provide the initial sound bearing for the attack. It had some limitations, though. For the guidance system to work, the torpedo had to run quietly, and for that to happen it had to run at low power. This reduced its speed to 20 knots (37 km/h; 23 mph), which meant the torpedo could only chase slow-moving merchant vessels. Furthermore, to avoid acoustic confusion the submarine had to turn off its own engines during the attack.

These problems were addressed in an improved type of homing torpedo, the G7es Type V *Zaunkönig* ('Wren'), which went into service in August 1943. It became known by the Allies – and eventually even

Chapter 10

among the Germans – as the GNAT (German Navy Acoustic Torpedo). The GNAT could be fired when the submarine was either surfaced or submerged and the technology allowed torpedo launch while the submarine was still running its engines, although cautious U-boat commanders still preferred to shut down their powerplants. (Some research suggests that one U-boat, *U-972*, was in fact destroyed by its own G7es Type V torpedo returning home after launch.) The weapon also had a longer range of 5.7 km (3.5 miles) and, critically, it ran fast enough to catch escort vessels.

The GNAT bit the Allies hard: data suggests the torpedo was responsible for sinking a total of 77 Allied ships. The Kriegsmarine, naturally, worked diligently throughout the war to keep the weapon a secret. But there were enough cracks in the system for information to slip through. Specifically, data about the torpedo was shared with Germany's ally Japan. The US intelligence community had cracked Japanese diplomatic and military ciphers and codes; thus details of the GNAT were in Allied hands even as it was coming into service. Information in itself is not a countermeasure, but the Allies soon created one. The 'Foxer' device, which entered production in June 1943, was basically a large perforated metal pipe towed singly or in pairs about 200 m (656 ft) behind a ship. It created an acoustic disturbance in the water louder than the cavitation produced by the ship's propellers. Its downside was that it couldn't be towed faster than 14 knots (26 km/h; 16 mph), or it would interfere with the ship's sonar.

ALLIED ANTI-SUBMARINE WEAPONS

The Germans were not the only players in the game when it came to homing torpedoes. In fact, they were also on the receiving end of them. In March 1943, the same month as the Germans began introducing the *Falke*, the United States began issuing the Mark 24 mine, code-named by the OSRD as 'FIDO'. The word 'mine' was really a deception; the weapon was actually an air-dropped anti-submarine homing torpedo. It had been under development since the late 1940s, through a collaboration between Bell Telephone Labs and Harvard Underwater Sound Lab (HUSL). It was every bit as ingenious as the German torpedo. Once released into the water in the vicinity of the detected U-boat position, the Mark 24 would begin an automatic circular search pattern; if submarine propeller sounds were detected, the hydrophone array would guide the torpedo through rudder and elevator commands to the submarine's location.

The Mark 24 was used in combat against both the Germans and the Japanese, with 37 submarines sunk and 18 more damaged. As with all World War II guided weapons, however, we should not expect unfailing precision guidance. In fact, the Mark 24 was launched some 340 times in combat, giving it a hit rate of just 16 per cent. It nevertheless contributed to the overall hostility of the environment for U-boats. While the FIDO was deployed from Liberator or Catalina aircraft, the United States also developed a submarine-launched acoustic homing weapon, the Mark 27, which went on to see service until the 1960s.

The British came up with further secret innovations in their effort to kill the U-boats. In the early years of the war, the Royal Navy's Directorate of Miscellaneous Weapons Development set its collective mind to addressing two tactical problems: 1) the ASDIC blind spot as it approached a U-boat's location; 2) the challenge of co-ordinating a depth-charge drop with the submarine's position, i.e. you could identify the submarine's position, but by the time you got there it had moved on.

The spiky solution was called the 'Hedgehog'. It consisted of a launcher unit, mounted on the deck of an escort vessel, holding 24 contact-fuzed bombs. If a submarine was detected, the escort could engage it at a range of about 250 m (270 yd) with the Hedgehog, which fired the bombs forward in a pronounced arc in a two-at-a-time rippling salvo. The bombs were arranged in the launcher to produce an elliptical pattern about 60 m (200 ft) in diameter on the water (in the Mk II version), delivering the equivalent of an aquatic shotgun blast. The

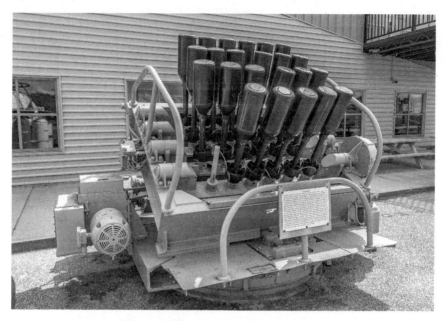

A Mk 15 hedgehog launcher on display at the USS Silversides museum in Muskegon, Michigan. Note how the banks of rockets are angled to achieve a wide distribution on the water. Credit: Aaron Headly

bombs sank through the water at about 7 m/sec (23 ft/sec). Being contact fuzed, if one exploded then it almost certainly meant that you had hit a submarine, unlike depth charges.

The Hedgehog entered service in 1942, and the following year the naval researchers added a related weapon to the arsenal, the 'Squid'. Again it used a powerful bomb launcher, but this time it had three 305 mm (12 in) mortar barrels firing 177 kg (390 lb) projectiles, each with far heavier warheads: 94 kg (207 lb) of Minol, compared to the 16 kg (35 lb) held in the most potent Hedgehog bomb. Being heavier, the Squid bombs had a faster sink rate of 13.3 m/sec (45 ft 6 in/sec) and instead of the contact fuze they were set to detonate at a certain depth via a clockwork time fuze; this could be continuously adjusted up to the final moment of launch. The range was about the same as that of the Hedgehog, and the pattern on the water was triangular, about 37 m (121 ft) along one side of the triangle. Two Squid units would often be mounted to one escort vessel, so six bombs would be launched in a single attack. Each unit would set different detonation depths, however, in the attempt to bracket the submarine and destroy it with pressure waves from multiple directions.

Squids and Hedgehogs gave the Allies a far more accurate means of targeting submerged U-boats, and one that raised the chances of a decisive effect. Some statistics bear out this point. Looking at British anti-submarine warfare (ASW) efforts between January 1943 and May 1945, 5,174 depth-charge attacks produced 85.5 submarine kills, meaning a kill ratio of 60.5 to 1. Hedgehogs, however, were used in 268 attacks for 47 kills, increasing the attack-to-kill ratio to 5.7 to 1. A double Squid arrangement was used in just 27 attacks, but it yielded 11 kills, taking the ratio to just 2.45 to 1. It was clear that the Allied secret weapons were no mere frustrating diversions; they were killing subs.

HUFF-DUFF AND CENTIMETRIC RADAR

As if this picture wasn't bad enough for the Axis submarines, from late 1941 their ability to hide from their enemies faced additional erosion. The new threat came in the form of High Frequency/Direction Finding (HF/DF). The British, seemingly incapable of letting a bare abbreviation stand, called it 'Huff-Duff'.

HF/DF was a detection equipment designed to plot the position of an enemy submarine from its high-frequency radio transmissions, the data plotted visually on an oscilloscope. The system had been through a long gestation period since the 1920s, at first used for navigation purposes but from 1940 applied by the British to detecting enemy aircraft heading for the British Isles. The pioneer of its core technology was Scottish radio engineer Robert Alexander Watson-Watt, but development had taken place on both sides of the Atlantic, including in the hands of the US Naval Research Laboratories.

HF/DF began to appear in escort vessels specifically for ASW from late 1941. It opened yet another window on to a submarine's location.

Chapter 10

When a U-boat discovered a convoy, it would typically shadow it while radioing the location at intervals to other U-boats, guiding the wolf pack to its prey. Even though the encrypted message took only about 20 seconds to broadcast, that was enough for Huff-Duff's aerials to pick up the signal and triangulate the position of the broadcaster. The goal then was a rapid response, using escort vessels and aircraft to attack and sink the lead submarine.

It worked, devastatingly so; about 24 per cent of U-boat sinkings involved the tactical use of HF/DF.[62] It took many flooded U-boats and dead crews before the U-boat fleet learned that radio silence was imperative. There were some tactical countermeasures. For example, a U-boat commander might spot a convoy, sprint away for its position to a distant location, make the broadcast from there, then dash back to the convoy. The Kriegsmarine also pushed its boffins to find a technological answer. They found one, but just too late to make a difference. They developed the Kurier burst transmission system, which clipped radio transmission time down to between 250 and 450 milliseconds, which was faster than the Allies' detection times using HF/DF. It came so late in the war, however, that it never went into widespread operational use.

The Allies also came to win the detection war by their use of centimetric radar. Building on critical improvements in the design of the cavity magnetron (a high-power vacuum tube, used to generate microwaves) centimetric radar operated in the SHF radio frequency band from 3 to 30 GHz, at wavelengths of 10 cm to 1 cm (3.9 in to 0.39 in). This meant that it could detect an object the size of a submarine conning tower when the vessel was surfaced. (As mentioned, submarines spent far more of their operational life on the surface rather than submerged, and would often make attacks from this position, particularly at night.) Air-to-surface vessel (ASV) radar had been available in early forms since 1940, but until centimetric models arrived in service in March 1943 these had significant limitations for detecting submarines.

A U-boat comes under unsparing air attack, with depth charges exploding near the hull and machine-gun fire rippling across the ocean surface. Many U-boats ended their operational careers in this way. Credit: Historical/Getty

The new technology appeared in a variety of types: the British ASV Mark III (a modified version of Bomber Command's H2S radar) and the American DMS-1000 (British ASV Mk IV), Western Electric SCR-517 and Philco ASG (ASV Mk V). From May 1943 they were aboard the Very Long Range (VLR) Liberator bombers, which finally had the range to close the Atlantic air gap – the middle section of the Atlantic in which Allied ships had previously been beyond the reach of air cover. The Liberators, however, were just one of the predatory ASV-radar equipped aircraft that came to hunt over the Atlantic, equipped with a bristling array of anti-submarine weapons, including air-dropped mines and torpedoes, depth charges, rockets and cannon.

Chapter 10

The use of centimetric radar resulted in the so-called 'Battle of the Seconds', the ultimate exercise in human urgency. A U-boat's best defence against an aircraft bearing down on its position was to dive. But an emergency dive typically took 30–40 seconds to clear the decks and put the submarine underwater. So the air crew were sprinting to make a kill in this window, while the U-boat crew were desperately using the same seconds to get submerged. If they lost this race, the submarine would likely be destroyed.

Another Allied secret weapon in this engagement was the Leigh Light, named after the man who conceived the idea, RAF Squadron Leader H. de Verd Leigh. It was an ultra-powerful 610 mm (24 in) searchlight fitted in a retractable 'dustbin' beneath the fuselage of a maritime patrol aircraft. At the selected moment, it could be deployed and switched on to produce a 22-million candlepower beam of light, illuminating a patch of sea as if it were daylight. The Leigh Light was originally designed to compensate for limitations in detecting surfaced submarines at night by the ASV Mk II radar. When combined with the new centimetric radars, the effect was devastating. The pilot would use the radar to make a close approach to the target, then at the last moment throw on the light, make visual identification, and open fire with the weaponry. The situation became so bad that U-boat commanders started surfacing more during the day; at least this way they might be able to spot the incoming aircraft, although this also increased their vulnerability to surface gunnery.

The Kriegsmarine promoted some technology countermeasures in the detection war, particularly a range of ASV radar detectors that would, hopefully, give advance warning of an enemy contact. The first of these was the FuMB 1 Metox 600A, developed in response to the German capture of an ASV Mk I set aboard a downed RAF Wellington bomber. The Metox was fielded from August 1942, but it gave poor performance, being easily confused by other signal traffic. It was also incapable of detecting centimetric radar. When this came into use, the Germans were puzzled over the reason behind the sudden escalation in U-boat losses. Their confusion was amplified by the cunning of a captured British bomb-aimer, who said that losses were due to the Allies detecting Metox transmissions. This deception delayed the invention of the FuG 350 Naxos I, which operated between 2,500 MHz and 3,750 MHz (wavelengths of 12 cm to 8 cm; 4.7 in to 3.1 in) and was capable of detecting centimetric signals to a range of approximately 8 km (5 miles). The Naxos I was superseded by the Naxos Ia, which had an improved antenna.

The Naxos systems shifted the advantage momentarily back towards the U-boats. But the Allies soon became aware of what was happening and built attenuators into the new generations of ASV radars, which reduced the signal output to produce false readings aboard the U-boat. Neither side rested in the detection war until the war itself ended.

THE LAST U-BOATS

By 1943, as in other domains of the German war effort, Hitler began encouraging naval secret weapon projects and pinning his hopes upon the output. In the development of submarines, Germany made some final and seminal leaps forward, a forlorn experimentalism that nevertheless laid the foundations for post-war submarine design.

One ambitious innovation focused on advancing submarine propulsion, in the form of a closed-cycle powerplant. Designed from the mid-1930s by Professor Hellmuth Walter at the Germaniawerft shipyard in Kiel, his air-independent propulsion (AIP) powerplant was designed to run without reliance upon atmospheric oxygen, as required by a diesel engine. Instead it used a form of stabilized hydrogen peroxide called Perhydrol. This underwent decomposition via a potassium permanganate catalyst and the resulting gas was burned with fuel oil to create a gas and steam mix that drove a turbine.

When applied to submarines, the Walter propulsion system was heavy with promise. It provided significantly more power than electric propulsion, which meant faster and longer submerged performance. The first production submarine to take the powerplant was a coastal vessel, the Type XVIIA. But the design and production process revealed as many

Chapter 10

problems as it solved. Chief among these was the promethean volatility and the production issues surrounding the fuel, as explained here by naval historian Anthony Preston:

> *The chief difficulty was in the manufacture and storage of the fuel, known as 'Ingolin'. This was highly unstable, and any impurity in the storage tanks led to decomposition and spontaneous combustion; only clinical sterility would do, and eventually synthetic rubber was discovered to be the least dangerous material for lining the tanks. Ingolin was also very expensive to make, costing about eight times as much as oil, and was consumed at a prodigious rate, so that a Type XVIIA boat could only travel 80 miles at top speed – which put the clock back to about 1900 as far as operational radius was concerned.*[63]

Preston illustrates that innovation often comes with trade-offs, and sometimes those threaten the sustainability of the programme. While at this stage of the war, an industrial giant such as the United States could throw almost limitless money and man hours at a project (as we shall see in the final chapter), for a buckling Germany, R&D was often an indulgent strain.

Only three Type XVIIAs were produced. It was also planned to construct an ocean-going version, the Type XVIII, but this programme was eventually suspended to focus efforts on an extraordinary new secret submarine type, the Type XXI *Elektroboot* ('Electric Boat').

The Type XXI represents an entirely new generation in submarine design. It was a large craft, with an overall length of 76.7 m (251 ft 8 in) and a beam of 8 m (26 ft 3 in). The size allowed the upper half of the craft to be fitted with huge banks of batteries to extend underwater endurance and power. Surface power came from conventional MAN M6V40/46KBB geared supercharged six-cylinder diesel engines; gone was the affection for the Walter system. The whole craft was designed for exceptional efficiency on top of and below the waves. The hull profile and fin-shaped conning tower were streamlined for hydrodynamic efficiency. Combined with the additional battery reserves, this meant that the Type XXI attained underwater speeds of 17.2 knots (31.9 km/h; 19.8 mph). Using its SSW GV232/28 'creep motors' – designed for silent running and for energy efficiency while recharging batteries – it could maintain a speed of 5 knots (9 km/h; 5.6 mph) while staying submerged for more than two days. The designers invested in improving the living accommodation and food storage/preparation areas for the five officers and 52 enlisted men, who had to endure months of overseas operations.

Recharging U-boat batteries while submerged had also been made possible by the incorporation of the *Schnorchel*. This was an air intake pipe that extended up from the conning tower of the submarine, providing ventilation for both engines and crew while allowing the submarine to stay at periscope depth. The *Schnorchel* was actually a Dutch design; the Germans appropriated it from the Netherlands following the occupation in 1940 and subsequently applied it to several U-boat types, including the Type XXI. It was a good idea, compromised somewhat by reality. When deployed, the *Schnorchel* slowed the submarine down (to prevent breaking the mast off), created a more visible wake, and was prone to blocking up. These issues notwithstanding, the *Schnorchel* on the Type XXI meant that the submarine could recharge its batteries in just five hours.

Another advance in the Type XXI was the weaponry. The submarine had six 533 mm (21 in) torpedo tubes with 17 reloads. The torpedo crew also had the luxury of a mechanical loading device, to speed up the rate of fire.

The Type XXI was one of the most impressive submarines to emerge from World War II. A total of 118 were completed, but by the time they went into service the German war effort was overstretched and collapsing. Instead of concentrating on the Type XXI to the exclusion of other types, Hitler tried to keep production going on the Type VIIC, overloading a manufacturing base already suffering from shortages in manpower, raw

Chapter 10

materials and plant capacity. The Allied bombing of Valentin submarine pens also deprived the new submarines of a final assembly plant. Ultimately, only two Type XXI vessels – *U-2511* and *U-3008* – actually went to sea on combat patrols, but scored no victories. Despite six years of ingenuity, the Germans lost the submarine war.

Chapter 11

Fat Man and Little Boy – The End of Secret Weapons

***

For millennia, humanity has been drawn to apocalyptic visions. Eschatological impulses have commonly emerged from religion, a yearning for the 'last times' when divine powers would finally, sometimes destructively, establish their dominion on earth and in heaven. Unfortunately for humanity, during the 20th century new weapons technologies emerged that made global, or at least regional, destruction physically possible. World War II, furthermore, revealed the appetite to use them.

From the 1930s, certain corners of the military-scientific and theoretical physics communities began to explore the possibilities of weapons that might destroy entire armies, even entire nations, at a stroke. Some of these were improbable sci-fi dreams. During the 1920s, for example, the German physicist Hermann Oberth, a leading theorist in rocket science and space exploration, proposed the development of a 'death ray' device. It consisted of an orbiting space station with a huge metallic sodium reflector, 9 km^2 (3.4 square miles) in area, that could collect and channel the Sun's rays to a lethally destructive point on the Earth's surface, powerful enough to burn out a city. He just needed up to 100 years to develop it.

Oberth's vision for a death ray was, in essence, a well-informed fantasy. But other minds tackled what seemed, at first, scientific and engineering challenges well beyond the capability of the human race. They, however, broke the boundaries between possibility and reality, their success measured in two towering mushroom clouds on a Japanese horizon.

CHEMICAL AND BIOLOGICAL WARFARE

World War I had witnessed the unapologetic use of chemical agents in warfare. Clouds of lethal gases were wafted around the battlefields – mustard, phosgene, chlorine, bromine, and others. The return of these weapons was much feared during the 1930s, not least because France, Spain, Italy, Russia and Japan all applied gas weaponry in various colonial or internal conflicts during this decade. Furthermore, the new generations of strategic bombers could distribute gas bombs far and wide, even, potentially, over the big cities.

As it turned out, the combatants of World War II largely turned their backs on the large-scale use of chemical weapons in conventional warfare. But such weapons remained waiting in the wings. On the Allied side, for example, the United States built up considerable stockpiles of the blistering agents mustard gas and Lewisite (the latter lovingly nicknamed the 'Dew of Death') and maintained an active research programme into chemical weaponry. The fact that these weapons were not used was actually a close-run thing. On 2 December 1943, German aircraft bombed and destroyed the US merchant ship SS *John Harvey* in the harbour at Bari, Italy. Many other Allied ships were sunk that day, but inside *John Harvey* was a secret consignment of 2,000 M47A1 mustard-gas bombs. The fumes released, inhaled by oblivious rescue crews and nearby service personnel, hospitalized 628 people, with 83 deaths. Only in 1959 were records relating to this incident fully declassified, but the fact that live gas bombs were shipped from the United States to an active war zone indicates that their use was an option.

Some combatants, however, dropped all decency in their experiments with chemical and also biological agents. In benighted parts of Japanese-occupied China, for example, special military-scientific units (most infamous, Unit 731) were given unrestrained access to human beings for dreadful experiments. Thousands were herded into camps, there to be poisoned, shot, burned, blasted, contaminated, cut. Japanese aircraft even released diseases such as cholera, plague and anthrax over populated areas. The effects of this unseen campaign, according to estimations published in 2002, included as many as 580,000 deaths.

The Nazi regime, as we now know, was also open to ghastly experimentation, this mostly directed at POWs, Jews and other enemies of the state in the network of concentration and, eventually, extermination camps operated between 1933 and 1945. Dr Joseph Mengele stands as the nightmarish representative of this barbarity, but there were others. It is dreadful what can happen when curious, intelligent people are given unrestricted power over fellow human beings.

We should be thankful, therefore, that Germany's scientific investment in new generations of nerve agents didn't reach operational status. Nerve agents are substances that interfere with the transmission of nerve impulses in the body, a dry description that belies the rapid and agonizing death involved. The pioneer of German nerve agent development was insecticide specialist Dr Gerhard Schrader, who worked for the Bayer AG division of industrial giant I.G. Farben. He discovered the Tabun nerve agent quite accidentally during his research but having become aware of its suffocating effects he reported it upwards. (He and his assistant were poisoned by a miniscule spillage and required three weeks to recover.) A sample of what was at this time called Preparation 9/91 found its way to the Chemical Warfare Department, Wa Prüf 9, in May 1937, where its military potential was quickly recognized. A research centre was established at Wuppertal-Elberfeld and by 1940 full production facilities were in operation at Dyhernfurth-am-Oder, today in Poland. The chemical was called 'Tabun', after the German word for 'taboo'.[64]

Tabun took only about 20 minutes to kill a healthy human being. But by this time, Schrader and a wider team had excelled themselves and produced an even more lethal agent, initially called 'Substance 46' but eventually known as Sarin, after the names of the leading scientists involved: Schrader, Otto Ambros, Gerhard Ritter and Hans-Jürgen von der Linde. It was a clear, colourless liquid, without smell or taste. Even the smallest drop on the skin would produce effects within seconds; larger doses would lead to loss of consciousness, seizures, respiratory and cardiac failure, and death within minutes. In 1943, construction began on a Sarin factory at Falkenhagen, in Brandenburg, Germany.

By the end of the war, the Nazis had produced 12,000 tonnes (11,810 tons) of Tabun and up to 10 tonnes (9.8 tons) of Sarin, the much lower Sarin figure reflecting the later start date and the inherent challenges involved in its production and storage. The Tabun, however, was installed into tens of thousands of artillery shells and bombs, thankfully never fired or dropped. Hitler, a man who had himself been gassed in World War I, likely understood the retaliatory consequences of using these weapons.

THE GERMAN ATOMIC PROGRAMME

The fact that the United States transparently won the atomic arms race in 1945 can obscure the fact that the scrabble began in the first place in Germany. In 1938, the German physicists Otto Hahn and Fritz Strassmann began conducting experiments in which they fired neutrons at uranium atoms. In January the following year, they published and shared their results, and fellow physicists Otto Frisch and Lisa Meitner recognized that the experiments revealed the possibility of atomic fission – splitting the atom – with the enormous release of energy that could theoretically produce. Atomic fission might be harnessed for nuclear power. It also, others quickly realized, might be the foundation of a weapon unlike all others that came before it.

It is useful at this point to give a basic scientific overview of how World War II-era atomic bombs worked. They relied upon the process of fission, splitting the atoms of two elements: uranium and plutonium. Uranium has two isotopes: U-238 comprises the vast majority of the element, while U-235 constitutes only 0.7 per cent. Only the atoms of U-235 are fissile, capable of being split under the impact of neutrons, when that process is forcibly initiated. Under the impact, two or three free neutrons are released, striking other neutrons, which in turn release free neutrons, and so on. As this process happens, quite enormous energy is released in the form of heat and gamma radiation. Control the process, it provides productive atomic power; let the process run free and uncontrolled, it is an atomic bomb. To ensure that the chain reaction is viable, however, there needs to be enough of the element present to achieve 'critical mass', that is, the minimum amount of fissionable material that will ensure the chain reaction is self-sustaining. For U-235, the critical mass is around 47 kg (104 lb), although for practical purposes more is required, as the isotope is never pure. For Pu-239, the primary fissionable isotope of plutonium, the critical mass is around 10 kg (22 lb). During an atomic explosion, when the number of fission events increases with each generation of fission events, the bomb becomes 'super-critical' and will produce the explosive event. There are two primary scientific and engineering challenges in here: 1) manufacturing enough of the fissionable isotope sufficient for critical mass; 2) creating the means to initiate the chain reaction. At the time the bomb was conceived, neither was remotely practically possible.

In April 1939, the Reichswehrministerium (RKM) facilitated the formation of the Uranverein ('Uranium Club'), a group of scientists working from the prestigious physics institute in Göttingen University to investigate the possibility of developing an atomic weapon. The following autumn, with war underway, the Heereswaffenamt formed an atomic programme under German military authority, headed by physicist Kurt Diebner. By the end of the year, the great physicist Werner Heisenberg had put more theoretical flesh on the bones and demonstrated how an explosive chain reaction could be produced using the U-235 isotope. Furthermore, uranium oxide production had begun in a factory at Oranienburg, controlled by the industrial firm Auergesellschaft. The plant provided cubes of uranium to the Kaiser-Wilhelm Institut für Physik (KWIP; 'Kaiser Wilhelm Institute for Physics') in Berlin, which began working on an early form of nuclear reactor.

The pieces of the puzzle were coming together. Research into the theoretical foundations of the atomic bomb progressed throughout 1940 and 1941. Separation of the U-235 isotope, albeit at agonizingly slow pace, was being performed using a centrifugal method. At the Vemork plant in Rjukan, Norway, operated by Norsk Hydro, the Nazis also established a facility for the production of heavy water (deuterium oxide), a neutron 'moderator' used to slow down neutrons and enable controlled fission in reactors. This was significant because a fissionable material was plutonium, which was actually a by-product of uranium used as a reactor fuel.

From 1942 onwards, however, the story of the Nazi atomic bomb programme becomes muddled and open to interpretation. The conventional theory (which is not to say that it is wrong) is that the atomic research from this point became fragmented and diluted as the Nazi hierarchy lost faith in its viability. Other reasons behind the waning interest include: the flight of valuable Jewish nuclear physicists from Germany and Europe in the late 1930s and early 1940s; scientists being diverted into military service or research on other weapon systems; scientific errors that set back progress beyond practical timelines; the inability to produce viable quantities of enriched uranium or plutonium; Allied sabotage and bombing interference with the heavy water programme; and Hitler's lack of comprehension about the technology. Regardless of the various reasons, the atomic research appears to have been cancelled officially in July 1942 and was only pursued further by nine different agencies.

In recent years, however, contrary, and often disputed, evidence has been presented to the effect that the Nazis went much further with the atomic bomb programme in secrecy. The evidence is a patchwork of tantalizing trails and suggestions. Certainly, there is an extant German schematic of a complete implosion-type plutonium weapon, the diagram in a report compiled just after the war. Some have argued that the elevated electricity consumption and huge funding that went into the Monowitz Buna-Werke concentration camp (a sub-camp of Auschwitz, run by I.G. Farben), went not into the production of Buna synthetic rubber, but rather the enrichment of uranium. (Tellingly, no synthetic rubber was produced.) More sensationally, historian Carter Plymton Hydrick has argued in detail (including with some high-level endorsements) that immediately after its surrender in Europe in May 1945, Germany transferred 509 kg (1,120 lb) of enriched uranium to the United States, this transfer enabling the United States to complete its own atomic weapons.[65] In the later years of the war, designs seem to have emerged for both modified V-1 and V-2 missiles, adapted to take an atomic or nerve-agent warhead, and for plans to conduct a nuclear attack on the United States from a super-long-range bomber. Finally, we can add the apparent eye-witness accounts to what might have been a German atomic bomb test conducted on the island of Rugen in the Baltic in October 1944. The two testimonies come from Luigi Romersa, an Italian war correspondent, and a He 111 pilot, Hans Zinsser. From the latter, his log book recounts:

> *In early October 1944 I flew away 12-15km from a nuclear test station near Ludwigslust (South of Lübeck). A cloud shaped like a mushroom with turbulent, billowing sections (at about 7000 metres) stood, without any seeming connections over the spot where the explosion took place. Strong electrical disturbances and the impossibility to continue radio communication as by lighting turned up.*[66]

Chapter 11

The reference to the 'electrical disturbances' adds to the authenticity, as atomic explosions generate powerful electromagnetic interference.

Given such seductive and partial evidence, it seems that the story of the German atomic programme will likely remain only partly told. But one truth is absolute – the Germans did not produce and deliver an atomic bomb in combat. That terrible honour would be left to the Americans.

THE MANHATTAN PROJECT

The overall contours of the Manhattan Project – the US government's programme to develop a fully functioning atomic weapon – are largely well known, at least notwithstanding Hydrick's research. Here, therefore, I will only pull out the main points in the chronology, before selecting some of the salient points for our story of secret weapons.

The journey to the US atomic bomb began in August–October 1939, when none other than Albert Einstein presented a letter to President Roosevelt. The letter was written by eminent, concerned European scientists, warning of the dangers of emerging German atomic research and urging the US government to get involved in what could be the most important arms race in the history of humanity. The beginning of the European war in September 1939 gave the warning more urgency, and various research efforts were commissioned to explore the theory and the potential practice. On 6 December 1941, just a day prior to the Japanese attack on Pearl Harbor, the collective atomic research work was placed under the authority of the OSRD.

The year 1942 was the change point. By this year, the research was pointing to the real-world viability of an atomic weapon. The War Department now became a co-owner of the project, and the 'Corps of Engineers' Manhattan District' was established in August. This dull administrative heading was the cover for the huge multi-location effort to build a bomb that could be tested, then, if necessary, deployed in combat. The main scientific research and testing centre was the Los Alamos Laboratory, New Mexico, under the directorship of the now-

The American physicist Norris Bradbury sits thoughtfully alongside the 'Gadget', the atomic bomb that delivered the 'Trinity' test on 16 July 1945. Bradbury was in charge of the device's final assembly. Credit: Historical / Getty

legendary scientist J. Robert Oppenheimer. The Clinton Engineer Works, or Oak Ridge, in Tennessee conducted uranium enrichment while the Hanford Engineer Works, Washington, manufactured plutonium. Other research activities took place at Columbia University, New York, focusing particularly on the nuclear reaction process. Collectively, the 'Manhattan Project' – as it came to be known – was under the leadership of the driving, formidable persona of Brigadier General Leslie Richard Groves Jr., described by US Army officer Kenneth D. Nichols as 'the biggest S.O.B. I have ever worked for'.[67]

The Manhattan Project drew in the greatest scientific and engineering minds of a generation, including Edward Teller, Leo Szilard, Enrico Fermi, Ernest Orlando Lawrence, Otto Frisch, Niels Bohr, Felix Bloch, James Franck, Emilio Segrè, Klaus Fuchs, Hans Bethe and John von

Chapter 11

Neumann. Although brainpower was never wanting, the scientific and technical challenges faced by the tens of thousands of people who worked on the project were legion.[68] The programme fell on to two tracks: the development of a uranium 'gun-type' bomb and of a plutonium 'implosion' bomb. The theoretical and engineering problems of making either work were immense, as was the industrial effort to produce enough plutonium and uranium to form a critical mass. Nevertheless, on 16 July 1945 a 20,000-kiloton implosion bomb (equivalent to 20,000 tons of TNT) named 'Trinity' was successfully detonated on an isolated range at the Alamogordo air base 193 km (120 miles) south of Albuquerque, New Mexico.

Trinity was the biblically titled proof that the age of the atomic bomb had arrived. Japan would discover this truth on 6 August and 9 August 1945, when the cities of Hiroshima and Nagasaki respectively were flattened by the God-like hand of two atomic weapons, given the irreverent names 'Little Boy' and 'Fat Man'. The war ended just days later with the formal Japanese surrender.

The Manhattan Project is, undoubtedly, the greatest of our secret weapons projects. Indeed, its secrecy is something of a miracle of information management. We must be clear – the core science and the practical possibility of an atomic weapon was not a secret, but rather was widely known. But the creation of the device, and the progress being made in the United States, certainly was. At its peak, some 130,000 people were working on the programme in thousands of different roles. The total financial cost of building the bomb was $2 billion, equivalent to $35 billion in 2025. And yet, the Japanese seemed unaware of what was heading their way. It is akin to keeping the Apollo space mission hidden from the Soviet Union. The secrecy was obtained through rigorous compartmentalization of research and individual projects, so only a select few individuals had a picture of the overall progress of outcomes. There was also rigorous surveillance and monitoring of staff, the spotlight shining on everyone without exception.

This being said, we now know that many atomic secrets were leaked from the Manhattan Project and from associated British research out to the Soviets, some of the famous names being John Cairncross, Klaus Fuchs, David Greenglass, Theodore Hall, Clarence Hiskey, Russell McNutt, Melita Norwood and Oscar Seborer. The 1940s and '50s were an age of ideology. Many scientists had either socialist or communist leanings, while others felt it their moral duty to share the secrets of the bomb with America's allies. Duly aided in their research, the Soviet Union exploded its own atomic weapon on 29 August 1949.

Once the American atomic bombs went from secret to visible mushroom cloud, the world changed. At the tactical level, this was a weapon of a different order of magnitude than anything else before it, a device that could literally destroy cities. As a reminder of its power, the following is an excerpt from the official 'United States Strategic Bombing Survey: The Effects of the Atomic Bombs on Hiroshima and Nagasaki', published on 30 June 1946:

A single atomic bomb, the first weapon of its type ever used against a target, exploded over the city of Hiroshima at 0815 on the morning of 6 August 1945. Most of the industrial workers had already reported to work, but many workers were enroute [sic] and nearly all the school children and some industrial employees were at work in the open on the program of building removal to provide firebreaks and disperse valuables to the country. The attack came 45 minutes after the 'all clear' had been sounded from a previous alert. Because of the lack of warning and the populace's indifference to small groups of planes, the explosion came as an almost complete surprise, and the people had not taken shelter. Many were caught in the open, and most of the rest in flimsily constructed homes or commercial establishments.

The bomb exploded slightly northwest of the center of the city. Because of this accuracy and the flat terrain and circular shape of

Chapter 11

the city, Hiroshima was uniformly and extensively devastated. Practically the entire densely or moderately built-up portion of the city was leveled by blast and swept by fire. A 'fire-storm,' a phenomenon which has occurred infrequently in other conflagrations, developed in Hiroshima: fires springing up almost simultaneously over the wide flat area around the center of the city drew in air from all directions. The inrush of air easily overcame the natural ground wind, which had a velocity of only about 5 miles per hour. The 'fire-wind' attained a maximum velocity of 30 to 40 miles per hour 2 to 3 hours after the explosion. The 'fire-wind' and the symmetry of the built-up center of the city gave a roughly circular shape to the 4.4 square miles which were almost completely burned out.

The surprise, the collapse of many buildings, and the conflagration contributed to an unprecedented casualty rate. Seventy to eighty thousand people were killed, or missing and presumed dead, and an equal number were injured.[69]

Given such descriptions, and the growing potential for future Armageddon, in June 1947 key members of the *Bulletin of the Atomic Scientists* set running the 'Doomsday Clock', a metaphorical timepiece updated regularly to illustrate how close human beings are to midnight, i.e. total global catastrophe. It is still ticking.

At times throughout this book, some secret weapons have been so laughably implausible I have treated them with the levity they deserve. And yet, all the weapons here represent a fundamental failure in human society. Whether bat bombs or nuclear bombs, rocket planes or Panjandrums, mini submarines or explosive coal, all share the common purpose of killing human beings or destroying the things they make or the buildings in which they live and work. Such is the tragedy of weapons in general, including secret ones.

If we were to find some light in the darkness, however, it would be that the secret weapons programmes reveal the heights to which human intelligence and ingenuity can ascend. We might therefore wonder, in our present times, which secret weapons are under current development, hidden in shaded corners of the military-industrial complex. We might also wonder what their effects will be when they make an appearance.

Endnotes

INTRODUCTION

1. Martin van Creveld, 'Technology and War: to 1945', in Charles Townshend (ed.), *The Oxford History of Modern War* (Oxford: Oxford University Press, 2000) p.20

2. Eugene T. Jensen, 'Something I Will Never Forget', *The Phoenix Gazette*, 6 January 1997. See also 'First Encounter with the Me-262', 100th Bomb Group Foundation: https://100thbg.com/first-encounter-with-the-me-262/

3. Ibid.

4. Ibid.

5. Winston Churchill, Memorandum, Churchill Papers: 13/27 (1917)

6. Marek Thee (ed.), Armaments, Arms Control and Disarmament: A UNESCO reader for disarmament education (Paris: UNESCO, 1981) p.101

7. John F. Victory, Executive Secretary of NACA, Draft Act of Congress for setting up a National Defense Research Committee (NDRC) (1940)

8. This famous quotation was recounted by Hugh Dalton, Minister of Economic Warfare, in a diary entry for July 1940.

CHAPTER 1

9. Quoted in National Army Museum, 'Origins of the Special Forces' (accessed 7 April 2025): https://www.nam.ac.uk/explore/special-forcesWW2

10   James F. Gebhardt, *Soviet Front Special Purpose Troops: An Historical Perspective* (Fort Leavenworth, KS: Department of the Army, Soviet Army Studies Office, 1990) p.5

11   Office of Strategic Services, *OSS Weapons: Special Weapons and Devices* (Washington DC: Research and Development Branch, OSS, June 1944) p.3. The catalogue is available to view at: https://www.nas.gov.sg/archivesonline/private_records/record-details/dd346d60-82cb-11ea-8566-001a4a5ba61b

12   Captain W.E. Fairbairn, *Get Tough! How to Win in Hand-to-Hand Fighting* (Boulder, CO; Paladin Press, 1996) p.104

13   International Churchill Society, 'Ungentlemanly Warfare', Bulletin #126 (December 2018): https://winstonchurchill.org/publications/churchill-bulletin/bulletin-126-dec-2018/ungentlemanly-warfare/

14   Adam Kline with Robin Dexter, 'Secret Weapons, Forgotten Sacrifices: Scientific R&D in the Second World War', NARA, *Prologue Magazine*, Vol. 48, No. 1 (Spring 2016): https://www.archives.gov/publications/prologue/2016/spring/office-scientific-research-development-world-war-ii

15   Philip H. Dater, 'SAR Tests the .32 caliber Welrod', Small Arms Review (August 2002): http://www.smallarmsreview.com/display.article.cfm?idarticles=2335

16   Historical Firearms, 'Silence Stens': https://www.historicalfirearms.info/post/141056060049/silenced-stens-the-first-suppressed-sten-was-built

17   The closed-bolt configuration meant that the bolt was closed up and locked to the breech; only the firing pin moved when the trigger was pulled. The low shift of mass meant that the rifle was very accurate in this mode. The open-bolt configuration meant that the entire

bolt was held to the rear between bursts of fire. Pulling the trigger released the bolt to strip, feed, chamber and fire a cartridge in one go; the shift of mass was greater, making the weapon less accurate, but it promoted better cooling of the weapon and the full-auto bursts compensated for the diminution in accuracy.

18 US War Department, 'New German Rifle for Paratroopers', Intelligence Bulletin (June 1944)

19 Office of the Chief Ordnance Officer, 'U.S. Ordnance Report' (18 July 1945). Quoted in Tom Laemlein, 'Nazi Secret Weapon: The Krummlauf StG44', *The Armory Life* (10 November 2020): https://www.thearmorylife.com/nazi-secret-weapon-the-krummlauf-stg44/

CHAPTER 2

20 Quoted in Richard Norton-Taylor, 'How exploding rats went down a bomb – and helped British boffins win the second world war', *Guardian* (27 October 1999): https://www.theguardian.com/uk/1999/oct/27/richardnortontaylor

21 Ibid.

22 Ibid.

23 SOE, Descriptive Catalogue of Special Devices and Supplies (1944)

24 David Welker, 'Explosive Coal: Bombs Hiding in Plain Sight', *Studies in Intelligence*, Vol. 66, No. 1 (March 2022) pp.41–7; p.45

25 Bill Miles, 'Dad's Army', WW2 People's War, BBC (28 December 2003): https://www.bbc.co.uk/history/ww2peopleswar/stories/93/a2159093.shtml

26 The original quotation, in German, came from von Moltke's *Kriegsgeschichtliche Einzelschriften* ('Individual Studies on Military History'), 1880.

CHAPTER 3

27 Christopher A. Lawrence, 'Comparative Tank Exchange Ratios at Kursk', The Dupuy Institute (26 December 2018): https://dupuyinstitute.org/2018/12/26/comparative-tank-exchange-ratios-at-kursk/

28 John Ellis, *The World War II Databook: The Essential Facts and Figures for All the Combatants* (London: Aurum Press, 1995) p.230

29 Ian Hogg, *German and Allied Secret Weapons of World War II* (London: Phoebus, 1976) p.34

30 Ibid. p.35

CHAPTER 4

31 Quoted in Donald Caldwell and Richard Muller, *The Luftwaffe Over Germany: Defense of the Reich* (London: Greenhill, 2007) p.189

32 At first, it was intended to fit the Me 262 with BMW engines, but reliability problems with these led to the switch to Junkers Jumo 109-004B-4 powerplants for the production model.

33 Quoted in Robert Forsyth, *Luftwaffe Mistel Composite Bomber Units* (Oxford: Osprey Publishing, 2001)

CHAPTER 5

34 Brian Ford, Secret Weapons: Death Rays, Doodlebugs and Churchill's Golden Goose (Oxford: Osprey Publishing, 2013) p.43

35 Dan Hart, 'The Politics, Pickle Barrels, and Propaganda of the Norden Bombsight', Museum of Aviation (23 April 2016): https://museumofaviation.org/general/the-politics-pickle-barrels-and-propaganda-of-the-norden-bombsight/

36 Quoted in Carroll V. Glines, 'The Bat Bombers', *Air & Space Forces Magazine* (1 October 1990): https://www.airandspaceforces.com/article/1090bats/

CHAPTER 6

37 Stanley Baldwin, speech before the House of Commons of the United Kingdom (10 November 1932).

38 Frank Winter, 'Hs 117 Schmetterling (Butterfly) Missile', NationalAir And Space Museum (accessed 24 February 2025): https://airandspace.si.edu/collection-objects/missile-surface-air-henschel-hs-117-schmetterling/nasm_A19890595000

39 Dan Johnson, 'EMW C2 Wasserfall', Luft46.com (accessed 25 February 2025): http://www.luft46.com/missile/wasserfl.html

40 Ibid. and Hogg, *Secret Weapons*, p.108

41 Albert Speer, *Inside the Third Reich*, translated by Richard and Clara Winston (New York: Simon & Schuster, 1997) p.492

42 US Naval Technical Mission to Japan, 'Description and Operation of the Japanese Type 3 photoelectric fuse: "Intelligence Targets Japan" (DNI) of 4 September 1945' (San Francisco, CA) p.3

43 Michael W. Robbins, 'The Allies' Billion-dollar Secret: The Proximity Fuze of World War II', HistoryNet (19 October 2020): https://www.historynet.com/proximity-fuze/

44 Ibid.

45 Hogg, *Secret Weapons*, p.122

46 Both quoted in Peter R. Kolakowski, 'Naval Proving Ground at Dahlgren and the Hidden History of the VT Fuze', *Naval Sea Systems Command* (accessed 25 February 2025): https://www.navsea.navy.mil/Home/Warfare-Centers/NSWC-Dahlgren/Who-We-Are/History/Blogs/VT-Fuze/

CHAPTER 7

47 Albert Speer: *Inside the Third Reich*: The Classic Account of Nazi Germany by Hitler's Armaments Minister, 7th edition (London: Phoenix, 2002) pp.323–7.

48 Alfred Price, 'V-weapons', *The Oxford Companion to the Second World War* (Oxford: Oxford University Press, 1995) pp.1249–53

49 Air Ministry, 'A Forecast of Air Developments in 1945: A Study prepared by the German Air Historical Branch, (8th Abteilung) and dated 22nd September, 1944' (London: Air Ministry, 2 November 1946)

50 National Air and Space Museum, 'Bomb, Guided, Fritz X (X-1)': ttps://airandspace.si.edu/collection-objects/bomb-guided-fritz-x-x-1/nasm_A19840794000 accessed 28 February 2025

CHAPTER 8

51 Marine Aircraft Experimental Establishment, Helensburgh, Upkeep – Reculver trials 14.4.43 to 16.5.43', Report No. H/Arm/104 (24 June 1943). For wider report, see https://sussexhistoryforum.co.uk/index.php?topic=2325.0

52 For video footage and narrative of this event, see Dark Footage, 'Bouncing a Bomb Back Into the Tail of Your Own Plane', YouTube (11 March 2021): https://www.youtube.com/watch?v=FEgbi6n1C0E

53 Ford, *Secret Weapons*, p.214

CHAPTER 9

54 H.I. Sutton, 'Mignatta', Covert Shores (8 November 2018): http://www.hisutton.com/Mignatta.html

55 In his authoritative website Covert Shores, H.I. Sutton explains that many sources incorrectly title the boat the Siluro a Lento Corsa ('Slow-Running Torpedo'). See H.I. Sutton, 'The famous CosMos CE2F chariot', Covert Shores (29 February 2016): http://www.hisutton.com/The%20famous%20CosMoS%20CE2F%20chariot.html

56 H.I. Sutton, 'Chariot Mk II', Covert Shores (24 May 2017): http://www.hisutton.com/Chariot_Mk2.html

57 Geoff Galway, *Geoff's Opus* (Self-published, 1992) pp.104–05; quoted at https://www.coppsurvey.uk/latest-news/x-craft-training

58 MSW, 'The Explosive Boats of the Kriegsmarine', WarHistory.org (22 November 2016): https://warhistory.org/@msw/article/the-explosive-boats-of-the-kriegsmarine

59 Vincent P. O'Hara, 'Risk vs. Reward Off the Italian Riviera', *Naval History*, Vol. 27, No. 5 (September 2013): https://www.usni.org/magazines/naval-history-magazine/2013/september/risk-vs-reward-italian-riviera

60 Ibid.

CHAPTER 10

61 Hugh Martyr, 'Die Torpedokrise: The problems of the malfunctioning German Torpedoes in early WWII', World War II database (Jan 2019): https://ww2db.com/other.php?other_id=47

62 Arthur O. Bauer, 'HF/DF an Allied weapon against German U-boats 1939–1945' (Diemen, Self-Published, 2004): https://aobauer.home.xs4all.nl/HFDF1998.pdf

63 Anthony Preston, *Submarines: The History and Evolution of Underwater Fighting Vessels* (London: Octopus, 1975) p.90

CHAPTER 11

64 Sarah Everts, 'The Nazi origins of deadly nerve gases', *Chemical and Engineering News* (17 October 2016): https://cen.acs.org/articles/94/i41/Nazi-origins-deadly-nerve-gases.html

65 Carter Plymton Hydrick, *Critical Mass: How Nazi Germany Surrendered Enriched Uranium for the United States' Atomic Bomb* (Trine Day, Chicago, 2016)

66 Quoted in Fiona Keating, 'Discovery of radioactive metal points to "success" of Nazi atomic bomb programme', *Independent* (23 September 2017): https://www.independent.co.uk/news/world/europe/radioactive-nazi-atom-bomb-bernd-thalmann-germany-amateur-treasure-hunter-a7963521.html

67 Atomic Heritage Foundation, 'Leslie R. Groves': https://ahf.nuclearmuseum.org/ahf/profile/leslie-r-groves/, accessed 7 April 2025

68 For a fuller examination of the Manhattan Project, see Chris McNab, *J. Robert Oppenheimer: The Man Behind the Atom Bomb* (London: Arcturus, 2024)

69 Chairman's Office, *United States Strategic Bombing Survey: The Effects of the Atomic Bombs on Hiroshima and Nagasaki* (Washington, DC: U.S. Government Printing Office, 30 June 1946) p.3

Bibliography

Air Ministry, 'A Forecast of Air Developments in 1945: A Study prepared by the German Air Historical Branch, (8th Abteilung) and dated 22nd September, 1944' (London: Air Ministry, 2 November 1946)

The Armourer's Bench, 'SOE Sabotage - Plastic Explosive' (26 July 2020), YouTube: https://www.youtube.com/watch?v=0UO3_TG5nGM

The Armourer's Bench, 'SOE Sabotage - Explosive Coal' (28 July 2020), YouTube: https://www.youtube.com/watch?v=BqMh-KBIHrE

Atomic Heritage Foundation, 'Leslie R. Groves': https://ahf.nuclearmuseum.org/ahf/profile/leslie-r-groves/, accessed 7 April 2025

Bauer, Arthur O., 'HF/DF an Allied weapon against German U-boats 1939–1945' (Diemen, Self-Published, 2004): https://aobauer.home.xs4all.nl/HFDF1998.pdf

Brunner, Dr John W., *The OSS Crossbows* (Williamstown, NJ: Phillips Publications, 1990)

Chairman's Office, *United States Strategic Bombing Survey: The Effects of the Atomic Bombs on Hiroshima and Nagasaki* (Washington, DC: U.S. Government Printing Office, 30 June 1946)

Caldwell, Donald and Richard Muller, *The Luftwaffe over Germany: Defense of the Reich* (London: Greenhill, 2007)

Creveld, Martin Van, 'Technology and War: to 1945', in Charles Townshend (ed.), *The Oxford History of Modern War* (Oxford: Oxford University Press, 2000) p.201

Dabbs, Will, 'Welrod Pistol: Allied Assassination Tool', *The Armory Life* (9 May 2023): https://www.thearmorylife.com/welrod-pistol/

Dater, Philip H., 'SAR Tests the .32 caliber Welrod', *Small Arms Review* (August 2002): http://www.smallarmsreview.com/display.article.cfm?idarticles=2335

Ellis, John, *The World War II Databook: The Essential Facts and Figures for all the combatants* (London: Aurum Press, 1995)

Fairbairn, Captain W.E., *Get Tough! How to Win in Hand-to-Hand Fighting* (Boulder, CO: Paladin Press, 1996) p.104

Felton, Mark (Mark Felton Productions), 'Ungentlemanly Weapons: WW2 Secret Agent Special Guns' (3 July 2023), YouTube: https://www.youtube.com/watch?v=pziMTCzMGMg

Ford, Brian, *Secret Weapons: Death Rays, Doodlebugs and Churchill's Golden Goose* (Oxford: Osprey Publishing, 2013)

Ford, Roger, *Germany's Secret Weapons in World War II* (Staplehurst: Spellmount, 2000)

Forsyth, Robert, *Luftwaffe Mistel Composite Bomber Units* (Oxford: Osprey Publishing, 2001)

Galway, Geoff, *Geoff's Opus* (Self-Published, 1992)

Gebhardt, James F., *Soviet Front Special Purpose Troops: An Historical Perspective* (Fort Leavenworth, KS: Department of the Army, Soviet Army Studies Office, 1990)

Glines, Carroll V., 'The Bat Bombers', *Air & Space Forces Magazine* (1 October 1990): https://www.airandspaceforces.com/article/1090bats/

Hart, Dan, 'The Politics, Pickle Barrels, and Propaganda of the Norden Bombsight', Museum of Aviation (23 April 2016): https://museumofaviation.org/general/the-politics-pickle-barrels-and-propaganda-of-the-norden-bombsight/

Historical Firearms, 'Silence Stens': https://www.historicalfirearms.info/post/141056060049/silenced-stens-the-first-suppressed-sten-was-built

Hogg, Ian, *German and Allied Secret Weapons of World War II* (London: Phoebus, 1976)

Hogg, Ian, *German Artillery of World War Two* (London: Greenhill, 1997)

Hydrick, Carter Plymton, *Critical Mass: How Nazi Germany Surrendered Enriched Uranium for the United States' Atomic Bomb* (Chicago: Trine Day, 2016)

International Churchill Society, 'Ungentlemanly Warfare', Bulletin #126 (December 2018): https://winstonchurchill.org/publications/churchill-bulletin/bulletin-126-dec-2018/ungentlemanly-warfare/

Johnson, Dan, 'EMW C2 Wasserfall', Luft46.com (accessed 25 February 2025): http://www.luft46.com/missile/wasserfl.html

Kline, Adam, with Robin Dexter, 'Secret Weapons, Forgotten Sacrifices: Scientific R&D in World War II', NARA, *Prologue Magazine*, Vol. 48, No. 1 (Spring 2016): https://www.archives.gov/publications/prologue/2016/spring/office-scientific-research-development-world-war-ii

Kolakowski, Peter R., 'Naval Proving Ground at Dahlgren and the Hidden History of the VT Fuze', Naval Sea Systems Command (accessed 25 February 2025): https://www.navsea.navy.mil/Home/Warfare-Centers/NSWC-Dahlgren/Who-We-Are/History/Blogs/VT-Fuze/

Lawrence, Christopher A., 'Comparative Tank Exchange Ratios at Kursk', The Dupuy Institute (26 December 2018): https://dupuyinstitute.org/2018/12/26/comparative-tank-exchange-ratios-at-kursk/

Ludwigsen, Karl, *Professor Porsche's Wars: The secret life of legendary engineer Ferdinand Porsche who armed two belligerents through four decades* (Barnsley: Pen & Sword, 2014)

Marine Aircraft Experimental Establishment, Helensburgh, 'Upkeep – Reculver trials 14.4.43 to 16.5.43', Report No. H/Arm/104 (24 June 1943)

Martyr, Hugh, 'Die Torpedokrise: The problems of the malfunctioning German Torpedoes in early WWII', World War II database (January 2019): https://ww2db.com/other.php?other_id=47

McNab, Chris, *J. Robert Oppenheimer: The Man Behind the Atom Bomb* (London: Arcturus, 2024)

Miles, Bill, 'Dad's Army', WW2 People's War, BBC (28 December 2003): https://www.bbc.co.uk/history/ww2peopleswar/stories/93/a2159093.shtml

MSW, 'The Explosive Boats of the Kriegsmarine', WarHistory.org (22 November 2016): https://warhistory.org/@msw/article/the-explosive-boats-of-the-kriegsmarine

National Air and Space Museum, 'Bomb, Guided, Fritz X (X-1)': https://airandspace.si.edu/collection-objects/bomb-guided-fritz-x-x-1/nasm_A19840794000 accessed 28 February 2025

National Army Museum, 'Origins of the Special Forces': https://www.nam.ac.uk/explore/special-forcesWW2, accessed 7 April 2025

Norton-Taylor, Richard, 'How exploding rats went down a bomb - and helped British boffins win the second world war', *Guardian* (27 October 1999): https://www.theguardian.com/uk/1999/oct/27/richardnortontaylor

Office of Strategic Services, *OSS Weapons: Special Weapons and Devices* (Washington DC: Research and Development Branch, OSS, June 1944) p.3. The catalogue is available to view at: https://www.nas.gov.sg/archivesonline/private_records/record-details/dd346d60-82cb-11ea-8566-001a4a5ba61b

O'Hara, Vincent P., 'Risk vs. Reward Off the Italian Riviera', *Naval History*, Vol. 27, No. 5 (September 2013): https://www.usni.org/magazines/naval-history-magazine/2013/september/risk-vs-reward-italian-riviera

Porter, David, *Hitler's Secret Weapons: Facts and Data for Germany's Special Weapons Programme* (London: Amber Books, 2018)

Preston, Anthony, *Submarines: The History and Evolution of Underwater Fighting Vessels* (London: Octopus, 1975)

Price, Alfred, 'V-weapons', *The Oxford Companion to the Second World War* (Oxford: Oxford University Press, 1995) pp.1249–53

Rigden, Dennis (introduction), *SOE Syllabus: Lessons in ungentlemanly warfare, World War II* (Richmond: Public Record Office, 2001)

Robbins, Michael W., 'The Allies' Billion-dollar Secret: The Proximity Fuze of World War II', HistoryNet (19 October 2020): https://www.historynet.com/proximity-fuze/

Special Operations Executive, *Descriptive Catalogue of Special Devices and Supplies* (London: M.0.1 (S.P.) The War Office, 1944)

Speer, Albert, *Inside the Third Reich: The Classic Account of Nazi Germany by Hitler's Armaments Minister*, 7th edition (London: Phoenix, 2002)

Stubblebine, David, 'G7es Type V Torpedo', World War II Database (November 2021): https://ww2db.com/weapon.php?q=389

Sutton, H.I., 'Chariot Mk II', Covert Shores (24 May 2017): http://www.hisutton.com/Chariot_Mk2.html

Sutton, H.I., 'The famous CosMos CE2F chariot', Covert Shores (29 February 2016): http://www.hisutton.com/The%20famous%20CosMoS%20CE2F%20chariot.html

Thee, Marek (ed.), *Armaments, Arms Control and Disarmament: A UNESCO reader for disarmament education* (Paris: UNESCO, 1981) p.101

US Naval Technical Mission to Japan, 'Description and Operation of the Japanese Type 3 photoelectric fuse: "Intelligence Targets Japan" (DNI) of 4 September 1945' (San Francisco, CA)

Welker, David, 'Explosive Coal: Bombs Hiding in Plain Sight', *Studies in Intelligence*, Vol. 66, No. 1 (March 2022) pp.41–7

Winter, Frank, 'Hs 117 Schmetterling (Butterfly) Missile', National Air And Space Museum (accessed 24 February 2025): https://airandspace.si.edu/collection-objects/missile-surface-air-henschel-hs-117-schmetterling/nasm_A19890595000

Index

.22 Caliber Automatic Pistol 40

A-10 *America-Rakete* (rocket) 149
Aberdeen Proving Ground 17
Adams, Lytle S. 116–17, 118
Aeronautical Research Committee 135
air defence 119–37
Ambros, Otto 224
Anerometer (explosive trigger) 61
Anglo-German Naval Agreement 16
anti-tank weapons 78–83
Apparatus Air Defence Type L (air defence system) 122
Arado Ar 234 (aircraft) 96–8
Artillery Research Station 145
ASDIC (submarine detector) 205–7
Assault Vehicle Royal Engineers (AVRE) 75–6
ASM-N-2 Bat (guided bomb) 158–9
atomic weapons 224–33
AZON (guided bomb) 157–8

Bachem Ba 349 Natter (aircraft) 91, 93–4
bat bombs 116–18
Bawdsey Research Station (BRS) radar research group 18
Bell P-59 Airacomet (aircraft) 110–11

Bell, T.I.S. 184
Bensusan-Butt, David 112
Bethe, Hans 229
Biber (submarine) 189
Big Joe 5 (crossbow) 44–5
Black Prince (A43) (tank) 75
Bloch, Felix 229
Blohm und Voss Bv 246 Hagelkorn (guided bomb) 156
Bohr, Niels 229
bolt-action rifles 45–6
bombing raids 111–18
Bonham-Carter, Sir Maurice 108
bouncing bombs 160–5
Brandenburgers 30
Burney gun (anti-tank weapon) 82–3
Burney, Charles Dennistoun 82
Bush, Vannevar 31
Bushmaster (booby trap trigger) 40

Caccolube 62
Cairncross, John 231
Campbell, Levin H. 137
Campbell, Sir Malcolm 43
Central Aerohydrodynamic Institute (TsAGI) 20
Chadwick, Roy 163
Chamberlain, Joseph 115
Chapman, Edward Arnold 59
Chariots (torpedo) 181–3
chemical weapons 222–4

249

INDEX

Churchill, Winston 14, 19, 27–8, 34, 62, 181, 202
Clarke, Cecil Vandepeer 174
coal bomb 57–8
Combined Operations Pilotage Parties (COPP) 28, 182
Committee for the Scientific Survey of Air Defence (CSSAD) 18
Cönders, August 150
Creveld, Martin van 9
CTV-N-2 Gorgon IIC (guided bomb) 159

de Havilland Vampire (aircraft) 110
De Lisle carbine gun 43
depth charges 204–5
Diebner, Kurt 226
Dinsdale, Walter 104
Directorate of Miscellaneous Weapons Development 168, 170, 211
Disney Bomb 168–70
Dolphin, John 183
Dönitz, Karl 201
Dornberger, Walter 145–6
Dreadnought, HMS 12, 13
Dunn, John 104

Edgeworth, Thomas 57
Einstein, Albert 228
Elefant (tank) 22
Enzian (air defence system) 130–1
Everett, Douglas 42

Explosive No. 808 54
Fairbairn, William Ewart 32, 33

Fairbairn–Sykes (fighting knife) 32–3
Fermi, Enrico 229
FG 42 (rifle) 47–8
Fiesler Fi 103R (flying bomb) 101–2
firearms 35–52
First Special Service Force (FSSF) 28–9, 33
Fisser, L.F. 117
Fliegerfaust (air defence system) 126
Focke-Wulf *Triebflügel* (aircraft) 94–5
Ford, Brian J. 171
Franck, James 229
Frederick, Robert T. 33
Frisch, Otto 224, 229
Fritz-X (guided bomb) 154, 155–6
Fuchs, Klaus 229, 230
Fukuryu (kamikaze frogmen) 30, 195–6

Galland, Adolf 88
Galway, Geoff 184–5
Gammon Bomb 62–5
G7 (torpedoes) 207, 209–10
GB-1 (guided bomb) 159
Gerlich, Hermann 79
Gloster E.28/39 (aircraft) 108
Gloster meteor (aircraft) 109–107
GNAT (torpedo) 209–10

Goebbels, Joseph 140–1
Göring, Hermann 98, 120
Gotha Go 229 (aircraft) 99
Grand Panjandrum 170–2
Grand Slam (bomb) 166–8
Greenglass, David 231
Griffith, Alan Arnold 108
Grillo (boat) 177–8
Grote, Edward 70, 74
Group for the Study of Reactive Motion (GIRD) 20
Groves, Leslie Richard 229

Hahn, Otto 224
Hall, Theodore 231
Harris, Sir Arthur 112
Hart, Dan 114–15
Hartmann, Fred 51
He 111 H-2 (aircraft) 143
He 162 *Salamander* (aircraft) 90–1
He 178 (aircraft) 86–7
He 280 V1 (aircraft) 87
Hedgehog (anti-submarine weapon) 211–13
Heeresversuchsanstalt Peenemünde (HVP) 19, 125
Heereswaffenamt (HWA) 19
Heinkel 86
Heisenberg, Werner 226
Hiroshima bombing 231–2
Hiskey, Clarence 231
Hitler, Adolf 15, 19, 54, 69, 70, 72, 73, 88, 139, 140, 150
Hobart, Sir Percy Cleghorn Stanley 76

Hogg, Ian 81
Horten Ho IX (aircraft) 98–9
Horten, Reimar and Walter 98
Hs 117 *Schmetterling* (air defence system) 127, 128
Hs 293 (guided bomb) 152–5
Hs 297 *Föhn* (air defence system) 125
Huff-Duff (submarine detector) 213–14
Hussey, George F. 137
Hyde, George 36
Hydrick, Carter Plymton 227, 228

Identification Friend-or-Foe (IFF) system 17
IL-2 *Sturmovik* 22
incendiary devices 59–60
Incendiary Packet 60
Industrial Revolution 11–12

Janeček, František 80
Jefferis, Millis 62, 173–4, 181
Jensen, Eugene T. 9–11
jet aircraft 86–100, 108–11
Joint Psychological Warfare Committee 36
Ju 287 (aircraft) 99–100

Kairyu (submarine) 190–1
Kaiten torpedoes 30
Kammler, Hans 131
KAN Little Joe (air defence system) 131
Kennedy, Joseph P. 105

knives 32–5
Kramer, Max 154
Krummlauf attachment 50–2
Kurier burst transmission system 214
Kurt (bouncing bomb) 165
Kurzzeitsperre (air defence system) 126–7
KV-2 (tank) 74–5

Landkreuzer P1000 Ratte (tank) 70–1
Landkreuzer P1500 Monster (tank) 71
Lawrence, Ernest Orlando 229
Lee-Enfield Mk III (rifle) 43
Leichtgeschütz 40 (anti-tank weapon) 82
Leigh Light (submarine detector) 216
LeMay, Curtis Emerson 115
Liberator pistol 35, 36–7
limpet mines 173–6
Linsen (boat) 191–4
Lippisch, Alexander 91
Little Joe Penetrometer (crossbow) 44–5
Littlejohn Adapter 80
Lockheed P-80 Shooting Star (aircraft) 111
Lovell, Stanley 57
Ludendorff, Erich 21

M3 gun 39–40

M20 RCL Rifle (anti-tank weapon) 83
Macrae, Robert Stuart 174
Maiale (submarine) 176
Main Artillery Directorate (GAU) 19–20
Manhattan Project 18, 228–31
Marinewaffenamt (MWa) 19
Mark 24 (torpedo) 210–11
McNutt, Russell 231
Me 163 *Komet* (aircraft) 91–3
Me 262 (aircraft) 10–11, 87–90
Me 321 (aircraft) 105–6
midget submarines 183–91
Meitner, Lisa 224
Mignatto (torpedo) 178–9
Military Intelligence (Research) department 19
Ministry of Defence 1 (MD1) 62
Mistel (aircraft) 103–5
Mk 1 Limpet Mine 174–5
Molch (submarine) 188
Mole (explosive trigger) 61
Muck, Otto 151
Mussolini, Benito 42

National Defense Research Committee (NDRC) 31, 44, 135
Naval Research Laboratory (NRL) 17
Naxos systems (submarine detection) 217
Neger (torpedo) 188
Nichols, Kenneth D. 229
NKVD 29

Nobel, Alfred 54
Norden bombsight 112–16
Norden, Carl Lucas van 112
Norwood, Melita 231
Nuffield Mechanisation & Aero Ltd 77

Oberkommando der Marine (OKM) 19, 70
Oberth, Hermann 221
Office of Scientific Research and Development (OSRD) 17–18, 31
Office of Strategic Services (OSS) 29, 32, 33, 36–40, 41, 59–62
Ohain, Hans Pabst von 86
Operation *Anvil* 105
Operation *Aphrodite* 105
Operation *Catechism* 167
Operation *Chastise* 164–5
Operation *Crossbow* 144, 148
Operation *Frankton* 176
Operation *Husky* 182
Operation *Jaywick* 175–6
Operation *Meetinghouse* 112
Operation *Neptune* 183
Operation *Overlord* 186
Operation *Pastorius* 59
Operation *QWZ* 183
Operation *Source* 185–6
Oppenheimer, J. Robert 228–9

P-51D Mustang 10
Panther (tank) 22, 23
Panzer III (tank) 22
Panzer IV (tank) 22

Panzerbüsche 41 (anti-tank weapon) 79–80
Panzerfaust (anti-tank weapon) 79
Panzerjägerkanone 41
Panzerschreck (anti-tank weapon) 79
Paolucci, Raffaele 178–9
Patton, George S. 137
Peenemünde Army Research Centre 155
penetrator bombs 166–70
piggyback aircraft 103–6
plastic explosives 54–9
Porsche 72–3 (anti-tank weapon) 80
Power Jets Company 108
precision-guided munitions (PGMs) 151–6, 157–65
Preston, Anthony 218
Prien, Günther 208
Projector, 3-inch Mk 1 (air defence system) 123–4
Puff, Carl 79
PzKpfw VII *Löwe* (tank) 71–2
PzKpfw VIII *Maus* (tank) 72–4

radar 119–20, 214
rat bombs 56–7
RDX explosives 54
Reactive Scientific Research Institute (RNII) 20
Reeves, Hugh Quentin Alleyne 41, 42
Reichsluftfahrtministerium (RLM) 19

INDEX

Research Department, Woolwich Arsenal 18, 80, 121
Rheinocter (air defence system) 130
Rheinmetall-Borsig 81
Richmond, William 181
Ritter, Gerhard 224
rocket-powered weapons 100–3
Roosevelt, Franklin D. 29, 31, 117, 228
Rossetti, Raffaele 178–9
Royal Air Force Special Duties (SD) Service 28
Royal Arsenal Woolwich 18
Royal Marines Boom Patrol Detachment (RMBPD) 28
Russo-Japanese War (1904–05) 12

Sarin (chemical) 224
Schaede, Hans 51
Schrader, Gerhard 223, 224
Seborer, Oscar 231
Secret Weapons: Death Rays, Doodlebugs and Churchill's Golden Goose (Ford) 171
Seehunden (submarine) 188
Segrè, Emilio 229
Sherman tanks 22, 23, 76
Shintani, K. 195–6
Shinyo (boat) 194–5
Sieber, Lothar 94
Silbervogel (aircraft) 100–1
Siluro a Lunga Corsa (SLC) (torpedo) 179–81
Skorzeny, Otto 42

Sladen, Geoffrey 181
Small Thermit Well 60
Smatchet (knife) 33–4
SMG rifles 46–7
Special Air Service (SAS) 28, 32, 41
Special Boat Service (SBS) 28
Special Operations Executive (SOE) 19, 28, 29, 32, 34–5, 54, 55–9, 62
special-purpose weaponry 60–5
Special Service Brigade 28
Speer, Albert 71, 73, 129–30, 139
Squid (anti-submarine weapon) 212–13
SS-Jäger-Bataillon 502 30
SS-Panzer Brigade 150 30
Station IX (Research Section) 31, 41
Station XII 31
Station XVb 31
Stauffenberg, Claus von 54
Sten gun 42
StG 44 (rifle) 49–50
Sticky Bomb 62–5
Stinger (pistol) 37–8
Strassmann, Fritz 224
submarine detection 205–6, 211–17
submarine warfare 200–4, 217–20
Surface-to-Air, Lark (air defence system) 131
Sykes, Eric Anthony 32
Szilard, Leo 229

INDEX

T9 Recoilless Howitzer (anti-tank weapon) 83
T15 RCL [Recoilless] Rifle (anti-tank weapon) 83
T28 (super-heavy tank) 77–8
T-34/85 (tank) 22, 23
T-42 (super-heavy tank) 74
Tabun (chemical) 224
Taifun (air defence system) 125–6
Tallboy (bomb) 166–7
tanks 68–78
Teller, Edward 229
Terrell, Edward 168
Tesei, Teseo 179
Thiel, Walter 129
Tiger tanks 22, 23, 69–70
Tizard, Henry 18, 135
Tizard Mission 135
torpedoes 176–86, 207–10
Tortoise heavy assault (tank) 77
Toschi, Elios 179
Tuve, Merle 135
Type A *Ko-hyoteki* (submarine) 189–90

U-boats (submarines) 200–4, 214–20
Udet, Ernst 87
Unit 9903 29

V-1 (flying bomb) 141–5, 156
V-2 (ballistic missile) 145–9
V-3 (multi-chamber cannon) 149–51
V-42 (knife) 33
Varley, C. H. 184
Versailles Treaty 14, 15, 201
Volkssturm-Flugabwehr-Raketenwerfer (air defence system) 125
von Braun, Walter 146, 148–9
von der Linde, Hans-Jürgen 224
von Neumann, John 229–30
VT fuse 135–7

Wallis, Barnes 160–1, 162, 166
Walter, Hellmuth 217
Washington Naval Treaty 15
Wasserfall (air defence system) 128–9
Welman (submarine) 183–4
Welrod pistol 41
Welwand 'sleeve gun' 42
Wendel, F.H. 192
Whittle, Frank 108
Who, Me? spray 38–9
Whyte, Lancelot Law 108
Wiley, Wilford J. 105
Wocke, Hans 99

X-Craft (submarine) 184–6

Yokosuka MXY7 Ohka (flying bomb) 102–3

Zinsser, Hans 227–8

255